THE GOOD FUNERAL

ALSO BY THOMAS G. LONG

HOMILETICS
Preaching from Memory to Hope
Preaching In and Out of Season
The Senses of Preaching
The Witness of Preaching

BIBLICAL COMMENTARIES
Hebrews (Interpretation: A Bible Commentary for Teaching and Preaching)
Matthew (Westminster Bible Companion)

WORSHIP
Accompany Them with Singing—The Christian Funeral
Beyond the Worship Wars: Building Vital and Faithful Worship

THEOLOGY
Testimony: Talking Ourselves into Being Christian
What Shall We Say? Evil, Suffering, and the Crisis of Faith

COLLABORATIONS
Preaching as a Theological Task: World, Gospel, Scripture (with Edward Farley)
Teaching Preaching as a Christian Practice: A New Approach to Homiletical Pedagogy (with Leonora Tubbs Tisdale)

ALSO BY THOMAS LYNCH

ESSAYS AND MEMOIRS
The Undertaking: Life Studies from the Dismal Trade
Bodies in Motion and at Rest: On Metaphor and Mortality
Booking Passage: We Irish and Americans

POEMS
Skating with Heather Grace
Grimalkin & Other Poems
Still Life in Milford: Poems
Walking Papers: Poems
The Sin-eater: A Breviary

FICTION
Apparition & Late Fictions: A Novella and Stories

DRAMA
Lacrimae Rerum

THE GOOD FUNERAL

Death, Grief, and the Community of Care

THOMAS G. LONG

THOMAS LYNCH

First edition
Published by Westminster John Knox Press
Louisville, Kentucky

13 14 15 16 17 18 19 20 21 22—10 9 8 7 6 5 4 3 2 1

Scripture quotations, unless otherwise indicated, are from the New Revised Standard Version of the Bible, copyright © 1989 by the Division of Christian Education of the National Council of the Churches of Christ in the U.S.A., and used by permission.

Scripture taken from *The Message.* Copyright © 1993, 1994, 1995, 1996. Used by permission of NavPress Publishing Group.

Excerpts from "What I Learned from My Mother," from *Sleeping Preacher,* by Julia Kasdorf, © 1992. Reprinted by permission of the University of Pittsburgh Press. Excerpts from "Local Heroes," from *Walking Papers,* by Thomas Lynch. Copyright © 2011 by Thomas Lynch. Used by permission of W. W. Norton & Company, Inc. and the Random House Group Limited. Excerpts from "Brother to a Dragonfly," by Will Campbell, © 1977. Reprinted by permission of Bloomsbury Continuum. Excerpts from Edna St. Vincent Millay, "Dirge without Music," from *Collected Poems.* Copyright 1928, © 1955 by Edna St. Vincent Millay and Norma Millay Ellis. Reprinted with the permission of The Permissions Company, Inc., on behalf of Holly Peppe, Literary Executor, The Millay Society. www.millay.org. Excerpt from Jane Kenyon, "Twilight: After Haying," from *Collected Poems.* Copyright © 2005 by the Estate of Jane Kenyon. Reprinted with the permission of The Permissions Company, Inc. on behalf of Graywolf Press, www.graywolfpress .org. Chapter 7 is a revised and expanded version of Thomas Lynch's "The Holy Fire," copyright © 2010 by the *Christian Century.* "The Holy Fire" by Thomas Lynch is reprinted with permission in a modified version from the April 6, 2010, issue of the *Christian Century.* Chapter 9 is a revised and expanded version of Thomas G. Long's "Faith Matters: Grief without Stages," copyright © 2011 by the *Christian Century.* "Grief without Stages" by Thomas G. Long is reprinted with permission in a modified version from the June 28, 2011, issue of the *Christian Century.* Some portions of Thomas G. Long's "A Chronicle of a Death We Can't Accept" were first published in the *New York Times.*

Book design by Erika Lundbom
Cover design by designpointinc.com
Cover illustration: View from the Grave, © *Emilia Unger/shutterstock.com*

Library of Congress Cataloging-in-Publication Data

Long, Thomas G., 1946-
   The good funeral : death, grief, and the community of care / Thomas G. Long, Thomas Lynch.—First edition.
     pages cm
   Includes index.
   ISBN 978-0-664-23853-7 (alk. paper)
   1. Funeral rites and ceremonies—United States. 2. Mourning customs—United States. 3. Death—United States. 4. Bereavement—United States. I. Title.
   GT3203.L66 2013
   393.0973—dc23

                                                                                          2013003068

Most Westminster John Knox Press books are available at special quantity discounts
when purchased in bulk by corporations, organizations, and special-interest groups.
For more information, please e-mail SpecialSales@wjkbooks.com.

In memory of Wes and Betty Rice
In paradisum deducant te Angeli

And in memory of Edmund A. Steimle and Ernest T. Campbell
verbum Domini manet in aeternum

CONTENTS

Funeral Directors and Clergy

The Funeral

The Grieving

FOREWORD

Patrick Lynch

MY BROTHER TOM AND I GREW UP IN A HOUSEHOLD PARENTED by Rosemary O'Hara and Edward Lynch, wherein discussions about heavy topics—the inevitability of death and dying; the significance of grief and mourning; the value of liturgy, ritual, and ceremony; and the fundamental belief that God is ever present during our earthly journey—were commonplace. We were blessed to have a father who, because of his work as a funeral director, saw the intrinsic value of all faiths as people navigated their way through the sorrows of death and dying. We were taught to think ecumenically before ecumenism was fashionable.

For example, returning from St. Columban Catholic School as a third or fourth grader, I reported that one of the nuns had instructed us, "Never go into the church next door": Our Shepherd Lutheran. My father assured me that the good nun was wrong. At any time, I could go into Our Shepherd to pray and God would hear me. Furthermore, he explained, if I wanted to ask the pastor of Our Shepherd, the Reverend Howard Allwardt, to assist me in prayer, it would not be a bad thing. Pastor Allwardt and my father had a relationship that went far beyond pastor and funeral director. They were friends. Similarly, all the local clergy—Baptist, Catholic, Congregational, Episcopal, Methodist, Orthodox, Presbyterian, and Unitarian—were my father's friends and regular visitors in our home. While conscious of their differences, Tom and I and the rest of our siblings were more intrigued by their similarities. Like our father, we had been blessed by these holy people and made the better for it.

Thus, it seemed fitting that in February 1992, on the eve of my father's Mass of Christian Burial, his body was prayed over by clergy from all denominations. Perhaps the most touching of these prayers was offered by our close family friend, the Very Reverend Fr. Laurence Lazar, Dean of St. George Romanian Orthodox Cathedral. Following the traditional Trisagion Service, which includes those beautiful ancient refrains, "Lord Have Mercy" and "Memory Eternal," Fr. Laurence read the following:

> In the name of the Father and of the Son and of the Holy Spirit.
>
> Brothers and Sisters-in-Christ, Our Family.
>
> In his profession your father, Edward, served the final needs of thousands and thousands of people in this community, and, because God had blessed him, he helped and supported many parishes of different faiths. But, the fact that you have invited us, from St. George Romanian Orthodox Cathedral, to be with your family tonight (for which we thank you), and to share with you this final farewell of your father, will always remind us of the special relationship and friendship he shared with us and we shared with him and your family.
>
> And so, on behalf of the Cathedral clergy and our faithful parishioners, I offer you our sincere condolences. And we do so with the same hand of compassion that your father offered

our people and so many others over the decades. And finally we do so with the prayer that, as St. Paul the Apostle said, "You do not grieve as if there is no hope"; because we believe that "Jesus Christ died and rose from the dead, and it will be the same for all those who love Him."

May God forgive him, and give him rest.

Amen.

This letter speaks to the relationship our father developed over many years with the members of the clergy in our community. As young funeral directors working under his tutelage, Tom and I were made acutely aware of the ministerial partnership shared by funeral directors and the clergy. We learned that both parties were critical to the care of the dying, dead, and bereaved, and that by serving the living while caring for the dead, we brought an added measure of dignity to life itself. This partnership, which in later years extended beyond funeral directors and the clergy to include hospice workers, social workers, and other caregivers, has been a gift to our professional lives.

For years, our father had a habit of asking Tom, "When are you going to write something about what we do?" He was, of course, talking about funerals, and while at the time Tom had published a few volumes of poetry, he had never written a book directly addressing his life as an undertaker. He promised our father that he would get to it someday. Then our father died. Determined to keep his promise, Tom began collecting his thoughts, and in 1997 *The Undertaking: Life Studies from the Dismal Trade* was born. Recipient of the American Book Award and a finalist for the National Book Award, *The Undertaking* catapulted Tom into the international spotlight. He quickly became one of the most sought after speakers for funeral directors, clergy, and health-care professionals around the world. Meeting and speaking with people he would have otherwise never met, Tom soon recognized the extensive impact he could make on the way our culture thinks about death, dying, grief, and funerals. As passionate as he was about his work as a funeral director, he became equally dedicated to his life as a writer and lecturer. I believe this career combination, while certainly rare and at times difficult to manage, has borne more fruit than Tom will ever know.

As Tom continued to travel and lecture following the release of *The Undertaking*, another gifted Tom, Dr. Thomas Long, a theologian and Presbyterian clergyman, was writing extensively on the same topics. Thus, it comes as no surprise that "the Toms" began reading each other's books and presenting to the same audiences. They soon met and, recognizing in the other a kindred spirit, they began corresponding on a regular basis. Over the course of many conversations, my brother learned that Tom Long was taking theological exception with the increasing willingness of funeral directors and clergy alike to turn good funerals, which he considers acts of sacred community theater, into convenience-based and spiritually empty "celebrations of life." My brother's message has been nearly identical. He has openly criticized funeral directors, clergy, and the culture at large for allowing funerals to become anything less than an existential experience possessing certain basic elements: someone who has died, someone to whom that death matters, and someone to broker the message between them. An event, he insists, which lacks these fundamental components does not fulfill the real obligation of a funeral: "to get the dead where they need to go and the living where they need to be."

My brother and I decided years ago to share with as wide an audience as possible our belief that grief is inevitable; public mourning is healthy; and that funerals, when done properly, are immeasurably valuable to the bereaved. We theorized that Tom, who is not only a funeral director but a well-known writer, could influence a diverse audience through his writing and lecturing. His was an independent, credible, and articulate voice, and because he was not tied to any trade group or professional association, we believed media outlets would more readily solicit his opinion. Our theory was correct. Tom was soon contacted by newspapers, magazines, and Web sites around the world. Everyone wanted to know what this small-town undertaker had to say.

While Tom continued to write and lecture, he and I agreed it would be best if I sought leadership positions in our state and national associations of funeral directors. In this way, I could directly influence thousands of funeral professionals who may or may not be going about their work the best way. In the course of my association journey I have met many professionals who understand exactly what Tom and I mean when we talk about good funerals. I've also met people who have become terribly misguided. Tom has influenced those outside our profession and I've done my best to influence the profession from within. For both Tom and me this collective endeavor has been time-consuming, tedious, and, at times, even thankless. But we have been motivated in large part by the memory of a twelve-year-old boy who, in 1936, after seeing funeral directors quietly dress and casket his dead uncle, a priest, decided at that very moment that he would do the same with the rest of his life. That twelve-year-old boy was our father. As soon as he came home from the war, he became a funeral director. The first twenty-five years of his career he worked for others. But in his fifties, along with his sons, he founded Lynch & Sons Funeral Directors, which now operates seven locations serving about 1,500 families a year. Tom and I have spent our entire professional lives in thanksgiving for what that twelve-year-old boy saw and the legacy he left behind.

In 2003 our efforts began to merge. It was my year as president of the Michigan Funeral Directors Association and I was overseeing the coordination of our annual convention.

Tom and I began discussing potential programming for the attendees and immediately thought of Dr. Long. To this end, "the Toms" led a panel discussion about trends in contemporary funeral practices and were absolutely masterful in their ability to communicate with each other and the audience. I knew immediately that their collective insights could benefit a much broader audience. Thus, six interdisciplinary seminars were scheduled for late October through early December 2003. Titled "The Good Death, Good Grief, Good Funerals: Finding Our Place on the Continuum of Care," these statewide programs were attended by over 1,500 funeral directors, clergy, hospice workers, social workers, and students. The response was overwhelmingly positive.

Several years later I was elected President of the National Funeral Directors Association (NFDA), the leading and largest association of funeral directors in the world. Among my hopes was to bring the same program we had in Michigan to the national audience. NFDA's executive board recognized the value of such programming and approved the first regional Clergy/Funeral Director seminars sponsored by NFDA in over a decade. With the cooperation of over a dozen state funeral director associations, "The Good Death, Good Grief, Good Funerals" program was presented in Pennsylvania, Massachusetts, Indiana, and Georgia. The response was the same: when it comes to death, dying, grief, and funerals, Long and Lynch were producing the best scholarship in the world.

This book is the culmination of the countless hours Tom Lynch and Tom Long have spent together at these meetings and others, listening to and speaking with thousands of funeral directors, clergy, and health-care professionals. I cannot stress its importance enough as we investigate the meaning of death, dying, grief, and funerals in our own lives. It will be the book of record for generations to come.

FOREWORD

Barbara Brown Taylor

WHEN PEOPLE ASK ME WHAT I MISS MOST ABOUT PARISH ministry, the answer is easy. I miss baptisms and funerals, the bookend rituals in which life and death point to one another, linking birth to death and death to new life. I miss standing by stone bowls full of water and open graves full of dirt, reading from a prayer book that gave me magnificent words to say while I handled water, flesh, oil, and earth in ancient, sacred ways. Even now I can easily turn to those pages because they are the most wrinkled in the book—the baptismal pages pocked with dried water and oily thumbprints, the funeral pages smeared with rain, tears, and mud. In my Episcopal tradition, both rituals are sacraments, which means that there is no separating the spiritual truth in them from the physical truth in them. The magnificent words and the sacred handling both require human bodies; there is no other way to address human souls.

The two Toms—Long and Lynch—make that point so well in this book that the hardest part of writing a foreword is resisting the urge to quote them nonstop. Early on they speak of the power of language to name and transform reality, and that is one of the chief virtues of this book. The authors have spent decades thinking about their topic, settling more deeply into it than most of us are comfortable doing. More than that, they have spent decades bodily invested in the practice of burying the dead, so that what they say grows from the ground of long experience. On page after page they say what they know so gorgeously that it strikes the heart like a gong. Those of us who have buried our own dead know the truth too; we simply did not know how to say it half as well.

That is the other standout virtue of this book: the authors embody the truth they tell with such rich narratives that their real-life stories call forth the reader's own. When Tom Lynch recalls an episode of the television hit *Six Feet Under*, in which an Episcopal priest uses a ritual shaker to sprinkle dirt on a dead man's coffin, I am taken straight back to the first funeral I ever did. The church service was over. The family and a large number of friends had followed the hearse to the cemetery, where we had parked our cars and processed behind the coffin to the grave. I had rehearsed everything ten times over to make sure that there were no undignified surprises, but nothing prepared me for the vial of sand that the funeral director held out to me after the coffin had been lowered into the ground. My next lines included the phrase "earth to earth, ashes to ashes, dust to dust," but what was in the vial did not look like any of those. It looked like something from a child's sandbox, or a nice beach in Florida. The sacrament required more.

I did a quick visual search for real dirt but the entire gravesite had been covered with artificial turf. With no time to waste, I lifted the corner nearest my feet and rummaged around under the green plastic grass for some red Georgia dirt. The damp clump sat in my hand during the final prayer. Then I dropped it on the beautiful casket at the bottom of the hole, where it made an unseemly mess and a very final sound. Since none of us had rehearsed that part we all sat silent for a moment while we registered the incongruity of what had just happened, which was also the reality of what had just happened: earth to earth, ashes to ashes, dust to dust. The next time the funeral director and I did a graveside service together, he had a handful of dirt ready for me. I never saw another vial of sand.

⸎

One gifted storyteller would be enough for a volume like this, but this one has two. When Tom Long tells the story of the Buddhist undertaker who cared for the bodies of those lost in a tsunami, I am back at the funeral home where my father was cremated. Because I was the one who was with him when he died, I wanted to be the one to carry his remains back home, which meant finding something to do for the three hours it took his ashes to cool. The funeral home was one of Atlanta's oldest, situated in a part of town that had become affordable for a number of new immigrant communities. The family who owned it had ignored the trend toward furnishing such establishments as blandly as possible. This place was full of old grandfather clocks, carved wooden mantelpieces, and pieces of furniture so large and dark that they looked like sleeping buffalos—an effect heightened by the dim lighting, which came mainly from antique ceiling fixtures with painted glass globes.

After my husband Ed and I had identified my father's body and signed all the papers we lingered in the lobby, walking past the rooms set aside for visitations. Two of them had open caskets in them but no visitors yet. In the last room, three sticks of incense burned in a vase on a table at the entrance. Everyone inside was dressed in white. When I stepped back to look

xviii   Foreword by Barbara Brown Taylor

at the name of the deceased, it seemed likely that he had been a Theravada Buddhist, or had at least come from the part of the world where that tradition is dominant. I could not have asked for a better reminder that what felt like my singular loss was in fact my sure bond to everyone else on earth. Whether death comes by cancer or tsunami, grief is a language everyone speaks.

With hours left to go, Ed and I walked outside into a gray December day. I wanted to head down the sidewalk to find a place for lunch; Ed wanted to circle the building. As soon as we rounded the first corner I knew why. Three tall chimneys rose from a wing attached to the back of the funeral home, with smoke coming out of the center one. A red-tailed hawk climbed upward on the spiral of heat produced by the furnace below. We stood and watched until the air stopped rippling and the hawk flew away. Later, when we signed again for the urn of my father's ashes, they were still warm to the touch.

We did not carry out all of his wishes, which included being dressed in his tuxedo for an open-casket funeral. We did the best we could at an Episcopal church with the urn, and I remain deeply grateful to the clergy friends who stepped in so I could sit in a pew and weep. Now that I have read this book, I wish we could do it all over again. I would insist on the body, if not on the tux. But since we cannot do it all over again, I will do the next best thing: I will use what I have learned from this book to make some suggestions to my next of kin. Whether they know it or not, they will benefit from going the distance with me, bearing as much of the burden of me as they can stand—for, as both Toms say more than once in this book, it is by getting the dead where they need to go that the living get where they need to be.

The authors say that they have written this book for pastors and funeral directors, to help those first responders remember what their jobs really are. I have no doubt that this book will be helpful to such people. But if my reading of it is any indication, then the questions the two Toms raise and the counsel they offer will go much deeper than that. It will remind anyone with a body what a means of grace that is, and how important it is to handle the sacrament of flesh with reverence all the way to the end. If we get our hands dirty, so be it. There is no better way to touch the soul.

ACKNOWLEDGMENTS

THOMAS LYNCH WISHES TO MAKE KNOWN HIS INDEBTEDNESS TO the editors of the following publications where some of this work first appeared, often in much different form: *The Christian Century, The New York Times, The American Funeral Director, Commonweal Magazine, The Director Magazine, Mortuary Management, Michigan Quarterly Review,* and *The Times of London.*

PREFACE

SEVERAL YEARS AGO, AT THE KIND INVITATION OF THE MICHIGAN Funeral Directors Association, the two of us spent a few weeks traveling like troubadours around that state's pleasant peninsulas. Our assignment was to speak to gatherings of funeral directors and clergy in various locations around Michigan on the theme of the "good funeral." We were, in some ways, an odd pair—one of us a funeral director and the other a seminary professor and ordained minister; one of us raised Catholic and the other Protestant; one of us a composer of poems, short stories, and plays and the other a writer of seminary textbooks and church homilies. But the more we traveled and talked, the more we realized that we were kindred spirits on many things, especially matters funereal.

We discovered that both of us are persuaded that the rituals and practices around death are a window into the soul of a culture. And we also discovered a mutual concern that our cultural soul is currently troubled on this very score. A society that is unsure about how to care for the dead and is confused about what to do with grief and loss is a society that is also uncertain about life. We found a common passion to work to reclaim wise ways of addressing death, both as an end in itself and also as a means toward recovering wise ways of simply being more alive as human beings.

Since those days in Michigan, we have had many other opportunities to work and speak together. Along the trail we have swapped stories and jokes about clergy and funeral directors, exploring both the foibles and the virtues of our two professions. We have talked, studied, and collaborated, our thoughts striking fire like flint against steel, so that over time we have refined our ideas of what makes for good death practices. Sometimes we have lost track of whose ideas were whose as our understanding has been deepened and brought closer through our conversations.

This book is the result of, and an expression of, those conversations. Because death, grief, and funerals are never impersonal topics, and how one views them is inevitably shaped by experience, we open this book with two autobiographical chapters, one by each of us. One of us grew up to be a funeral director, and one of us grew up to be a theologian. These are not simply our jobs; these are the places that we have come on our life's journey. So we spend a few pages recounting how we got to those places and hoping these chapters will be an invitation to our readers to contemplate their own journeys.

In the remaining chapters we examine the themes of death, the body, the nature of a funeral, cremation, grief, the proper role of funeral directors and religious leaders, and the current perplexities of the culture about these issues. Because we have written from our separate perspectives—clergyman and funeral director—we have identified which of us wrote each chapter.

Many people today are interested in and concerned about

funerals and death rituals, and we had all such readers in mind as we wrote. In particular, though, we had clergy and funeral professionals, including seminarians and mortuary science students. If our practices around death are to become more grounded, more humane, and, indeed, more faithful, it will require wise leadership from those who most closely care for families at the time of loss.

Thomas G. Long
Thomas Lynch

Why We Do This

What I Learned from My Mother

I learned from my mother how to love
the living, to have plenty of vases on hand
in case you have to rush to the hospital
with peonies cut from the lawn, black ants
still stuck to the buds. I learned to save jars
large enough to hold fruit salad for a whole
grieving household, to cube home-canned pears
and peaches, to slice through maroon grape skins
and flick out the sexual seeds with a knife point.
I learned to attend viewings even if I didn't know
the deceased, to press the moist hands
of the living, to look in their eyes and offer
sympathy, as though I understood loss even then.
I learned that whatever we say means nothing,
what anyone will remember is that we came.
I learned to believe I had the power to ease
awful pains materially like an angel.
Like a doctor, I learned to create
from another's suffering my own usefulness, and once
you know how to do this, you can never refuse.
To every house you enter, you must offer
healing: a chocolate cake you baked yourself,
the blessing of your voice, your chaste touch.

Julia Kasdorf

Chapter 1

HOW WE COME TO BE
THE ONES WE ARE

Thomas Lynch

IN THE SUMMER OF 2012, GUS NICHOLS, ONE OF DUBLIN'S great undertakers and the President of FIAT-IFTA, the International Federation of Thanatologists Associations, invited me to Ireland to speak on a subject of my choosing. FIAT-IFTA is a congress of funeral directors from around the world and at this, their twelfth international convention, there would be representatives from thirty nations, two hundred and fifty registrants in all, from places as far-flung as Malaysia and Sierra Leone, Argentina and Australia, Canada and China and Columbia. My brother Patrick was the immediate past president of our National Funeral Directors Association and traveled with me as a delegate from the United States to thank Gus, Finbarr O'Connor and, indeed, several members of the Irish Association of Funeral Directors for having traveled to Chicago the year before to participate in Pat's convention. There would be a gala banquet and golf outing, tours of Glasnevin Cemetery and the Titanic Exhibition in Belfast, and plenty of good shopping in Grafton Street. The conference was held in Dublin Castle, a huge, walled compound in the center of that ancient city, with turrets and towers, dungeons and courtyards, dating to early in the thirteenth century—eight hundred years of history oozing from its stones. And I found myself constructing a line for the obituary I am always editing in my head that would someday in the long-distant future read, "He had presented to funeral directors from around the world." Travel and castles will do that to you. I was grateful for the invitation.

I had been to the castle once before. Indeed, I'd been to Ireland dozens of times in the forty-some years since my first visit there in the winter of 1970, in search of my roots and my future, as twentysomethings are wont to do. But my first visit to Dublin Castle was in the late 1980s, to the offices of Poetry Ireland, which were housed there in Bermingham Tower, to arrange for a reading tour of the country after my first book of poems was published.

And now, twenty-five years and several books later, rising to speak about our common calling to a room full of mortuary sorts from Asia and Africa and the Americas, from Europe and the Antipodes and just down the road, it seemed as if my life's works and preoccupations—poetry and funerals, the literary and the mortuary arts—were finally melding into one. They were, in many ways, the same but different: equal tributaries of the one enterprise. So much so, in fact, that I had titled my presentation after a poem I intended to read them called "Local Heroes." How many funeral directors from small-town, middle America, I asked myself, get to hold forth their ideas and recite their poems to colleagues from around the world in Dublin Castle in the middle of June? It felt like a gift and I felt lucky and exceptionally fortunate and it made me wonder, as Gus Nichols was giving me a generous introduction and I was gathering my papers and thoughts together and readying to rise to the august occasion, and praying, as we do, not to make the huge fool of myself that I have in me to do, I wondered *what exactly am I doing here?*

How do we come to be the ones we are?

I was raised by Irish Catholics. Even as I write that it sounds a little like "wolves" or some especially feral class of creature. Not in the apish, nativist sense of immigrant hordes, rather in the fierce faith and family loyalties, the pack dynamics of their clannishness, their vigilance and pride. My parents were grandchildren of immigrants who had mostly married within their tribe. They'd sailed from nineteenth-century poverty into the prospects of North America, from West Clare and Tipperary, Sligo and Kilkenny, to Montreal and Ontario, upper and lower Michigan. Graces and O'Haras, Ryans and Lynchs—they brought their version of the "one true faith," druidic and priest-ridden, punctilious and full of superstitions, from the boggy parishes of their ancients to the fertile expanse of middle America. These were people who saw statues move, truths about the weather in the way a cat warmed to the fire, omens about coming contentions in a pair of shoes left up on a table, bad luck in some numbers, good fortune in others. Odd lights in the nightscape foreshadowed death; dogs' eyes attracted lightning; the curse of an old woman could lay one low. The clergy were to be "given what's going to them," but otherwise, "not to be tampered with." Priests were feared and their favor curried—their curses and blessings opposing poles of the powerful medicine they were known to possess. Everything had meaning beyond the obvious. The dead were everywhere and their ghosts inhabited the air and memory and their old haunts, real as ever, if in an only slightly former tense, in constant need of care and appeasement. They were, like the saints they'd been named for, prayed over, prayed to, invoked as protection against all enemies, their names recycled through generations, reassigned to new incarnations.

My mother thought I might become a priest. Not because I was especially holy; rather, as a devout and Catholic mother of six sons and three daughters, she would've known the expected ecclesiastical surtax on so many healthy babies would be a curate or two and maybe a nun to boot. "Be stingy with the Lord and the Lord will be stingy with you," was the favorite wisdom of her parish priest and confessor, Father Thomas Kenny, of the Galway Kennys in Threadneedle Road.

∞

I was named for a dead priest, my father's uncle. Some few years after surviving the Spanish flu epidemic of 1918, he got "the call." "Vocations follow famine," an old bromide holds. No less the flu? He went to seminary in Detroit and Denver and was ordained in the middle of the Great Depression. We have a photo of his First Solemn High Mass on June 10, 1934, at St. John's Church in Jackson, Michigan, a block from the clapboard house he'd grown up in.

His father, my great-grandfather, another Thomas Lynch, did not live to get into this photo of women in print dresses and men in straw boaters on a sunny June Sunday between world wars. My great-grandfather had come from the poor townland of Moveen on the West Clare peninsula that forms the upper lip of the gaping mouth of the river Shannon—a treeless sloping plain between the ocean and the estuary, its plots of pasturage divided by hedgerows and intermarriages. He'd come to Michigan for the work available at the huge penitentiary there in Jackson where he painted cellblocks, worked in the laundry, and finished his career as a uniformed guard. He married Ellen Ryan, herself an immigrant. Together they raised a daughter who taught, a son who got good work with the post office, and another who would become a priest—like hitting the trifecta for poor Irish "Yanks," all cushy jobs with reliable pensions. He never saw Ireland again.

In the middle of the retinue of family and parishioners posed for the photo at the doors to the church around their freshly minted, homegrown priest, is my father, Edward, aged

ten years, seated next to his father and mother, bored but obe-
dient in his new knee breeches. Because the young priest—he
has just gone thirty—is sickly but willing, the bishop in Detroit
will send him back out West to the bishop in Santa Fe, who will
assign him to the parish of Our Lady of Guadalupe, in Taos, in
hopes that the high, dry air of the Sangre de Cristo Mountains
might ease his upper respiratory ailments and lengthen his days.

The young curate is going to die of pneumonia just two
years later at the end of July, 1936. The Apache women
whose babies he baptized, whose sons he taught to play
baseball, whose husbands he preached to, will process his
rough-sawn coffin down the mountains from Taos, along
the upper reaches of the Rio Grande, through landscapes
Georgia O'Keeffe will make famous, to the Cathedral in Santa
Fe where Archbishop Rudolph Gerken will preside over his
requiems, then send his body back to his people, C.O.D., on a
train bound for Michigan and other points east.

A moment that will shape our family destiny for generations
occurs a few days later in the Desnoyer Funeral Home in Jackson. The dead priest's brother, my grandfather, is meeting with
the undertaker to sort details for the hometown funeral at St.
John's. He brings along my father, now twelve years old, for reasons we can never know. While the two elder men are discussing plots and boxes, pallbearers and honoraria, the boy wanders
through the old mortuary until he comes to the doorway of a
room where he espies two men in shirtsleeves dressing a corpse
in liturgical vestments. He stands and watches quietly. Then
they carefully lift the freshly vested body of his dead uncle from
the white porcelain table into a coffin. They turn to see the boy
at the door. Ever after my father will describe this moment—
this elevation, this slow, almost ritual hefting of the body—as
the one to which he will always trace his intention to become a
funeral director. Perhaps it aligned in his imagination with that
moment during the masses he attended at St. Francis De Sales

when the priest would elevate the host and chalice, the putative body and blood of Christ, when bells were rung, heads bowed, breasts beaten in awe? Might he have conflated the corruptible and the incorruptible? The mortal and immortality? The sacred and the profane? We have no way to know.

"Why," we would often ask him, "why didn't you decide to become a priest?"

"Well," he would tell us, matter-of-factly, "the priest was dead."

It was also true that he'd met Rosemary O'Hara that year, a redheaded fifth-grader who would become the girl of his dreams and who would write him daily when he went off to war with the Marines in the South Pacific; who would marry him when he came home and mother their nine children and beside whom he'd be buried half a century later.

"God works in strange ways," my mother would remind us, smiling, passing the spuds, all of us marveling at the ways of things.

And so these "callings," such as they were, these summons to her life as a wife and mother and his to a life as a father and under-taker—a life's work he would always describe as "serving the living by caring for the dead," or "a corporal work of mercy," or "not just a living, but a way of life." And his sons and daughters and their sons and daughters, who now operate half a dozen funeral homes in towns all over lower Michigan, were all called to a life of under-taking. And all are tied to that first week of August, 1936 when a boy watched two men lift the body of a dead priest into a box.

How we come to be the ones we are seems a useful study and lifelong query. Knowing how we got to where we are pro-vides some clues to the perpetual wonder over what it is we are doing here—a question that comes to most of us on a regu-lar basis. Indeed, a curiosity about one's place and purpose keeps one, speaking now from my own experience, from going too far astray.

"Listen to your life," the writer and minister Frederick Buechner tells us. "See it for the fathomless mystery that it is."[1]

Thus a book that endeavors to say what I've learned from forty years as a funeral director might well be improved by some notes on how I came to be one.

"In the boredom and pain of it," Buechner continues, "no less than in the excitement and gladness: touch, taste, smell your way to the holy and hidden heart of it because in the last analysis all moments are key moments, and life itself is grace."[2]

All these years later it feels like grace—life itself—chancy as any happenstance, and yet we get these glimpses of a plan and purpose behind how we come to be the ones we are.

Possibly my father was trying to replicate that moment from his boyhood for me in mine when he took me to work with him one Saturday morning when I was eight or ten.

The old funeral home in Highland Park was a storefront chapel on Woodward Avenue that served mostly a Romanian clientele because the owner, William Vasu, was part of that immigrant community. There was an apartment upstairs, offices that flanked the parlors, caskets in the basement, and, at the rear of the building, the embalming room. We parked behind the building and entered from the back door whereupon I found myself for the first time in the presence of a dead human body. My father had not prepared me for this with any memorable warning or precaution. He did not tell me what I was about to encounter. I was simply going to the office with him on a Saturday morning. The tall, old man on the table was covered with a sheet except for his face. His bald head caught the sunlight from the transom over the door. The room was quiet and smelled like the doctor's office. He had large earlobes, a pointed nose, and thick glasses, though it was clear he would not be reading any more. In my memory of it my father is standing just beside me. And so I asked what the man's name was, how old he was, how did he die? The tense shifts are intuitive and provisional. What the answers were are long since forgotten, but that I was given answers and told further that I should pray for the dead man and for his family were apparently sufficient on the day, because near as I can figure I was neither damaged nor traumatized by the experience, only certainly aware of the change of gravity embodied in the dead man on the table. And there was, ever after, the sense that my father's work had importance and purpose, however imponderable it might have been at the time.

That was another received truth of my father's nunnish upbringing and my own—that life and time were not random accretions of happenstance. On the contrary, there was a plan for each and every one of us, and ours was only to discern our vocation, our calling, our purpose here. No doubt this is how the life of faith, the search for meaning, the wonder about the way of things first sidles up to the unremarkably curious mind.

When I was seven, my mother sent me off to see the priest to learn enough of the magic Latin—the language of ritual and mystery—to become an altar boy. Father Kenny, our parish priest, had been at seminary with my father's uncle and had hatched a plan with my sainted mother to guide me toward the holy orders. This, the two of them no doubt reckoned, was in keeping with the will of God—that I should fulfill the vocation and finish the work of the croupy and tubercular young man I'd been named for. I looked passably hallowed in cassock and surplice, had a knack for the vowel rich acoustics of Latin, and had already intuited the accountancy of sin and guilt and shame and punishment so central to the religious life. This tuition I owed to *Father Maguire's Baltimore Catechism* and the Sister Servants of the Immaculate Heart of Mary, who had prepared me for the grade school sacraments of Confession and First Holy Communion. I had learned to fast before communion, to confess and do penance in preparation for the feast, to keep track of my sins by sort and number, to purge them by prayer and mortification, supplication and petition. To repair the damage done by impure thoughts or cursing at a sibling, a penance of Our Fathers and Hail Marys would be assigned. *Mea culpa, mea culpa, mea maxima culpa* became for me the breast thumping idioms of forgiveness and purification, atonement, reconciliation and recompense that are so central to the holy sacrifice of the Mass we Catholic school kids daily attended. Thus were the connections early on established between holiness, blight and blessedness, contrition and redemption; and these powerful religious metaphors gathered themselves around the common table. It was all a way to be ever ready for the unpredictable death that might suddenly claim us. This theater replayed itself each night at our family meals where our father and our blessed mother would enact a home version of the sacrifice and feast, the brothers and sisters and I returning prodigals for whom the fatted calf, incarnate as stew or goulash, meatloaves or casseroles had been prepared. On Fridays my father brought home bags of fish and chips. Whatever our sins were, they seemed forgiven.

Likewise were we made aware of the assistance we might lend the dead in their pilgrimage between this life and the next. Purgatory was the way station between the joys of heaven and this "vale of tears"—a place where sinners were purged of the guilt of their trespasses by the cleansing of temporary flames. Our prayers, it was well known, could shorten this purging for "the suffering souls," and on certain days, notably the Feast of All Souls, we could pray them immediately into their eternal reward by coming and going into church with the proper combination of Our Fathers, Hail Marys and Glory Bes. There was a meter and mathematical aspect to our rituals and observances, and the dead, though gone, were not forgotten in our talk or daily rounds.

We were not alone in this. A version of my ethnically flavored religious training played out in the homes of my Lutheran friends and Methodists, Jews and Buddhists, Muslims and Humanists—each had a narrative about life and death, right and wrong, sickness and health, goodness and evil, life's endless litany of gains and losses, joyful and sorrowful mysteries.

∞

For all of my mother's and the priest's well-intentioned connivances, and though I kept my ears peeled for it, I never ever heard the voice of God. I remember seeing the dead priest's cassock hanging from a rafter in my grandparents' basement, a box with his biretta and other priestly things on a shelf beside it. I tried them on but nothing seemed to fit, and over time my life of faith came to include an ambivalence about the church that ranged from passion to indifference—a kind of swithering brought on, no doubt, by mighty nature. A certain sense awakened in me when I was twelve or thereabouts that among the Good Lord's greatest gifts to humankind were the gifts he gave us of each other. Possibly it was meditating on the changes I could see in bodies all around me and sense in my own body, late in my grade school years, that there were aspects of the priestly life that would be, thanks be to God, impossible for me.

If pubescence foreclosed any notion I might have had of the celibate priesthood, it was the early sense of mortality and of my father's association with it that shaped my adolescence.

I remember the neighborhood celebrity my brothers and sisters and I enjoyed because our father was an undertaker. And though it would be years before I understood that word, I knew it meant that he had a lot to do with dead bodies, which would eventually find their way "under" the ground.

As my brothers and I got older we were given jobs at the funeral home. Cutting lawns and painting parking blocks at first, then washing cars. When the first of our sisters was a teenager, she was put in the office to learn bookkeeping. And while she went on to become bookkeeper and comptroller of my father's business, my brothers and I matriculated to removals from homes and hospitals, dressing and casketing bodies, swinging the door during visitations, and working funerals.

We were dressed up in black suits, white shirts, and grey ties, shod in wingtips and barbered like men of another generation rather than the pimply boys we actually were, and we were paid by the hour to do whatever came up: cover the phones, work visitations, carry flowers, set up chairs, valet cars. It was a job. And it paid for our own cars, gas and maintenance, and left us enough money to go out on dates and other adventures. The summer days were long ones and we'd pile up a lot of overtime and lived like moguls. During the school year we would work shorter hours—evening visitations and Saturday funerals.

I think it was swinging the door where I first learned the powers of language and of presence. It was standing in the lobby of my father's funeral home that I first heard bereaved humans shaping the narratives that would carry them through their particular sorrow.

There were abridged versions:

"We couldn't wish him back, the way he was suffering."

"He sat in the chair and smiled at me and was gone."

"She never would have wanted to trouble any of us."

"She just slept away and never felt a thing."

"At least he died doing what he loved to do."

And longer renditions, which touch on existential themes:

> She woke in the middle of the night complaining of a pain in her back. And it was hard to know what to do or what she needed. I got her the heat pad and plugged it in. She asked me would I bring her a glass of water and one of her pills. But by the time I got back to the bed, she wasn't breathing. She'd rolled on her shoulder and her face was blue. It's as if the switch was thrown and the power was off. I still can't believe she's gone. I just always assumed I'd be the first and she'd outlive me by years.

Or the father of a dead soldier:

> God must just have looked down and said that Ben had learned everything life on the earth is supposed to teach you, even though he was only twenty-two years old, and we'll always treasure every day we had with him, so God must have said, "Come on home to heaven, Ben," and that was that. My son was a hero, and everyone enjoying freedom tonight has boys like Ben to thank for it all.

Or the daughter of a woman dead of cancer:

> She fought the good fight against it—surgery, chemo, radiation, even holistic cures—but in the end it just overcame her. But her courage, her stamina, her relentless passion for life has been an example to all of us.

Beyond the colloquies of the bereaved and the sympathies of family and friends, beyond the obituaries and eulogies and testimonials, were the raised speech and sacred texts of ritual and rubric: the Orthodox *saracustas* (prayers for the dead), the Blue Lodge services of the Masonic orders, the Catholics with their rosaries and wake services, and the inevitable obsequies and committals—ceremonies laden with Scripture and poetry, hymns and plainchants, psalms and litanies of praise. Both as helpless humans and as people of faith it was evident that language, with all its powers and nuances, became the life raft that kept the bereaved afloat in the unfamiliar seas of immediate grief.

It is nearly impossible to overestimate the balm that language can be. The familiar prayer, even to the lapsed and apostate, evokes a nearly protective order in an otherwise unspeakable circumstance. It became clear to me, early on, that a death in the family presented both the most faith shaking and religiously charged among life's many changes. And it is certain that many souls have been irreversibly won and irretrievably lost because of something said or read or sung over the dead in earshot of the living.

My fascination with language and its powers began very early. Sundays were, in particular, a feast of nothing so much as the various and best deployments of the lexicon. We'd go to church at St. Columban's in the morning, where the Latin liturgy was full of mystery and intrigue and the sense that we were communing in a supernatural and magical tongue. Father Kenny's homiletics—often red-faced and passionate disquisitions on the obligations of stewardship—were tirades in which the priest played every part of the conversation and always won the arguments he'd set up for himself, albeit ten or fifteen minutes after most of his parishioners had ceased to listen. The liturgy, laden with religious and spiritual metaphors that could be cyphered by the interlinear translations in the missal, gave even the most indifferent witness a sense of how the word did, indeed, become flesh. Sunday afternoons were spent at home with our large extended family. Often the aunts and uncles and cousins came, but always my two widowed grandmothers were there. My father's habit was to get them both a little liquored up and sit them in the living room and set them to arguing about something the priest failed to cover in his sermon, invariably involving religion or sex or politics— subjects that were studiously avoided in more refined families were just as studiously pursued in ours. When I would question my father on his motives, he would simply advise that I listen closely to "those old women," and I would learn more from their contretemps than I'd ever learn in school.

Of course, the sharpness of their discourse proceeded from the fact that they were opposites. My mother's mother, Marvel Grace O'Hara, it might be safely assumed, never suffered any low self-esteem. She was punctilious, grandiloquent, a rabid Democrat and union organizer. She became, eventually, superintendent of music in the Detroit Public Schools, raised three daughters and a son, outlived her harried husband by nearly thirty years, never discussed her age, and voiced her opinion on each and every one of her grandchildren whether she was asked to or not. She did everything in the faintly idolatrous style of the Irish-American Catholic for whom *The Bells of St. Mary's* and *The Quiet Man* were the principal studies.

My father's mother, on the other hand, was a quiet, formerly Methodist woman, a fine cook, quilter, gardener, and Eisenhower Republican who, I am sure, voted for him well into the 1980s; she wore print dresses, sensible shoes, her hair in a bun, and kept her own counsel, never giving any offense or scandal until early in the 1920s when she fell in love with an Irish-American Catholic. This did not please her Methodist kin, nor did her decision, in keeping with the custom of the times and to appease his parish priest, to "convert" to what she would ever after call "the one true faith?" (appending a lilt of uncertainty to the end of that phrase, as if the doubting saint whose name I also share, his finger aquiver over the wounded palm of Christ, was none too certain when he was heard to ask, "My Lord, my God?").

My grandmother would describe her conversion experience to us saying, "Ah the priest splashed a little water on me and said, 'Geraldine, you were born a Methodist, raised a Methodist, thanks be to God, now you're Catholic.'"

Some weeks after the eventual nuptials she was out in the backyard of their bungalow in Northwest Detroit, grilling beefsteaks for my grandfather on the first Friday in Lent, when a brother-knight from the local Knights of Columbus leapt over the back fence to upbraid her for the smell of beef rising over a Catholic household during the holy season. And she listened to the man, nodding and smiling in her quiet, formerly Methodist way, and when he had finished with his sermonette, she went over to the garden hose, splashed water on the grill and pronounced, "You were born cows, raised cows, thanks be to God, now you are fish." Then she sent the nosy neighbor on his way.

"Ah surely we are all God's children," she concluded her narrative, "the same but different, but all God's children, either way."

This notion that we are all "the same but different," struck me, on the one hand, as quite impossible—like being short but tall, thin but fat, old but young, this but that—and on the other it rang entirely true. It remains among the most serviceable wisdoms of my life. As does the bromide advanced by my other grandmother, to wit: "The ridiculous and the sublime belly up to the one bar." I did not, as a boy, know the meaning of this, but it had nonetheless the ring of truth about it, and in the lifetime since has proven to be among the most useful of the verities.

This, of course, was my first brush with author(ity)—the power of language to name and proclaim and pronounce and transform. Words could change cows into fish, Methodists into Catholics, things that were different into things that were the same. They held the power to redeem and reclaim and remake the everyday objects and people and concepts I was surrounded by. The voices of those dearly departed old women, quibbling over whatever came to mind, occupy one section of the chorus of voices that call us to become the ones we are.

> Ideal and beloved voices
> of those who are dead, or of those
> who are lost to us like the dead.

Sometimes they speak to us in our dreams;
sometimes in thought the mind hears them.

And with their sound for a moment return
other sounds from the first poetry of our life —
like distant music that dies off in the night.[3]

So wrote the great Alexandrian, Constantine P. Cavafy in his poem, "Voices." And this is how I still hear now *the first poetry* of my life, not in the voice of God speaking to me out of a whirlwind or out of the sky or burning bush, but in the voice of my parents and people, my elders and ancients and imagined ones—"ideal and beloved voices, of those dead or lost to us like the dead"—speaking to me, as if in dreams, like distant music that dies off in the night.

Sundays ended as all other days did, with our mother or father tucking us into bed with the prayer we all were required to say:

Angel of God, my guardian dear
to whom God's love commits me here,
ever this night be at my side
to light, to guard, to rule and guide.

This prayer, said at bedside—a grim little plea for protection against darkness and death—was the first poetry of my life. Long before I ever understood its deeper meanings, I heard the memorable, and not incidentally, memorizable rhymes between "dear" and "here," "side" and "guide." And the thumping heart-beating iambic code of the last line—to *light*, to *guard*, to *rule* and *guide*.

Its acoustic pleasures were immediate. Before it made sense, it made "sound" to me. It rang true in my ear. There were others:

God is great.
God is good.
Let us thank him for our food.

That is how they prayed before meals at Jimmy Shryock's house. I loved the off-rhyming between "good" and "food." Or when I spent the night at Mark Henderson's I was taught:

Now I lay me down to sleep
and pray the Lord my soul to keep.
If I die before I wake
I pray the Lord my soul to take.

It was a Protestant version of my Angel of God—involving the same grim contingencies, the same hopes, the same sense, and slightly different sounds that were metrical cousins to the secular poetics the world seemed full of:

Twinkle twinkle little star.
How I wonder what you are.
Up above the world so high,
like a diamond in the sky.

Or

ABCDEFG
HIJKLMNOP

Or

Tyger! Tyger! Burning bright
In the forests of the night
What immortal hand or eye
Could frame thy fearful symmetry?[4]

Or

Irish poets learn your trade
Sing whatever is well made
Scorn the sort now growing up
All out of shape from toe to top[5]

That quatrain about the Irish poets is part of a longer poem, "Under Ben Bulben," written by the Irish master,

William Butler Yeats, some months before he died in late January of 1939.

When the English master, W. H. Auden, got word of the great man's death, he wrote his elegy, "In Memory of W. B. Yeats," which includes this homage quatrain:

Earth receive an honored guest
William Yeats is laid to rest
Let the Irish vessel lie
Emptied of its poetry.[6]

And all of these sounded the same but different to me—nursery rhymes, prayers, alphabets, and poems—little seven-syllable meters, seasoned with rhymes to make them memorizable formulas:

Twinkle, twinkle little star
Now I lay me down to sleep
ABCDEFG
God is great and God is good,
let us thank him for this food.
Irish poets learn your trade
Earth receive an honored guest
William Yeats is laid to rest.

It was William Yeats who wrote in a letter to a woman he was trying to impress that the only subjects of interest to a studious mind were sex and death. How nice for me, I remember thinking in my early twenties, because I was predictably fond of sex, and the dead, as it turned out, were everywhere.

Thus were the hours spent working wakes and visitations at my father's funeral home, listening to the colloquies of mourners we met at the door, a daily instruction in the way of things—life and death and the shape of relations that gave them meaning and the rituals that tried to make some sense of the existential mysteries of coming to be and being and ceasing to be.

"If God speaks to us at all . . . then I think that he speaks to us largely through what happens to us."[7] That's Frederick Buechner again, in *Now and Then: A Memoir of Vocation*.

◌※◌

What happened to me while working at my father's funeral home was that folks began to treat me like a hero. They were so grateful when we would show up at the hospital or nursing home or family home in the middle of the night, so grateful for the way we handled their dead carefully and with respect. Or leaving after a long day's visitation at the funeral home, when a widow would hold me by the shoulders and tell me how very comforting it was to have us parking the cars and holding the doors and taking the coats and casseroles, directing folks to the proper parlor and bringing the flowers and for "just being there." Or turning from the graveside once everything that could be done had been done, how they would shake my hand or hug me and thank me profusely because "we couldn't have done this without you . . . thank you. . . . God bless you . . ." or heartfelt words to that effect. Such effusions made me feel useful and capable and helpful, as if I'd accomplished the job well done and all I really did was show up, pitch in, do my part. Before long I began to understand that showing up, being there, helping in an otherwise helpless situation was made heroic by the same gravity I had sensed when I first stood in that embalming room as a boy—the presence of the dead made the presence of the living more meaningful somehow, as if it involved a basic and intuitively human duty to witness.

By now I was beginning to think about sex and death almost exclusively—the former because I was in my twenties, the latter because, as the son of a funeral director, death and the dead were part of our daily lives. I was twenty-two and casting about for my calling. A high number in the Nixon Draft Lotto had kept me out

of Vietnam, my college career had been spent reading poetry and
playing cards and traveling back and forth to Ireland and the Continent in search of diversion and direction, I suppose. My younger
brother Pat was starting mortuary school that fall and, possibly
sensing my dilemma, my father asked if I'd like to go with him to
the NFDA convention in Kansas City that year. They convened—
nearly five thousand of them from across the country—on Halloween in the Hotel Muehlebach where all the meetings would be
held in the Imperial Ballroom. There was to be a dinner on Sunday night with music "by Woody Herman, in concert" for dancing; a "Special Ladies' Program"; another dinner "with radio and
T.V. personality, Art Linkletter!"; the usual sessions to elect offi-
cers, conduct association business, and take reports from various
committees; and a list of morning educational seminars. There
was what they called an "educational display of funeral merchandise and supplies in the Municipal Auditorium" across the street.
This display involved more than a hundred manufacturers and
suppliers of caskets and hearses and other accessories to the trade:
vaults and embalming fluids, printers of holy cards and thank you
notes, suits and shrouds and gowns for burial, canned music, candles and plastic flowers, grave markers, flags and insignia—all the
stuff that can be bought at wholesale, sold at retail just like books
and burgers and pharmaceuticals. There was a deep shine to the
limousines and hearses and I remember the odd names of things,
"Frigid Fluid" and "Progress Caskets," "Con-O-Lite" and "Phoe-
nix Embalming." It was a bit bizarre to be spending Halloween
filling our bags with freebees and samples from suppliers to the
mortuary trade—yard sticks and tie clips shaped to look like shovels and models of headstones and horse-drawn coaches—something for everybody, trick or treat.

But the stars of the exhibits were the casket companies: Batesville and National, the biggest and best, and Marsellus, which
made the mahogany cabinet President Kennedy had been buried
in. Springfield, Aurora, Boyertown, Belmont, and Merit were

there along with local and regional jobbers like Artco, Chicago, Missouri, Boyd, Delta, Quincy, Royal, and Flint. Each came with an entourage of salesmen, always smiling and glad-handing, eager to add to their accounts. And each of the caskets had its own name too, "The President" or "Permaseal" or "Praying Hands," which became a kind of litany of mostly metal caskets in those days, and polished woods, with plush velvet and crepe and satin insides that gave the impression in their collective display that funerals were mostly about the boxes.

Of course this was precisely the argument that Jessica Mitford had made less than a decade before with the publication of her muckraking classic, *The American Way of Death*. Because I was his bookish son, my father gave it to me to read when I was fifteen years old and told me to tell him what was in it. I told him I thought the style would earn her a lot of readers and that she would change the way people thought about funerals and that much of what she wrote was true and much of what she wrote missed the point entirely.

It was on the Feast of All Souls—that Tuesday in convention week—that the stuff began to give way to substance and the ridiculous began to make room for the sublime. That morning, NFDA's educational consultant, Robert C. Slater, who taught at the mortuary school at the University of Minnesota, arranged for what was called a "Think Tank" of scholars and teachers and clergy, each of whom had served as a consultant to NFDA. Robert Fulton, a sociologist; Dr. Vanderline Pine, a funeral director and sociologist; Dr. William Lamers, a psychiatrist and hospice pioneer; Robert Habenstein, author of *Funeral Customs the World Over* and *The History of American Funeral Service*; and Roger Blackwell, the marketing and consumer guru who taught at Ohio State University's School of Business, were joined by clergy-authors Rabbi Earl Grollman, Pastor Paul Irion, and Reverend Edgar Jackson, along with NFDA's Howard C. Raether and Robert Slater, to carry on an open discussion about the place of the funeral and the funeral director in American culture. Much of the discussion was shaped by questions from the more than 1,200 funeral directors in the ballroom. It was the best-attended session of the convention. These were writers and thinkers and professors and preachers and, in ways that casket salesmen were not, these were men of studious minds whose version of my father's work was much more serious than the cartoon that Jessica Mitford and the display of mortuary goods across the street would give one to believe. If psychologists, sociologists, consumer gurus, statisticians, the reverend clergy, and historians all found the funeral worthy of study, possibly the literary and mortuary arts could be commingled. And their topic was the funeral, as an event unique to humankind, as old as the species. Whereas the exhibits across the street proclaimed that the chief product of the mortuary were the cars and caskets and vaults and urns, piped in music and embalming, this think tank viewed such things as accessories only to the fundamental obligation to assist with the funeral. A death in the family was not a sales op, rather it was an opportunity to serve, in concert with the community of civic and religious, neighborhood and family circles that endeavored to respond to the facts of death.

"Take care of the service," I can still hear my father's good counsel: "and the sales will take care of themselves."

That night I told my father I'd be going to mortuary school. Some months later I was enrolled at Wayne State University's Department of Mortuary Science. After which I graduated, got my license, and the following year moved to Milford to take up residence in and management of the funeral home that our family purchased to accommodate the growing number of our funeral directors.

My friend and fellow in this book's endeavor, Thomas G. Long, writes with insight and candor about the changing religious landscape of America and the place of the clergy in a nation that is increasingly secular. The remarkable changes in religious practice over the past half century are coincident with, correlated to, and in many instances, trafficked in cause-and-effect with changes in our mortuary customs. Unlike the clergy who have fallen from great heights of approval, funeral directors have never been generally popular. It is the same with poets. While many people might approve the idea of poetry and are passably glad that there are poets at work, only a fraction of a fraction of the population can tolerate actually having to read a poem. Thus, a funeral director who writes poems is the occupational equivalent of a proctologist with a sideline in root canals. No less a preacher with a specialty in final things. Folks are glad to see us coming when there is pain or trouble, and gladder still to see us gone with their good riddance in tow. It was ever thus.

Thus, for two such unpopular sorts as my coconspirator and me to take on the toxic and oxymoronic topics of good death, good grief, and good funerals presumes there are others like ourselves for whom such things might be of interest.

As it often is among writers, I read Thomas G. Long before I met him. He published an article titled "The American Funeral Today—Trends and Issues" in the *Director*, published by the National Funeral Directors Association (NFDA). It was thoroughly original, full of original notions and insights and real scholarship and written in a way that even I could get. Some months later, Mark Higgins, a friend and fellow funeral director from North Carolina, secured for me an e-mail introduction. Reverend Long and I met in New York on the twenty-fifth of June in 1998. I was between stops on a book tour and he was teaching at Princeton then. He picked me up at LaGuardia, took me to lunch in the city, and told me about the project, just underway, which would eventually become *Accompany Them with Singing—The Christian Funeral,* the most important book on the Christian response since Paul Irion's *The Funeral: Vestige or Value* was published in 1977. Our views, shared over salads, arrived at so many of the same conclusions—some provisional, some hard-earned, some in search of replication—from our different vantage points and professional experiences. It is safe to say that the years Dr. Long has spent in ministry and teaching, coincident with the years I have spent in funeral service, have seen more changes in the nation's religious and mortuary customs and practices than in any generation before.

We first began working together doing daylong multidisciplinary conferences sponsored by the Michigan Funeral Directors Association for hospice, clergy, and funeral directors. The public relations firm hired by the association to work up some advance publicity advised that we could never get an audience for a conference called "The Good Death, Good Grief, Good Funerals." They saw it as a triple dose of the dire and dismal. "Think, 'good war, good plague, good famine,'" I distinctly remembered one of them saying. They proffered other more welcoming, heartwarming titles involving health and healing, celebration and memories. But we insisted that people who played on the front line of final things, the ones you would find out in the middle of the night en route to a home where a death had occurred, were among those rare and indispensable local heroes—hospice volunteers, pastors, good neighbors, and funeral directors—who drove towards such trouble rather than away from it. They would understand quite readily, we told the PR firm, what could, in fact, be "good" about death and grief and funerals. And they knew what could be bad. It is just such an audience this book hopes to find, those local heroes who ante up the power of their presence, their words that ring true, the quiet they can keep through the difficult vigils, and all they have learned of compassion, in service to their fellow pilgrims among the dying, the dead, and the bereaved.

One more thing: named, as I am, for a sickly priest and a famous doubter, the life of faith for me is constantly in flux. Some days it seems like stating the obvious to say that God is good, whoever she is. Still on others it seems we are entirely alone. Years ago I quit going to church on Sunday. I found myself second-guessing the sermons and the society of it all. It is a character flaw of mine, I readily confess. But compared to what I had seen and heard at funerals, when faith and hope and love are really up for grabs, the Sunday routine seemed, well, routine. When there's a body in the box at the front of the room or the foot of the altar and a family gathered round with a fist about to be shaken in the face of their maker and the reasonable questions about why such sadness and grief always seems to attend this life, that's when ministers really earn their keep. Baptisms, weddings, Sundays with the full choir and fashions on parade are nothing compared to the courage it takes to stand between the living and the dead and broker a peace between them and God. And inasmuch as I was going to funerals six days a week and hearing the clergy bring their A-games to them, on Sundays I began going to one of those places where they do twelve steps and smarmy bromides like "one day at a time" and "fake it till you make it," "let go, let God"—things like that. In the way things happen as they are supposed to happen, I arrived by the grace of Whomever Is in Charge Here at a provisional article of faith, to wit: if there's a God, it is not me. In the years I've been working and writing with Reverend Long, my faith has been emboldened by his own fierce faith. I think it is what we are all called to do: to embolden, encourage, behold, ennoble, instruct, and inspire our fellow humans in troubling times. It's what Tom Long's faith does for mine. It is what I hope this book will do.

Forty years since deciding, at a conference in Kansas City, to follow my father into funeral service, and two months after addressing in Dublin an international confab of fellow funeral directors, I find myself presenting to several hundred attendees of the Greenbelt Festival in Cheltenham, in the Cotswalds in greeny England.

These are mostly Anglicans and Methodists and seekers after some truth who come for a long bank holiday weekend to listen to Christian rock music and talks by poets and priests, the lapsed and beleaguered and devout. After my remarks, a woman in the audience stands to ask how might we "redeem" the funeral—that is her word—how we might redeem it from its failed and fallen ways.

Her question is at the heart of this book. And my answer is the same as it was to the funeral directors in Dublin: that we are all called to become local heroes; that the dead and the bereaved are the same but different everywhere, in need of someone who answers the call to show up, pitch in and do their part, to serve the living by caring for the dead; to be what Tom Long calls "undertakers." Because just as a good death does not belong exclusively to doctors or nurses or hospice workers, nor good grief to therapists, psychologists, or social workers, a good funeral belongs to the species, all of us, not just the clergy and funeral directors. Each of us must reclaim these last things for our own and for each other. Then I thought I'd finish with a poem, so I gave them the one that I was asked to write for undertakers in my country who answered the call to care for the victims and families of the 9-11 attacks. It has come to be for me an homage to the men and women who serve on the front lines of dying, death, and bereavement: the first responders, police and firefighters, doctors and nurses, hospice volunteers and clergy, funeral directors, no less the family, friends, and neighbors. These are the folks who can be counted on in times of trouble; they go out in the middle of the night, in the middle of dinner, in the middle of the weekday and weekend, holiday and holy day. Theirs are kindnesses that can't be outsourced or off-shored or done online. They are hand-delivered, homemade, deeply human, do-it-yourself. These are the ones whose voices make up the chorus that calls each of us in our own way to serve the living by caring for the dead and they are the ones for whom this book is written.

Local Heroes

Some days the worst that can happen happens.
The sky falls or evil overwhelms or
the world as we have come to know it turns
towards the eventual apocalypse
long prefigured in all the holy books—
the end-times of old grudge and grievances
that bring us each to our oblivions.
Still, maybe this is not the end at all,
nor even the beginning of the end.
Rather, one more in a long list of sorrows
to be added to the ones thus far endured
through what we have come to call our history—
another in that bitter litany
that we will, if we survive it, have survived.
God help us who must live through this, alive
to the terror and open wounds: the heart
torn, shaken faith, the violent, vengeful soul,
the nerve exposed, the broken body so
mingled with its breaking that it's lost forever.
Lord send us, in our peril, local heroes.
Someone to listen, someone to watch, someone
to search and wait and keep the careful count
of the dead and missing, the dead and gone
but not forgotten. Some days all that can be done
is to salvage one sadness from the mass
of sadnesses, to bear one body home,
to lay the dead out among their people,
organize the flowers and the casseroles,
write the obits, meet the mourners at the door,
drive the dark procession down through town,
toll the bell, dig the hole, tend the pyre.
It's what we do. The daylong news is dire—
full of true believers and politicos,
bold talk of holy war and photo ops.
But here, brave men and women pick the pieces up.
They serve the living, caring for the dead.
Here the distant battle is waged in homes.
Like politics, all funerals are local.

Where can I go from your spirit?
    Or where can I flee from your presence?
[8]If I ascend to heaven, you are there;
    if I make my bed in Sheol, you are there.
[9]If I take the wings of the morning
    and settle at the farthest limits of the sea,
[10]even there your hand shall lead me,
    and your right hand shall hold me fast.

Psalm 139:7–10

Chapter 2

FALLING INTO MINISTRY, LEARNING ABOUT DEATH

Thomas G. Long

I AM A PRESBYTERIAN MINISTER.

In my grandfather's generation, such a declaration might have earned a tip of the hat on the street, a window table at the neighborhood eatery, perhaps a "clergy discount" at the local haberdashery. But now, at least among strangers, it mainly turns conversations awkwardly quiet and squelches colorful jokes on the golf course. Perhaps this is why clergy and funeral directors, especially when we get to know each other as friends, find ourselves to be kindred spirits. We both tend to radiate cones of silence. Let a pastor or an undertaker walk into a lively room full of people and the conversational temperature will sometimes drop as the shadow of death or God, or both, passes over.

Lately, we clergy, frankly, have been going through an especially rough patch in public regard. Once near the top of the list of most admired professions, the pastoral office has been knocked around recently as a tawdry parade of priestly pedophiles, duplicitous bishops, embezzling deacons, crazed evangelists calling down hurricanes on iniquity, and eyeball-rolling, Koran-burning bigots flash dancing regularly across the television screen. The rabbi who spends every Wednesday visiting a nursing home or the priest who establishes a neighborhood literacy action program gets little press, but let some minister dip a greedy hand into the offering plate or get caught in a seedy motel with a pole dancer, and the fallen reverend will be doing a perp walk on "News Alive!" According to the polls, only about four in ten Americans now find much to admire in the men and women of the cloth. Our approval rating in the polls keeps pace with the Congress.

But the tabloid scandals would be but a nettlesome distraction were it not for the deeper trouble swirling around us clergy these days. The larger culture is undergoing a sea change in regard to religion generally. Protestant, Catholic, Jew—these were once the stable franchises of the religious establishment. But like an iceberg breaking away from the Greenland shelf, American society is slowly fracturing and drifting free from traditional religious institutions, and we clergy are caught in the backwash. With astonishing swiftness, the old religious monopolies, and the certainties they stood for, have broken up, and society now blossoms with vastly more religious variety than ever before imaginable. Even in small communities, where the choices were once limited to a few churches and synagogues, religious pluralism is in full sway, and the options are dizzying—mosques, temples, storefront chapels, shrines, prayer cells, crystal shops, meditation groups, covens, home-baked nature spirituality, and more.

The term "heresy" springs from an ancient Greek word meaning "to choose." The old world was marked by religious uniformity. When the village staked off the limits of one's world, every villager subscribed to the same myth, recited the same creed, chanted the same mantra, appealed to the same totem. Anyone who dared to choose outside the village way was, by definition, a heretic. But now society is a cafeteria of religious and nonreligious options, and, as sociologist of religion Peter Berger has pointed out, we are all forced to take our trays down the line and to choose.[1] People are compelled by the sheer force of the readily available alternatives to commit heresy. What'll it be? Baptist or Catholic? Muslim or Jew? Unitarian, freethinker, theosophist, Buddhist, evangelical, atheist, or none-of-the-above? We are not so much free to choose as we are condemned to choose. We clergy used to work hard persuading people not to become heretics. Now we try to help them become good heretics, shrewd heretics, folk who choose their brand of heresy wisely.

The novelist Walker Percy once imagined a comic scene in which John Calvin, the sixteenth-century theologian and church reformer, is improbably thrust onto the stage of *The Phil Donahue Show,* a television talk program in vogue in the 1980s. After introducing Calvin, who is dressed in his familiar black cloak and cap, a man clearly out of his time and place, Donahue turns and says, "Don't go 'way, folks. We're coming right back . . . ."

When the show resumes, the camera catches Calvin, who naturally doesn't get the idea of television or commercials, in mid-speech about redemption, sacrifice, repentance, and the mercy of God. Donahue interrupts, "Now wait a minute, Reverend. Let's check this out. You're entitled to your religious beliefs. But what if others disagree with you in all good faith? And aside from that . . . what's wrong with two consenting adults expressing their sexual preference in the privacy of their bedroom or, ah, under a bush?"

Calvin blinks into the camera, clearly puzzled, and finally speaks. "Sexual *preference*?"[2]

Preference indeed. As with sexuality, so with religion. It would hardly have occurred to a fifteenth-century peasant that he should be choosing his religion, his sexuality, his trade, his worldview, his position in society, his mate, or much of anything else about his identity. Now the magazines in the supermarket checkout suggest that we should be mulling over all of these, and more, as we put the lettuce and the cheese on the scanner belt.

Not many years ago I went to a graveside funeral for the mother of a childhood friend. The service was led by the family's pastor, a studious, kindly Disciples of Christ minister. The grave was located at the edge of a small-town cemetery, right next to a public park. As we gathered under the cemetery tent, we were all surprised to discover, fully underway in the park not twenty yards away from the freshly dug grave, a noisy ceremony of witches, chanting and performing a ring dance. Quickly sizing up the situation, the pastor wisely folded his prayer book and waited, shifting his weight slowly from one foot to the other, until the other ceremony had concluded. Then he turned to his small flock and, a bit bemused, softly began, "For if we have been united with Christ in a death like his, we will certainly be united with him in a resurrection like his."

We could hardly have been treated to a more perfect parable of the new religious pluralism. As I sat with the others, I thought of the good woman lying before us, awaiting her proper obsequies and a decent burial. I remembered her as I had first known her, as a Little League mom, a young wife and mother raising her children in the South of the 1950s, a land of churches and revivals and all-day Sunday School picnics, a land where we joked that there were "more Baptists than people." If someone had whispered to her then of the unseen future, a vision that her own funeral years hence would be delayed by a circle of witches, prancing and chanting to the moon goddess, she would not so much have disapproved of it as she would have simply disbelieved the possibility of it.

Some people respond to this new religious diversity and the choices it puts before us by turning up the volume on zealotry, by shouting intolerance through a megaphone. Most people, though, simply retreat to their own corners and keep their mouths shut. In a way unthinkable to the *Mayflower* Pilgrims, who hoped to turn their religious faith into a shining "city upon a hill," many Americans now want to scramble off the hill altogether when it comes to religion. Faith, they say, is a personal thing, a private matter best left in the hidden recesses of the heart. An Episcopalian married to a Jew living across the street from a megachurch evangelical and next door to a Muslim is likely to conclude that the price of household and neighborhood peace is to step politely and silently around this whole risky business of religion. After all, religious opinions and convictions can seem like sticks of kindling laid one across the other atop a pile of dry leaves. One careless spark and Nebraska could turn into Baghdad. William F. Buckley once quipped that at a New York dinner party you can talk about anything you wish, no matter how controversial. But if you mention God more than once, you won't be invited back.

So, I am a Presbyterian minister in a time when the old sureties are up for grabs, when the traditional religious institutions are under deep stress, and when many people feel that faith is a purely private choice and the world would be a saner, more peaceful place if religious people, especially clergy, would make themselves scarce and just shut up already.

Actually, I wouldn't want it any other way.

I like being a minister in a time when I have to get out into the noisy public square of competing ideas and opinions and negotiate a hearing for what I want to say. The seat of authority once ceded to the clergy is now crowded with rivals—swamis, personal coaches, spiritual directors, secular celebrants, and all manner of gurus, healers, and psychotherapists. Novelist Peter De Vries once noted that there was a time when people were afraid of being caught doing something sinful in front of their ministers, but now they are afraid of being caught doing something immature in front of their therapists.[3] I am energized by this collision of claims and claimants in the realm of the spirit. I am not nostalgic for the time when people would hear our sermons as bland incantations of conventional wisdom. They would nod approvingly—"Whatever you say, Reverend"—but they were actually in the first stages of nodding off.

I like being a minister in full public view when writing a letter to the editor or posting a remark on a blog or showing up at a political rally; or maybe just crossing the street wearing a cross and a collar is enough to suggest the embarrassing truth that faith cannot be kept secret and personal. I mourn the clergy scandals, of course, but I like it that what makes these sordid events *public* scandals to begin with is that underneath it all people hunger for priests to be trustworthy and accountable to others and for religious action to be able to bear up under the full disclosure of the sun. I like it that religion at its best is like going to an Ash Wednesday service and then showing up afterward for lunch at McDonald's, sitting there munching a Big Mac and fries while wearing on one's forehead the dark smear of a cross drawn in ashes and oil. The sacred and the profane, life and death, all mixed together and all out there exposed, for all to see.

And like Rhett Butler escaping with the beautiful Scarlet O'Hara as a doomed Atlanta burns around them, I even find hope in the collapse of the traditional religious structures. The old denominations are hemorrhaging members and funds, and many of the faithful wonder why God doesn't put a stop to it. Well, maybe God doesn't stop it because, just maybe, God started it. Perhaps God is tearing down the old patterns in order to build up something new, more faithful, more responsive to human need.

A clergy friend and now a Methodist bishop, William Willimon, whimsically dates the collapse of the old religious world to a Sunday evening in 1963 when the Fox Theater in Willimon's home town of Greenville, South Carolina opened on Sunday, in defiance of the state's Blue Laws. Willimon and six other members of the Methodist Youth Fellowship, made an appearance at church that Sunday evening, and then quietly slipped out the back door to take in the movie at the Fox. Reflecting later, Willimon said,

> Only lately have I come to see how that evening symbolizes a watershed in the history of Christianity in the United States. On that night, Greenville, South Carolina—the last pocket of resistance to secularity in the Western world—gave in and served notice that it would no longer be a prop for the church. If Christians were going to be made in Greenville, then the church must do it alone. There would be no more free passes for the church, no more free rides. The Fox Theater went head-to-head with the church to see who would provide ultimate values for the young. That night in 1963, the Fox Theater won the opening skirmish.[4]

I prefer being a pastor in a culture that does not give out free passes to me and my faith. I like being a Christian minister and theologian when Christendom is in tatters and all the prerogatives challenged. Because the problem is not when the world doesn't quite know what to do with the clergy. The problem, rather, is when the world knows all too well what to do with us, and what it knows to do is to domesticate the ministry and to file the edges off the pastoral role by providing reserved parking spaces at the hospital, a prominent seat at the head table so that we can pray our ceremonial invocations, and free clergy memberships at the country club. Ironically, I like being a minister in a time when religion itself is thought to be at least a little dangerous, because, truthfully, it is. Religion is not about holding a teacup properly at a church social. It is standing on a wild and windy mountain in the presence of the great Mystery. It is a claim of the truth from which all other truths derive. It is a white-water ride down the river of life. It will cause the faithful to lie down in front of tanks in Red Square; it will summon the devout to face down the police dogs in Selma; it will send mystics into the parched desert in search of the pure vision.

Some try to keep this danger at bay with the tepid language of respect. "Well, you know, I *respect* all religions." Respect is better than contempt, I suppose, but as literary critic and *New York Times* columnist Stanley Fish points out, a secular culture "counsels respect for all religions and calls upon us to celebrate their diversity. But religion's truth claims don't want your respect. They want your belief and, finally, your soul."[5]

As for the claim on my own soul, like many other ministers, I have a deep sense of being called to this work by God. In other words, ministry for me is not an occupation, something chosen at a high school careers fair, but a vocation. Like those old "Uncle Sam Wants YOU!" posters, a finger pointed in my direction and summoned me. God did not take over my self-control, of course. I got into ministry the way everybody gets to important places in life, by making decisions, playing hunches, following intuitions, and dumb chance, but even so, it is clear to me in retrospect that ultimately I didn't exactly volunteer for this; I got recruited.

I believe I was called to ministry. That is the truth, but saying it feels discomforting. Nothing seems to put up a firewall between clergy and the rest of us, between pastors and ordinary, sane people more than this idea of call. It's as if normal people become stockbrokers, lawyers, or bricklayers for mundane, rational reasons like making money, saving society, or following the family trade—but not pastors. No, we are, it seems, spiritual tuning forks vibrating to divine reverberations missed by the ordinary round of folk. We are a special tribe who somehow get whispered to in the midnight hour by white-robed Star Wars figures with flaming swords who speak in sepulchral voices, "Go to seminary. The Force will be with you."

But this is misleading. The fact of the matter is that most people who end up as priests, ministers, and pastors are not religious virtuosi at all, bear few markings of saints, and have made no As in purity of heart. In fact, most of us clergy spend at least some time explaining to the astonished people who knew us in our youth just how someone with our temperament and track record ended up as one of God's sky pilots.

In his memoir *Brother to a Dragonfly*, the colorful Baptist minister Will Campbell describes a day spent quail hunting with Thad Garner. Campbell, just out of Yale, was the new, very eager, very green, pastor of a small Louisiana Southern Baptist congregation. Garner, on the other hand, was a veteran and legendary minister in those parts, the pastor of a large Baptist church, chaplain of the volunteer fire department, and a famous revival preacher. He was also, as Campbell says, "the most profane man I have ever met. And, I suppose, in a way he was also the most profound." He drank a lot of wine, smoked a pipe, cussed a lot, and was powerfully wise in the ways of life.

> The day's hunt had been disappointing; not one bird had been flushed. But late in the day, the dogs got lucky and began pointing at what promised to be a large covey of quail. As the dogs moved in and the birds lifted suddenly from the earth and began to fly away, Thad fired three rapid blasts from his shotgun, managing, however, to miss every single quail. Thad began to turn the air blue. "Though I had not led what one would call a sheltered existence during my life," Campbell writes, "and my own language did not always measure up to garden party standards, I was not familiar with some of Thad's words."
>
> For a full sixty seconds the big Louisiana field was filled with his expletives. At the dogs, and the birds, at me, at the gun, at the manufacturer of the shells, at the Almighty—all

were profaned and reviled because of this misfortune. When he had quieted down he sank backward onto an eroded levee. I sat on the ground not far away. It was an occasion for a question I had wanted to ask him for some time.

"Thad, why did you ever decide to be a Baptist preacher?"

He looked puzzled and not just a little hurt. He pondered my question for a long time, sighting and squinting down the barrel of his shotgun. Finally he looked me straight in the eye and answered my question: "'Cause I was *called,* you damn fool!"[6]

So, why am I a Presbyterian minister? Because I was called, dammit. Few enter the ministry because we are dazzled by the starting salaries or prefer driving green Honda Civics to Maserati convertibles or covet a life of Saturday nights spent administering CPR to unresponsive sermon manuscripts or really get a kick out of "Hey Rev, must be nice working only one day a week" jokes. Like Abraham, like Moses, like Paul, like Sarah and Lydia, we clergy are mostly folks who were minding our own business, happy to be goatherds, pharmacists, or hedge fund managers, when suddenly a bush burst into flames and a voice informs us that Plan B is now in effect.

That's another thing. Burning bushes, I have learned, are almost never as dramatic in actual experience as they seem in Scripture. The call to ministry is rarely a Star Wars moment. Instead, the burning bush turns out to be a book we read, a speaker we heard, a tugging at our heart that won't go away, a chance comment made by the person seated next to us on the flight to Akron, a random observation by a friend. And burning bush experiences are not confined to the clergy. There are burning bushes aplenty in the middle of every one of life's deserts. God, it seems, has everybody's number and is constantly making calls, summoning us all beyond ourselves to some holy vocation. Clergy are simply the visible icons of what is secretly true of all mortals. This is one reason, I think, that ministers are such easy marks in jokes. It's a form of adult "Pin the Tail on the Donkey," a way of keeping at bay the overpowering truth that, here and there, now and then, almost every single person sees a burning bush out there on the edges of life, and we are all being called to the work of God, dammit.

In my case, the call came, strangely, through watching another minister go down for the count. I was in college, a chemistry major, medical school and a career as an internist in my sights. On class days, I found myself in the lab, running the gas chromatograph. On Sundays, I found myself in the pew at the local Presbyterian church, where the pastor was a young, intellectually astute visionary who spent his days blowing futilely on the embers of a congregation grown cold. He sprinkled humor into his sermons; no one laughed. He made passionate appeals on behalf of the gospel; no one was moved. He tried to lead them in new directions; they shrugged their shoulders and shuffled off the opposite way.

His main problem was that this was the late 1960s, and his sermons spoke clearly of the gospel's demand for racial justice to a flock firmly entrenched in the segregationist views of the Jim Crow South. He preached out of fierce love; they gossiped about him at the post office. He visited the sick, consoled the troubled, and buried the dead. They whispered about his wife, criticized his sermons, and schemed about how to be rid of him. He knew, of course, that he walked every day over a mine field of sinister plots, but he repaid no one evil for evil.

I watched him suffer this rejection. It had to be a lonely life, a painful life, but it also seemed a brave life, an extraordinary life, a faithful life, a life worth living. He eventually moved to another congregation in a distant state and found, I

hope to God, better soil for his ministry. But he left behind an
uneasy conscience in the town, a breathtaking portrait of the
breadth of divine love, an apprehension of God's unfinished
business, and—in my case—a stirring sense of call. I wanted
to be like him. I wanted to stand as tall as he had stood. I
wanted to mold myself after him. That was it. There was no
message written in the sky, no angelic appearance, no shaft
of eerie light falling on a key passage in the Bible, but just an
admiration for a courageous pastor going down for the third
time in the deep end of the pool. But after wrestling with my
thoughts for weeks, I finally saw them for what they were, a
summons to ministry.

I traveled home to tell my parents. They sat silently as I
shared with them what I, like a farmer harrowing the soil, had
been turning over incessantly in my mind. I told them how
I had finally come to a decision. I was not going to become
a physician after all, but a minister. The words were rapidly
tumbling out of me, and then, just as quickly, they stopped.
After a moment of suspense, my father nodded, if not with
approval at least with understanding, but my mother burst into
uncontrollable sobbing. This was not what she had dreamed.
Her son a minister! It was more than sad news; it was for her
like a death in the family.

Her reaction was not due to a lack of faith; she had plenty
of that. She and my father had raised me in the cradle of the
church. We were at least twice-a-week worshipers. My parents
had seen to it that, as a child, I learned the catechism. My
mother was a firm Christian, one who trusted the gospel and
who viewed ministers of the gospel with esteem. Her tearful
response, as I now think back on it, came because she had
seen too much. She had witnessed many times what I had
seen but once, ministers wounded by congregations, ministers
who, as Jesus said of himself, had played the flute for people
who would not dance, who had wailed for people who would

not mourn. My mother wept not because she was weak but because she understood the issues. My father imagined his minister son preaching wisely in the pulpit and confidently presiding at the communion table and was proud; my mother imagined her son carrying a cross, and her heart was pierced through.

She was inconsolable for weeks, scarcely able to speak about my new calling. The only thing that broke the spell was a stern note she received from a pious friend of hers, who told my mother, in so many words, to knock it off and to accept the fact that God had a claim on her son's life. Her friend closed with a paraphrase of Scripture: "The Lord hath need of him. Loose him and let him go!" When my mother showed the note to my father, he remembered that part of this paraphrase alludes to the New Testament story about procuring a donkey for Jesus to ride into Jerusalem. With a chuckle, he wondered aloud, "The Lord hath need of him? Loose him and let him go? Wasn't that said about an *ass*?"

True in its own way. I was a donkey in the fold who, for whatever mysterious reason, God had tethered for Jesus' next trip down the Mount of Olives. I wasn't even sure I had a real call. Maybe it was just hero worship of a brave pastor. Maybe at that confused season of my life I just needed to draw close to a very human father figure and had gotten it all mixed up with the voice of God. When I finally arrived at seminary, I was surprised and comforted to learn that almost everybody else's call to ministry was at least as messy and confusing as my own. Very few of my classmates told of unambiguous Damascus Road experiences, few reported midnight visions of the risen Christ beckoning them to ministry with words like "hark!" and "verily." Those who did were mostly lying or crazy. The rest of us had teased our sense of call out of barely visible patterns in the weavings of everyday life. The blowing of the wind of the Spirit often looks like a mere rustling of leaves in the live oaks. Anyway, my fragile sense of call managed to sustain me through seminary, and at age twenty-four I knelt on the wooden floor of an old chapel while others laid hands on my head and shoulders and prayed. When I stood up, I was an ordained minister.

My first parish charge was, all things considered, a vast relief. I found that not all congregations are populated with parishioners whose faces are like hatchets dipped in vinegar. There were bumps in the road, of course, but it was all made more than bearable by the fact that my little flock of Georgia Presbyterians knew how to laugh heartily, eat potluck suppers with relish, and show longsuffering love toward each other and their new young pastor. They were people of faith, but unimpressed by their own piety. They welcomed me into their homes and into the deepest recesses of their lives, forgave my convoluted sermons and my fretful tinkering with their order of worship, did not insist that my wife behave like a "preacher's wife," and greeted the birth of my two children with as much joy as if they were their own.

When Presbyterian clergy take ordination vows, we promise "to serve the people with energy, intelligence, imagination, and love." It's a tall order, impossible really, and I soon learned that ministry pressed me beyond my limits in every one of those areas. But I also learned that a crucial part of ministry has nothing to do with my intellect or creativity. Much of ministry is not about clever repartee, theological innovation, or pastoral charm, but simply standing up in front of people at crucial moments and announcing in clear and simple language what God is up to here. The secret was to let my feet take me to the places that mattered and to let my mouth say the words that counted.

So, when my congregation confessed their sins, I would stand in the chancel and, in words borrowed from the Bible, assure them that they were forgiven. Of course, it was not my forgiveness they were concerned about, it was God's. And that's what I told them; God was right here, in our midst, forgiving and not condemning. I stood there when they gathered in prayerful support around brides and grooms, their grown-up sons and daughters now beaming and bursting with yearning and trembling, making promises so awesome only God could actually keep them. At the right moment I would pronounce that a transformation had taken place, that this man and woman were no longer merely a bride and a groom but now a husband and a wife, and that their joining together was God's own doing. When we gathered at graveside and lowered a coffin down into the gaping earth, I would tell them that, despite appearances, this was neither the end of the journey nor the final word but that God was already speaking a new word, already performing beyond our sight and our full knowing another mighty work of hope.

Theologian Karl Barth called all of this the "impossible possibility" of ministry, the foolish thought that little human beings could stand there and take God's very words on their merely mortal lips, could presume to act out in their frail bodies what they believe God to be doing in the world. Barth thought the miracle of it all was not simply the absurdity of the act but the fact that God did not instantly destroy those caught in the presumption. The Danish philosopher Søren Kierkegaard once said that Martin Luther always spoke and acted as if lightning were about to strike behind him at any moment. After a few months of ministry, of presuming to stand in God's place and to speak God's words, I quickly understood Luther's apprehension.

So I am, by dint of a combination of flailing and calling and falling, a minister. But I am also a minister with a deep interest in funerals. In some ways, this is not unusual. Many of us parsons find ourselves absorbed by the power of funerals because this is often where we find ourselves the most useful. Sunday sermons, baptisms, confirmations, weddings, welcoming new members to the community, watching sadly as others moved or drifted away. This is the stuff of ministry, and ministers soon discover that it's cumulative, that it builds toward the time when the lives given to us by God are given back. It surprised me, indeed it almost always surprises young pastors, to discover that faith's message about life is nowhere more clearly brought to completion than at the time of death. Years after I served that first church, I was interviewing pastors as part of my research for a book on funerals, and many reported that they thought they did their best ministry at funerals. I understood.

It's not that ministry is fundamentally different at a funeral; it's just that the urgency of it is more apparent. On other occasions there are distractions. At a baptism there is almost always an uncle with a video cam, beaming and circling the font; at a wedding, some bridal coordinator is often in the wings, barking orders and directing the choreography. But at a grave, the grinning uncles and know-it-all wedding consultants have vanished. This is death, and no one knows exactly what to say or do. But something must be said, something must be done, and the pastor is the one standing there. The physicians have snapped shut their black bags and put away their stethoscopes, and the attorneys have not yet arrived to parse the will. The minister is standing there alone beside the grave, at the brink of all that we fear. If faith has no word for this, it has no word at all. The moment calls for faith, for bravery, even for presumption. So the pastor stands in God's very place and announces God's very own words, "Behold I tell you a mystery . . ."

But the river of my interest in funerals is also fed by other streams. When I was teaching at Princeton Theological Seminary, I made a chance decision to use a sabbatical year to write a textbook on funerals for pastors. The last truly satisfying book on funerals had been written nearly a half century earlier, I routinely taught a course on worship leadership that included a section on funerals, and I thought the textbook market was ripe for a new entry. It was a moderately ambitious project, and I figured it would take me the whole year to research and write it. As it turned out, it took me fifteen years.

One of the reasons it took me so long was that my research drove me into a windstorm of new data and fresh insight. I found all of my assumptions challenged and my presumptions blown away, so much so that I ended up writing a book *against* the book I started out to create. I had headed out on the venture intending to pen a tame, respectable book on how the funeral could be a gentle and comforting form of grief management. Exploring the history and theology of Christian funerals, though, led me into a much vaster understanding of the purpose and potential of a funeral, one that grows out of the wisdom of ancient tradition but that initially struck me (and continues to strike many of my ministerial colleagues) as counterintuitive, one that includes comfort for the bereaved, to be sure, but only as a part of a much larger set of tasks. It is a view of funerals I continue to explore in these pages.

A fine gift indeed in those years of research came in the form of meeting a funeral director and poet from Milford, Michigan named Thomas Lynch. I had read his provocative book *The Undertaking* early on in my study, and I marveled that this was not only the wisest and wittiest book I had read on death and funerals but it was also, in its own way, the most theologically profound. Tom Lynch's Catholic heritage has provided him with a salty reverence, a sacramental vision, and a weight-bearing vocabulary. I have learned so much from him over the years, I sometimes forget where my ideas end and his begin.

The writing of this book, that would eventually be titled *Accompany Them with Singing—The Christian Funeral*, also put me in touch with forgotten memories that I am now aware also shaped my passion for understanding death rituals. One experience from my teenage years stands out in particular. My uncle Ed ran an American Oil service station in a small town in South Carolina. He hunted and fished and told loud, uproarious jokes, never forgot anyone's name, and would extend generous credit to people he knew were hurting—and people loved him. One morning at the station, while he was still in his 40s, he reached up to get a fan belt off a wall rack, and his big heart failed him. He died behind the counter, leaving behind a grief-stricken wife and kindergarten-aged son.

The family gathered for the funeral. The pastor at the church was on vacation several states away when Ed died, and despite assurances from the widow that he needn't trouble himself to interrupt his holiday to travel back for the service, he insisted on coming to be with us and to preside at the funeral. He drove hard all night and arrived just in time to come to the family home to accompany us to the church.

The moment of his arrival was unforgettable. Indeed, as I look back on it now, it created in me not only an awareness of the power of funerals but also one of the first stirrings toward ministry. The extended family was all together in the living room of Ed's home, jammed onto the sofa and scattered onto the piano bench and various chairs borrowed from the kitchen and dining room. Through the big picture window we saw the minister arrive. He pulled up in his stripped-down Ford, got out and walked toward the house, all spindle-legged, wearing a cheap blue suit, clutching his service book like a life preserver. Now that I am a minister myself, I think 1 know what was going through his mind as he approached: "What to say, dear God, what to say? What words do you speak when words seem hardly enough?"

What he did not know, could not know, is how the atmosphere in that room changed the moment we saw him step out of his car. It was anticipation, but it was more than that. His arrival was, in its own way, a disclosure of the holy hidden in the fragmentation of our grief. This frail human being, striding across the lawn in his off-the-rack preacher suit, desperately trying to find some words of meaning to speak, brought with him the grace of God, the sudden awareness that we were not merely there to bury a dead relative but to venture out on a sacred pilgrimage.

In the Bible, there is a revealing story about ministry. A band of Hebrew slaves has escaped the clutches of the Egyptian Pharaoh and are now runaway refugees, stumbling their way across the wilderness of Sinai toward the dream of a promised land. But out in the lonely, unforgiving desert, they run into more trouble. The Israelites grow hungry and thirsty and, to make matters worse, they are suddenly ambushed by a gaggle of tribal warriors led by a desperado named Amalek. Moses, the leader of the slaves, has no arsenal, no strategic plan of defense, so instead he exercises the only option available: an act of ministry. He stands in God's place, at the top of a hill, and does God's deed; he raises his arms in blessing over the children of Israel.

Sure enough, under the arms of blessing, the ragged Hebrew underdogs prevail over the warriors of Amalek, but only while Moses' arms remain uplifted. Eventually, of course, Moses grows weary. Like all ministers before and since, he is finally ill-equipped to play the role of God for long, and his body starts to sag and his arms begin to droop. When they do, the battle tide turns, and Amalek's warriors gain the advantage. So two of Moses' companions—Aaron and Hur—take positions at Moses' side, one on the right and one on the left, and they each hold up one of Moses' arms until the battle is won.

It has been my privilege over the years to meet and to work with a number of deeply committed funeral directors who have shared the ministry of caring for people in seasons of loss. Together we have held up each other's arms of blessing. In seminary we teach ministers-in-training that when the phone rings at 3:00 a.m. and the word comes that someone has died, the best pastors pull on their clothes and go immediately to be with the mourners. When they do go, they will be comforted to discover that the best of the funeral professionals are already there, waiting there for them. Good pastors and good funeral directors show up. It's the first act of care.

Dear friend Thomas Lynch, a funeral director, and I, a Presbyterian minister, have written this book out of the confidence that we have much in common beyond the willingness to show up at the doorstep of death at three o'clock in the morning. Over the years, Tom's words, writings, and friendship have often helped to hold up my arms in blessing, and he tells me that I have sometimes done the same for him. This book is about how funeral professionals and clergy can think together about death, grief, and funerals, and how they can strengthen their mutual work. It is also about how all of us who tend to the needs of families in the time of death are unequal to the task. Our bodies sag and our arms droop. So we need to stand at each other's sides and, in shared strength, hold our arms aloft in blessing.

Caring for the Dead

I will teach you my townspeople
how to perform a funeral
. . . .
you have the ground sense necessary.
William Carlos Williams, from "Tract"

Chapter 3

HUMANITY 101

Thomas Lynch

THAT FIRST WEEK OF APRIL 2005 WAS DOMINATED BY IMAGES OF the dead man's body vested in red, mitered and laid out among his people with bells and books and candles, blessed with water and incense, borne from one station to the next in what began to take shape as a final journey. The front pages above the fold of the world's daily papers were uniform in their iconography: a corpse clothed in sumptuous vestments from head to toe, still as stone and horizontal. Such images, flickering across ubiquitous screens no doubt gave pause to many Americans for whom the presence of the dead at their own funerals had gone strangely out of style.

For many bereaved Americans, the "celebration of life" involves a guest list open to everyone except the actual corpse, which is often dismissed, disappeared without rubric or witness, buried or burned, out of sight, out of mind, by paid functionaries such as me. So the visible presence of the Pope's body at the Pope's funeral struck many as an oddity, a quaint relic of old customs. How "Catholic" some predictably said; or how "Italian" or "Polish" or "traditional;" how "lavish" or "expensive," or "barbaric." Such things were said after the deaths of Princess Diana and Ronald Reagan. "When in Rome," the perpetually beleaguered cable TV commentators would say, et cetera, et cetera.

In point of fact, what happened in Rome that week followed a pattern as old as the species—it was "human," this immediate focus on the dead and this sense that the living must go the distance with them. Most of nature does not stop for death. But we do. Wherever our spirits go, or don't, ours is a species that down the millennia has learned to process grief by processing the objects of our grief, the bodies of the dead, from one place to the next. We bear mortality by bearing mortals—the living and the dead—to the brink of a uniquely changed reality: Heaven or Valhalla or Whatever Is Next. We commit and commend them into the nothingness or some-thingness, into the presence of God or God's absence. What-ever afterlife there is or isn't, human beings have marked their ceasing to be by going the distance with their dead—to the tomb or the fire or the grave, the holy tree or deep sea, what-ever sacred space of oblivion we consign them to. And we've been doing this since the beginning.

The formula for human funerals was fairly simple for most of our history: by getting the dead where they needed to go, the living got where they needed to be. By acting out the necessary tasks to rid ourselves of dead human bodies, we came to understand the meaning of death. The dispo-sition of the dead inured to the benefit of the living, and so, unlike other living, breathing, eating, breeding things that died and were ignored by others of their kind—cocker spaniels and rock bass, warblers and wombats—our kind has always felt somehow duty-bound to do something with or for or to or about it.

You can try this at home.

If you have a pair of goldfish or angora kittens, parakeets or Pomeranians, geraniums or cacti—just about any animate being will do—when it dies in its own good time, watch what the other of its own kind does. There may be some sniffing or circling in momentary scrutiny but little else will happen. The surviving half of the former duo will simply swim or slink or saunter away, keeping whatever thoughts they have to themselves. Dogs may howl and kittens grow listless, and elephants and chimpanzees keep a kind of vigil. They have the heart for grieving if not the language, but they fashion no shrines or sepulchers, heavens or hereafters.

We humans are different and it was ever thus.

This too can be tried at home. Few parents have gotten through their child's childhood without having to fashion a coffin out of a handy box for a fallen bird or dig a grave behind the garage for the pet rabbit or turtle or officiate at a graveside service for the family dog. Even when it is not one of our own we construct sweet obsequies to make sense of those things we find hardest to put into words.

All the same, our mortuary responses followed on from nothing more remarkable than the fact that we die. The numbers have always been convincing on this, hovering as they do around one hundred percent: everyone who was ever born has or will eventually die. It was ever thus. And long before we began to fashion heavens or hells or purgatories, gods or devils or the unspeakable abyss beyond our ability to fathom; long before any of that we had to figure out what to do with the everyday trouble of a corpse on the floor.

Ours is the species bound to the dirt, fashioned from it according to the book of Genesis. Thus *human* and *humus* occupy the same page of our dictionaries because we are beings "of the soil," of the earth. The lexicon and language is full of such wisdoms. Thus, our "humic density," as the scholar Robert Pogue Harrison calls it: the notion that everything human—our architecture and history, our monuments and cities—all rooted in and rising from the humus: the earth, the ground in which our dead are buried, is what eventually defines us.

> The awareness of death that defines human nature is insep-arable from—indeed it rises from—our awareness that we are not self-authored, that we follow in the footsteps of the dead. Everywhere one looks across the spectrum of human cultures one finds the foundational authority of the prede-cessor. . . . Whether we are conscious of it or not we do the will of the ancestors: our commandments come to us from their realm; their precedents are our law; we submit to their dictates, even when we rebel against them. Our diligence, hardihood, rectitude, and heroism, but also our folly, spite, rancor, and pathologies, are so many signatures of the dead on the contracts that seal our identities. We inherit their obsessions; assume their burdens; carry on their causes; promote their mentalities, ideologies, and very often their superstitions; and very often we die trying to vindicate their humiliations.[1]

Years ago I took to trying to imagine the first human widow awakening to the dead lump of a fellow next to her, stone still under the hides that covered and warmed them against the ele-ments. This might have been forty or fifty thousand years ago, somewhere in the Urals or Mesopotamia or the Dordogne. Or maybe it was Lebanon or Uganda or the Congo around seventy or eighty thousand years ago. The species' history is a work in progress. Anyway, this is long before alphabets or agriculture, or any of the later-day civilizers. The species evolves from upright foragers and carnivores to upright forag-ers and carnivores who begin to think in symbolic terms. They begin to wonder. Symbol and image and icon and metaphor become part of their reality. What was it—I ask myself—that first vexed them into contemplations?

I always imagine a cave and primitive tools and art and artifacts. They have fire and some form of language and social orders. This first human widow wakes up to find the man she's been sleeping with and cooking for and breeding with gone cold and quiet in a way she had not formerly considered. Depending on the weather, sooner or later she begins to sense that something about him has changed quite utterly and irreversibly. Probably she smells the truth of this within a matter of a day or two. And what makes her human is that she figures she'd better do something about it.

Let us, for a moment, consider her options.

Perhaps she gathers her things together and follows the nomadic herd of her group elsewhere, leaving the cave to him, in which case we could call it his tomb. Or maybe she likes the decor of the place and has put some of herself into the improvements so decides that she should stay and that the now unresponsive and decomposing lump of matter next to her should be removed. She drags him out by the ankles and begins her search for a cliff to push him over or a ditch to push him into or maybe she digs a pit in the earth to bury him because she doesn't want wild animals attracted to his odor. Or maybe she builds a fire, a large fire, around and atop his rotting body and feeds it with fuel until the body is all but consumed. Maybe she keeps one of the bones for a totem or remembrance. Or let's say she lives near a body of water and counts on the fish to cleanse his remains; or maybe she hoists him into a tree and figures the birds will pick him clean. Maybe she enlists the assistance of others of her kind in the performance of these duties who do their part sensing that they may need exactly this kind of help in the future.

And here is where, in my imagination of this, Humanity 101 becomes the course of our history. It has to do with that momentary pause before she turns and leaves the cave, or the ditch or the pit or the fire or the pond or the tree or whatever oblivion she has chosen for him. In that pause she stares into the oblivion she has consigned him to and frames what are the signature questions of our species: *Is that all there is? Why is he cold? Can this happen to me? What comes next?* Of course, there are other questions, many more, but all of them are uniquely human because no other species ponders such things. And they align with questions that might have formed the first time she had sex or the first time she gave birth or the first time she was frightened by something in the sky or the dark. This is when the first glimpse of a life before or beyond this one begins to flicker into the species' consciousness and questions about where we come from and where we go take up more and more of the moments not spent on rudimentary survival. Maybe the way the sun rises and sets or the seasons change or the tide ebbs and flows begin to replicate her own existence. And maybe whatever made the larger and the smaller lights in the night sky and great yellow disk that moves across the day sky had something to do with her and the man whose body she is after disposing of.

And this is the point that I am trying to make: that the contemplation of the existential mysteries, those around being and ceasing to be, is what separates humans from the rest of creation; and that our humanity is, therefore, directly tied to how we respond to mortality. In short, how we deal with our dead in their physical reality and how we deal with death as an existential reality define and describe us in primary ways. Furthermore, the physical reality of death and the existential contemplation of the concept of death are inextricably linked so that it can be said, in trying to define what might be among the first principals of humanity, that *ours is the species that deals with death (the idea of the thing) by dealing with our dead (the physical fact of the thing itself)*.

Insofar as our *Homo sapiens neanderthalensis*—our first human widow all those millennia ago—is concerned, it was by dealing with the corpse of her dead man that she began to deal with the concept of death. This intimate connection between the mortal corpse and the concept of mortality, it goes without saying, is at the core of our religious, artistic, scientific, and social impulses.

"No form of human life," writes the sociologist, Zygmunt Bauman, "has been found that failed to pattern the treatment of deceased bodies and their posthumous presence in the memory of the descendants. Indeed, the patterning has been found so universal that discovery of graves and cemeteries is generally accepted by the explorers of prehistory as proof that a humanoid strain whose life was never observed directly had passed the threshold of humanhood."[2]

I want to emphasize that Bauman finds two elements to this "threshold of humanhood." First, "to pattern the treatment of deceased bodies," and secondly, "their [the dead's] posthumous presence in the memory of descendants." And when we find evidence of ancient graves and cemeteries, crematories, or other sites of final disposition, we can assume that they are venues where humans sought to deal with death by dealing with their dead—by treating their deceased bodies in ways that said they intended to keep "their posthumous presence in [their] memory."

And this formula—dealing with death by dealing with the dead—defined and described and, by the way, worked for humans for forty or fifty thousand years all over the planet, across every culture until we come to the most recent generations of North Americans who, for the past forty or fifty years, have begun to avoid and outsource and ignore their obligations to deal with the dead. They are willing enough to keep "their presence in the memory of descendants," (the idea of the thing), so long as they don't have to deal with "the treatment of deceased bodies," (the thing itself). A picture on the piano is fine, but public wakes, bearing the dead to open graves or retorts, is strictly out of fashion.

The bodiless obsequy, which has become a staple of available options for bereaved families in the past half century, has created an estrangement between the living and the dead that is unique in human history. Furthermore, this estrangement, this disconnect, this refusal to deal with our dead (their corpses), could be reasonably expected to handicap our ability to deal with death (the concept, the idea of it). And a failure to deal authentically with death may have something to do with an inability to deal authentically with life.

It bears mentioning that while this estrangement is coincident with the increased use of cremation as a method of disposing of the dead over the same half century, and may be correlated to it, cremation is not the cause of this estrangement. Indeed, cremation (which will be treated at length in chapter 7) is an ancient and honorable and effective method of body disposition, but in most cultures where it is practiced it is done publicly in ceremonial and commemorative venues, whereas in North America very often it is consigned to an off-site, out-of-sight, industrial venue where everything is handled privately and efficiently. Only in North America has cremation lost its ancient connection to fire because it is so rarely actually witnessed. In North America, in the past fifty years, cremation has become synonymous with disappearance, not so much an alternative to burial or entombment, rather an alternative to having to bother with the dead body.

As Mark Duffey, who operates a "funeral concierge service" proclaimed:

> "Baby boomers are all about being in control," said Mr. Duffey, who started his company after running a chain of funeral homes. "This generation wants to control everything, from the food to the words to the order of the service. And this is one area where consumers feel out of control."
>
> What they want, he said, are services that reflect their lives and tastes. One family asked for a memorial service on the 18th green of their father's favorite golf course,

"because that's where dad was instead of church on Sunday mornings, so why are we going to church?" Mr. Duffey said. "Line up his buddies, and hit balls." Another wanted his friends to ride Harleys down his favorite road, scattering his ashes.

The biggest change, Mr. Duffey said, is that as more families choose cremation—close to 70 percent in some parts of the West—services have become less somber because there is not a dead body present. "The body's a downer, especially for boomers," Mr. Duffey said. "If the body doesn't have to be there, it frees us up to do what we want. They may want to have it in a country club or bar or their favorite restaurant. That's where consumers want to go."[3]

This, of course, is exactly what the British gadfly and writer, Jessica Mitford, envisioned when she wrote *The American Way of Death*—a funeral without the "downers," most notably a corpse and a creedal obligation.

In some areas of the country—the East and West Coasts notably—the dismissal of the dead from their own "memorial services" has become the new normal. For testimony on the East Coast variation on this theme, there might be no better text than the recent memoir by the poet, Megan O'Rourke. A studious child who grew into a bookish woman, for whom reading and writing made sense of a world full of mystery and happenstance, O'Rourke writes with arresting power.

"We read books on the porch all afternoon," she writes in the Prologue to *The Long Goodbye: A Memoir of Grief*, recounting the summers of her childhood. "I was a child of atheists, but I had an intuition of God. The days seemed created for our worship." The daughter of educators and a graduate of Yale, O'Rourke began her career, as her bio professes, as "one of the youngest editors in the history of *The New Yorker*,"[4] and later at *The Paris Review* and *Slate.com*. Her first book of poems, *Halflife*, published in 2007, earned good reviews in the best of places. So when her mother died, of metastatic colorectal cancer shortly before three p.m. on Christmas Day of 2008, little wonder that she would seek solace in books. Five pages of bibliography— from Phillip Aries to Virginia Wolf—attest to her thoroughgoing scholarship. She avoids Mitch Albom but dives headlong into John Bowlby, Erich Lindemann, and Geoffrey Gorer. Likewise, little wonder she'd be moved to write. *The Long Goodbye* and her most recent book of poems, *Once,* are both memorials to her mother's cancer and death and the attendant griefs.

Still, a death in the family is more than a readerly or writerly event, and if Barbara Jean Kelly O'Rourke had died at fifty-five on the west coast of Ireland rather than the East Coast of America, the obsequies would be entirely different. The dutiful services of daughters in West Clare involve the corpse—its dressing and laying out, its transport and disposition—whereas in Westport, Connecticut, the response to death is more, well, *conceptual*: more the idea of the thing than the thing itself.

The Long Goodbye is a record of two bereavements, one as old as the species, to wit: a child's parent dies; the other, oddly postmodern, special to the last couple generations. The first one is told with grace and candor: "Mainly, I thought one thing: *My mother is dead and I want her back.* I wanted her back so intensely that I didn't want to let go."[5] The writing is richly wrought, detailed, open-eyed, intuitive. But this is the oldest story in the book. Grief is, as O'Rourke concedes, quoting Hamlet's mother, "common."

The newer story, a fresh lament raised within the context of the old one, is the story of a culture and a family bereft of existential narratives and metaphors, gone ritually adrift and left clueless as to what to do when someone dies. "After my mother's death, I felt the lack of rituals to shape and support my loss. I found myself envying my Jewish friends the practice of saying Kaddish, with its ceremonious designation of time each day devoted to remembering the lost person. As I drifted through the hours, I wondered: What does it mean to grieve when we have so few rituals for observing and externalizing loss?"[6] What Megan O'Rourke missed, along with a couple generations of Americans, was the year of mourning or some version of it, which granted to the bereaved some time to grieve as well as outlining customs meant to assist the mourner.

In O'Rourke's Connecticut, death and grief are quite literally, disembodied:

> They took my mother's body away so quickly. There we all were, touching her, hugging her, kissing her, saying goodbye. A year ago. For twenty minutes she was warm and she didn't look dead. She didn't look alive either. But she didn't have the glazed, absent expression I had expected. Her being seemed present. I could feel it hovering at the ceiling of the room, changing, but not gone. I could have spent days with the body, getting used to it, loving it, saying goodbye to it.[7]

This inclination to "spend days with the body," much like her "intuition of God," are vestigial leanings towards the societal norms of wake and funeral, shiva and Kaddish—a primal obligation to witness or participate in the body's burial or burning or disposition—a version of which almost every human culture has observed since the beginning. These are customs that have only been abandoned in the last fifty years in favor of a more "virtual" or "convenient" commemorative event.

Her mother's body, for month's the cancerous center of energy and attention, recorded in detail in this memoir, is disappeared by functionaries on Christmas evening, cremated without witness or rubric and returned as ashes in a cardboard box that goes unnoticed in the household for another year. How far removed from any obligation to take part in the disposition of the dead is measured by O'Rourke without irony. It simply never occurred to her at the time to wonder what has become of the body that was taken from the home. One supposes that a phone call and a credit card are all that's required to affect the disappearance of what remains of the person around whom so much of the family's attention had circled for months before her final breath was taken. That it might never have occurred to the author to wonder about any of the adverbials—place, time, manner, cause, circumstance, degree—attached to the removal of her mother's corpse, and that her obliviousness could survive a year is breathtaking for its detachment.

> As I passed my father's open bedroom door, I saw a large, square white cardboard container on a side table. My heart started beating faster, I went in. The box bore a plain label that read, in neat type, BARBARA JEAN KELLY O'ROURKE. If the box had always been there, I had managed never to see it. Now, the morning of the anniversary of her death, I recognized it as the container of my mother's ashes.[8]

Had her mother died on the West Clare peninsula on the other side of the Atlantic, her daughter and her family would have had to mix their grief with dozens of duties and details to do with her final disposition. They would have to help lay her out, most likely in the bed she had died in. They might assist with the washing, dressing, and arrangement of the corpse—fresh linens for the bed, a rosary to hold her hands together, candles lit against any early putrefaction. Food and drink would have to be laid in for the wake, fresh clothes for the immediate family, trips to the airport for returning kin. There would be a visit with the priest or pastor to arrange things in church; talk of hymns and Scriptures and eulogists; a call to neighbors who might open the grave; and another call to the funeral director for a coffin, the hearse, newspaper notices, and memorial cards. There'd be a procession into town to lay out the dead for the larger community. And everything accomplished in a matter of days to match the urgency that nature assigns to death. Then a "month's mind" Mass in thanksgiving for the sympathies and kindness of friends and neighbors and to keep the conversation of mourning open, encouraged, approved of for the coming year. Then consultations with the stonecutters for a headstone to mark the place and the space assigned to the dead in the public landscape.

But for the O'Rourke's of Connecticut things are different. The body removed the Christmas before has been transformed to a downsized version of its former self. With no practical obligations to deal with her mother's dead body, O'Rourke has spent the intervening year searching out metaphors and resources and do-it-yourself ceremonials—the ubiquitous "celebration of life." No longer attached to any ethnic, religious, or regional culture that could be counted on for direction around a death in the family, she is left to reinvent the wheel that works the space between the living and the dead herself. She reads, she writes, she weeps, she tries to cope. Eventually there's a reading of Keats and a selection of wines at a service where the good laugh is approved while the good cry seems awkward.

> At the time the speedy removal felt natural, perhaps because I had no idea what to expect. Now, however, there is a blankness at the center that troubles me. We're too squeamish for the ritualistic act of cleansing and purifying, the washing of the body, that used to take place in other times, and still does, in other places, but I wonder if it might have helped me to take care one last time of the body I'd cared about my entire life.[9]

Grief work, as Geoffrey Gorer called it years ago, is not so much the brain's to do, as the body's. And it is better done by large muscles than gray matter; less the burden of cerebral synapse and more of shoulders, shared embraces, sore hearts.

Possibly, Meghan O'Rourke seems to say unambiguously, before the library or bookstore or Googling grief, we might better see them on their way, to the crematory or cemetery, where the first object lesson in grief is that by getting the dead where they need to go, the living get nearer where we need to be.

For the West Coast iteration of these issues there is, perhaps, no more reliable witness than Alan Ball, the creator and producer of the HBO series *Six Feet Under*, a black-comedy-drama that ran for five seasons and sixty-three episodes between June of 2001 and August of 2005.

Shot on location in Los Angeles and in Hollywood studios, the show won nine Emmy Awards, three Screen Actors Guild Awards, three Golden Globe Awards, and a Peabody Award. It followed the lives and times of the Fisher family, who operate their own Ma and Pa mortuary in L.A. Nathaniel Fisher, husband to Ruth and paterfamilias, is killed in the very first episode of the show. It is Christmas Eve when the brand new hearse he is driving to the airport to pick up his son Nate is broadsided by a bus. His children, the prodigal Nate, the dutiful David—who has followed his father into the family business—and Claire, his teenage daughter, must assist their mother with the funeral plans. This sets a pattern for the weekly episodes to follow, each of which will begin with a death, some sudden, some protracted, some ridiculous, some sublime, some shocking, some mundane. What is clear is that the show needs a corpse in every episode for the plot to accomplish its purposes, the denouement of which very often coincides with the disposition of the body.

When I heard Terry Gross interview Alan Ball on NPR's "Fresh Air," soon after the show's premier that June of 2001, I was flattered to hear him tell her that he had read my books on the subject of funerals and death.

There were so many similarities. Like David Fisher, I had taken up my father's business, and like David I had embalmed my father when he died, and like David, I still heard my dead father's counsel in difficult situations.

Needless to say I was a little starstruck, what with the Hollywood of it all and that an Oscar-winning artist and filmmaker had trained his attention on the quotidian work of morticians and their extended families. I also knew that what informed his vision were the experiences of death and grief in his own life, notably the horrific death of his older sister on her twenty-second birthday when he was thirteen and she was driving him to his music lesson when the car was broadsided on the driver's side. Terry Gross had questioned him in some detail during the "Fresh Air" interview on NPR about her death and funeral.[10] It was, by his account, a life-changing event.

"My life was very clearly separated into before and after at that moment," he tells Gross. "It was profoundly shocking . . . and I will carry deep scars until the day I die." He remembers the blood and the ambulance and the lie he was told by everyone about his sister being OK until the family physician, driving him home to his parents and telling him he'd "have to be strong" for his parents, let slip to Ball what actually happened. Ball could recall the physical feeling of "the bottom dropping out from under me," when he was told, and the surety that his life would never be the same.

Asked about how her funeral was he answers, "surreal . . . very surreal." Described as the "traditional open casket thing," he recounts, at his first sight of his sister in the casket, wondering "who's that?" They had given her "big boofey hair" and a lipstick color she would never have worn. "And I'm sorry," he says, "when they lay those bodies out in caskets, they look phony, like wax figures." He reports that for him this surreal event was "not at all comforting."

Worse still, he continues to Terry Gross, was that his mother's grief, her loud weeping, her "breaking down," was seen by the funeral home staff as problematic, and she was ushered into a side room behind a curtain where she might be expected to compose herself, as if amplified emotions were somehow inappropriate at the sight of your dead daughter's body in a box. As if "breaking down" was caused by some weakness or structural difficulty. Witnessing these reactions, along with the family doctor's well-intentioned but mistaken counsel about "being strong" for his parents, left the thirteen-year-old Ball no option for the authentic expression of his own deep hurt. The message he took from it was that grief should be quiet and private, muffled and subdued, hidden behind a curtain in an adjacent room. "That's a lie!" he tells Terry Gross, "what you need to do is scream, bang on the wall, tear at your hair, because grief is a primal thing and the only way out of it is through it." He describes his family's long term reaction: "Everyone splintered and went into their own little world, and there's a dynamic of that in the Fishers." And by his own account it took him another twenty-five years before really dealing with his sibling's death.

From the very first episode of the first season it was clear Ball wanted to change the conversation about funerals—a conversation that had, since the publication of Jessica Mitford's book in 1963 and its revision and reissue in 1998, revolved almost entirely around how much a funeral might cost. Such a dialogue, after a while, becomes tiresome—How much did you spend? How much did you save?—as if the math of caskets mattered most.

That said, Jessica Mitford changed my life. I was fifteen, working nights and weekends at my father's funeral home, greeting mourners at the door and moving flowers and caskets, when *The American Way of Death* was first published in 1963.

My father bought it and said I should read it. At first it seemed about funereal fashion—the boxes and cosmetics, the unctuous euphemisms of undertakers, their "beautiful memory pictures" and "grief therapy," the laughable sales pitches of cemetery moguls. Mitford took them all to task. In a culture that did not discuss these things, her willingness to do so was new. To an enterprise shrouded in darkness she brought her curiosity, wry humor, and wary indignation. So much of what we do when someone dies has been shaped by her commentary.

Whether or not they've ever read it, most of the families I've dealt with through the years have in their heads a version of Mitford's book. It has entered the conventional wisdom, seamlessly: that funeral directors are determined to sell you something you don't want for a price you can't afford, by preying on your grief and guilt—these are all articles of that conventional wisdom. Not only was this at odds with my experience and perceptions of my father's conduct, but they were at odds with a business model that relied on a community's good will as a guarantee of future business. Because most of the families who called us for help were those who had called us years before in similar circumstances, it made no sense that we could retain their confidence by abusing the trust they had placed in us. Serving a family in accordance with their wants, needs, and financial abilities was not only good ethical conduct, but good business as well. And where damage to one's building or rolling stock or equipment could be repaired or replaced, a stain on one's reputation would be permanent. And yet Jessica Mitford's book sold five million copies in the first summer after publication. My interest in her work and her impact on ours was keen and longstanding. Some months after their mother died, I secured an introduction to Jessica's daughter Constancia Romilly (whom Mitford nicknamed "Dinky") and Benjamin ("Benji") Treuhaft, who is Dinky's half brother and Jessica's youngest son. I had questions I wanted to put to them about *The American Way of Death Revisited,* published in 1998, a new edition of her best-selling book, which she had been working on at the time of her death, and which had been completed by some of her admirers. I also had questions about what was not in the books, but things I had heard from friends in the UK and America, so I invited them all to dinner in Manhattan's East Village.

"You should have seen my mother's funeral," Benjamin said. "Everybody loved it! They really, really liked it because there was no gloom." I asked if they thought their mother would approve, what with her celebrated preferences for simplicity and cost controls, of what turned out to be fairly elaborate transatlantic memorials. Her body had been cremated, the ashes scattered in the Pacific, but after that things got pretty pricey.

"The person who dies doesn't get to say anything about their funeral," Dinky said, "no matter how many books they might have written about it. The funeral is for the people who are left behind. They get to do whatever they want. No matter what the person wanted. So I used to tell Jessica, we're going to do whatever we want. We're going to have a New Orleans Band."

Jessica Mitford was born in the Cotswolds in 1917. Her parents were robustly right-wing aristocrats. One sister became a Nazi, another married Sir Oswald Mosley. Jessica rebelled by becoming what another sister, the novelist Nancy Mitford, called "a ballroom Communist," which is to say, someone who is at home in the free clinic with the other needy mothers and on the island in the Hebrides she will eventually inherit, the sort who tips well but likes to shoplift—an enigma, but a charming one. In 1937 Jessica ran off with a cousin, Esmond Romilly, a nephew of Churchill, to fight the fascists in Spain. They married. Her father disowned her. They returned to London, then left for America, where they worked in Washington and Florida. Esmond was killed in action during the Second World War, when the plane he was flying for the Royal Canadian Air Force was shot down over the English Channel, leaving her with the infant Constancia, and a job with the Office of Price Administration, "as close to the front-line of the war against fascism as anything in Washington,"[11] as she wrote in her second autobiography, *A Fine Old Conflict*. There she met Bob Treuhaft, a civil rights attorney. That he was handsome and brilliant and Jewish and from the Bronx, and well to the left, and that her father could be counted on to disapprove, all made the match the more dear. They married, settled in California, joined the Communist Party. He worked for the trade unions. They had two sons: Nicholas, then Benjamin. In 1954 Nicholas, age ten, was killed when a bus hit him as he was cycling near their home in Oakland. "We went dysfunctional," his siblings told me. "We couldn't talk to each other. We never talked about it again. It was as if Nicky was eradicated from the family." The dead boy's sister wore a red pleated dress to his memorial. She remembers the dress, people milling around, and a sense of total despair. "It's all blocked out," the younger brother says when asked what he recalls. Benjamin was seven and Constancia was thirteen when Nicky was killed. Jessica had been through the death of a child before, in London before the War. Her first daughter, Julia, died at age four months, of a fever during a measles epidemic. Jessica and Esmond chose the geographical cure. "The day after the baby was buried," she wrote, in the sad, solitary paragraph she devoted to her daughter's death in *Hons and Rebels,* her first autobiography, "we left for Corsica. There we lived for three months in the welcome unreality of a foreign town, shielded by distance from the sympathy of friends."[12] The sympathy of friends would have required the young bereaved parents to acknowledge that something of substance had happened, but Mitford seemed determined to keep the sadness out-of-sight and out of mind. Her first husband, her first daughter, her first son: disappeared at death, banished from family conversation and erased from the text of her biography lest they occasion feelings that might overwhelm.

As a Communist, Benjamin and Constancia explained to me, their mother did not believe in "that pie in the sky when you die thing" and, as a product of her class and times, had no faith in psychology. She embraced the unreality of California, and there was a ban on talk within the family. "We did our best," recalls Dinky, "but we didn't do very well."

"To trace the origins of this book," writes Jessica in the introduction to the revisited edition, "my husband, Bob Treuhaft, got fired up on the subject of the funeral industry in the mid-to-late Fifties."[13] Jessica joined in, mounting what she calls her "frontal assault on one of the seamier manifestations of American capitalism."[14] Her first article on the subject, called "St. Peter Don't You Call Me," was published in 1958. "The undertakers," she says, "were an easy target," and the topic allowed her to "give full rein to my subversive nature."[15] But it had more to do with dollars than with death. The math of caskets and the smarminess of casket peddlers and the unseemliness of fussing over bodies were her primary studies. Perhaps Evelyn Waugh, no sympathetic witness for the dismal trades, had it right when he wrote in his review of the book, "I sniff in Miss Mitford's jolly book a resentment that anyone at all (except presumably writers) should make any money out of anything. The presence of death makes the activities of undertakers more laughable, but I feel she would have the same scorn for hatters or restaurateurs."[16]

There was, nonetheless, a fundamental element of funerals that Jessica truly abhorred. For all her carping about boxes and embalming, it was the bodies of the dead that bothered her, those unwelcome realities whose stillness leaves us dumbstruck and bereft of punch lines. It is largely on her advice that we have become, in the decades since her book was first published, the first of our species to have our dead "disappeared," "banished," and "erased." What put her off most about the American way of death was our tendency to mark our losses and grieve for our dead in ways that—for intensely personal reasons, as it turns out—she could never understand.

"Decca would do anything for a laugh," her daughter told me. One can only speculate on what she'd think of the multimedia intercontinental extravaganzas in California and London that marked her death. Committees were formed and money was raised and halls were engaged and music selected and speakers arranged, and a good cause (Benjamin's "Send a Piana to Havana" project) named for memorial contributions. In London, the Lyric Theatre was rented at a cost, one reckons, exponentially higher than the average funeral. But for the hundreds who attended, from Maya Angelou and Salman Rushdie to her husband and daughter and son, the services had a meaning and comfort beyond the invoices because Jessica Mitford was a woman who was admired and loved, for all her passions and causes and foibles. To have done nothing would have been simpler, easier and cheaper—more convenient and cost-efficient—but something had to be done. Not because it matters to the dead, but because the dead matter to the living. That she hadn't the range for such contemplations does not lessen the impact she has had on the way we now respond to a death. A writer who offers two books called *The American Way of Death* and never mentions the names of her two dead children can be called quirky or eccentric or private or brave. But a woman who writes two volumes of autobiography—books on the subject of one's own life and times—and never reflects on the sad facts that her first husband, her first daughter, and her first son all died tragically and tragically young, can only be called sad and silent. That she never so much as writes the names Julia and Nicholas into the story of her life is a silence beyond any easy reckoning. After all her jaunty and good-humored banter, it is that silence that nearly deafens now.

Of course, regardless of Mitford's motivations, funeral directors unfailingly present a large and easy target for lampoon and ridicule. They are all too often their own worst enemies, which is one of the reasons why Mitford's book sold briskly in that first summer after publication and why things began to change in the mortuary marketplace. Almost immediately there was an increase in the cremation rate, which was below five percent before Mitford's book and has increased to nearly fifty percent in the decades since.[17] Whereas in Mitford's England, cremation is very much the norm and the living still accompany their dead to the crematory, in North America where the tendency is to separate the disposition of the body from commemorative rituals, the cremation is accomplished often out-of-sight, off-site, with convenience, cost containment, and industrial efficiency while the living gather later and elsewhere for their own purposes.

Here is where Alan Ball and Jessica Mitford differ. Mitford made much of caskets—how much they cost, how profitable they were, how devious or obsequious the sales pitch was. She disliked the boxes for their expense. But she especially disliked the bodies in the boxes for the untidy and unpredictable feelings they could be counted on to trigger. And while she wrote, often hilariously, about the foibles of morticians, she never wrote about the emotions she feared, about which life had provided her a substantial tuition. She recommended getting rid of both caskets and corpses, and letting convenience and cost efficiency replace what she regarded as pricey and barbaric display. Like Mitford, Ball sends up the smarminess and scams of those who see a death in the family as primarily a sales op or an altar call, and like Mitford, he abhors the wax figurines of overly "prepared" corpses. But whereas Mitford wants the bodies and all costly accoutrements banished, Ball unambiguously wants the body back, undisguised, its mortal nature manifest and the living welcome to their emotions, however raw; he wants to deal with the sad facts in the flesh. He rejects the virtual in favor of the real. He rejects ease and convenience in favor of the actual. He affirms the essential obligations of the funeral while dispatching the ridiculous accessories with grim drama and good humor. Nowhere is his intention to shift the conversation away from the Mitfordian, *what are we going to spend when someone dies?* and in the direction of his own more compelling, *what are we going to do?* than in the first episode of the first season of *Six Feet Under*.[18]

It is the first of the Fisher family funerals. The family is gathered at graveside to bury the hapless Nathaniel Fisher, husband and father, owner and director of Fisher & Sons of Los Angeles, California. The sunny day is at odds with all the paraphernalia of loss: the sprays of flowers, the black clad mourners, the reverend clergy with well-practiced Scriptures. As if on cue, one of the mortuary factotums flips the switch on the shining chrome lowering devise that slowly begins to lower the polished wood casket into the grave while the collared Episcopal priest dispenses some dirt from a kind of shaker onto the casket while pronouncing the words of committal, then passes the dirt shaker to the dead man's family in the front row of the graveside ensemble. First one, then another, then the next enacts this little symbolic punctuation of the "ashes to ashes, dust to dust" piety, while Nate, the prodigal, who did not go into his father's business, mutters under his breath but loud enough for all to hear, "It's like he's salting popcorn." There is some worried eye rolling among his family. Now the shaker comes to him and he cannot bring himself to comply. Instead he moves to the foot of the grave, bends to reach under the Astroturf and grabs a handful of actual earth—the "popcorn" shaker in one hand, a fistful of dirt in the other. The dutiful David, fearing the decorum will be terribly ruptured, hastens to his brother to advise that, "this is how its done," to which Nate responds, "well it's whacked," then launches into a brief and profanity-laden soliloquy on how awful it is that their father has died, how terrible it feels and how crazy it is to try to sanitize the feelings by "pumping him full of chemicals, propping him up in the 'slumber' room," and hiding it all behind the smoke and mirrors of Scripture and easy ritual. Better, he instructs his brother, to get your hands dirty and to tell the world how awful it is to have one's dad be dead. He swears and throws the dirt on the casket and turns from the grave to walk away, whereupon his mother, quiet up until now, says "Wait." She intuits the permission his outburst has given her and she goes to the end of the grave, kneels in the dirt and sobs with the full animality that is the voice of grief. While one son tries to stop her, the other affirms her rights to this. Both want to be a comfort and both are helpless. The scene is breathtaking in its gathering of truths about the human condition and announces Ball's willingness to place the full range of human emotions, from belly laughs to bone-wracking sobs into the dramatic service of his narrative. But as with everything, the truth is never as simple as black and white. Within moments it is David, as the brothers walk away from the grave, who is upbraiding Nate for his grandstanding, for pretending to be the rock the family can now depend on after he ran away from the family and the family business years before to become a clerk in a health food co-op in Seattle, leaving David holding the bag of the family business.

"You want to get your hands dirty?" David seethes at him. "You sanctimonious prick. Talk to me when you've had to stuff formaldehyde-soaked cotton up your father's ass so he won't leak." Here is a writer, I remember thinking of Alan Ball, who trades in nuance, ambiguity, and ambivalence; who knows how the good laugh and the good cry occupy, very often, the selfsame moment; how the wince and the grin look much the same. I was an immediate fan. I bought all five seasons when they came out on DVD and often review them again for what I can learn from the filmmaker's craft.

It was somewhere early in the second season, our little e-mail correspondence fairly well-established, that Ball wrote to say he had figured out the proper formula for the show's ability to bear a wide range of difficult narratives and never lose its edge. He said it was something "you funeral sorts always seemed to understand: *once you put a dead guy in the room you can talk about anything.*"[19]

And it is so: the presence of the dead so exponentially ups the existential ante that people generally feel the increased gravitas, the broadening of the emotional register, the increased sense of purpose and duty, the sense that we are somehow at swim in deeper water where the range of possible conversations and outcomes is broadened. The presence of the dead embodies, wordlessly, in utter stillness, the raison d'être for the gathering, for the nervous laughter and the tears, for the wailing and belly laughs, for the entire spectrum of responses and conversations—some holy, some hilarious, all of them focused on the dead and the ones to whom the death most matters.

The same lexicon that places *human* proximate to *humus* and *humic* does likewise with *grave* and *gravid, gravitas,* and *gravity.*

The very force of nature that keeps us "grounded" to the earth, the weighty and serious subject laden with meaning, the state of pregnancy weighted with expectancy, and the hole we open to bury our dead all share the same root word in all the ancient etymologies. And like the ancients, each new generation must find its way of dealing with death, bound as we are to its gravities.

Nowhere is the essential role that the body of the deceased plays in our responses to death felt more keenly than in those circumstances where bodies are lost or destroyed. Such was the case with most of the victims of the terrorist attacks of September 11, 2001. The terrible facts became all too clear as rescue and recovery teams worked through the rubble: that we would not get them back to let them go again. We would not be granted the little mercy to wake and weep over them, to look upon their ordinary loveliness once more, to focus all uncertainties on the awful certainty of a body in a box in a familiar room, borne on shoulders, processed through town, as if the borderless country of grief could be handled and contained, as if it had a manageable size and shape and weight and matter, as if it could be mapped or measured. If humans are the ones that consign their dead to oblivions of our own choosing—the grave or flames or tomb or sea or open air— and if the doing of these things is among the primary ways we deal with it because these hard duties have their comforts, then the further heartbreak and horror of that late-summer Tuesday's toll of the dead is that it would not be kin that scattered them, or friends who carry them or family ground that covers them, or their beloved who last whispers soft goodbyes. They were lost—too vastly buried, too furiously burned, too utterly commingled with the horror that killed them to get them back, to let them go again. We could not rescue very many. We recovered all too few. We were left with the dull facts of the matter: the names, the numbers, their backstories published in the papers, to which we cling the way we do to word of the weather, dates on the calendar, and all the happenstance we are helpless to undo.

Like funeral directors and clergy everywhere, I've waited with the families of abducted children, foreign missionaries, tornado victims, drowned toddlers, Peace Corps volunteers, firefighters overcome by flames, passengers in fallen planes, casualties of wars—waiting for their dead to be found and counted, identified and returned to them from whatever damage or disaster claimed them. I have witnessed the odd relief, elation, and thanksgiving at hearing that the lost are found and will be returned. I've stood with parents of children killed in crashes and other mayhems, viewing a body that cannot be restored to anything approximating its former appearance. And I've heard them give thanks for the recognizable limbs that are not gone missing, for the wounds that, however awful, did not dismember or decapitate even when they do disfigure. To have something, anything, unmistakably theirs to take leave of, say goodbye to, promise to remember—these are mercies in what often seem the most merciless of circumstances. This is why, in the weeks and months and years following the attacks of 9-11, the recovery, identification, and return of any remnant of the dead, however small, to their families was more often than not an actual comfort; and why, at long last, funerals were finally held for a portion of a portion of a body part pulled from the two million tons of Ground Zero rubble at Fresh Kills Landfill on Staten Island, which was used as a sorting ground after those attacks. Thousands of forensic experts spent more than a million hours there looking for remnants of the dead. A final tally of 4,257 human remains were recovered, from which three hundred people were positively identified before the remaining debris, which no doubt contains other human remains, was buried in a forty-acre portion of the site over which a permanent memorial will be placed. The notion of simply disposing of the dead loses its appeal when we have no alternative. Only people with options can opt not to deal with the bodies of the dead.

Likewise, I've heard no few well-meaning, though misguided, people suggest that the body in the box, there among the gladioli and hushed respects, was "just a shell" or "only the tent" or some other metaphor to minimize the loss. They mean, of course, to say that they believe our souls outlive us, that we are more than blood and bone and corporality. But to say that there is "something more," albeit unseen, is not to say that what we do see is "something less." The bodies of the dead are not "just" anything or "only" anything else. They are precious to the living who have lost them. They are the seeing—hard as it is—that is believing, the certainty against which our senses rail and to which our senses cling. They are the singular, particular sadness that must be subtracted from the endless mundane tally of sadnesses that are the everyday history of the world.

Ours is a species that deals with death (the idea, the concept, the human condition) by dealing with the dead (the thing itself, in the flesh, the corpse). Whatever our responses to death might be—intellectual, philosophical, religious, ritual, social, emotional, cultural, artistic, and so forth— they are firstly and undeniably connected to the embodied remnant of the person who was. And while the dead can be pictured and imagined and conjured by symbol and metaphor, photo and recording, our allegiance and our primary obligations ought to be to the real rather than the virtual dead. Inasmuch as a death in the family is primarily occasioned by the presence of a corpse, the emergent, immediate, collective, and purposeful response to that emergency is what a funeral is. In short, a funeral responds to the signature human concern, to wit, what to do about a dead human?

Thus, the presence of the dead is an essential, definitive element of a funeral. Funerals differ from all other commemorative events in that the presence of the dead and their subsequent disposition are primary concerns. Memorial services, celebrations of life, or variations on these commemorative events, whether held sooner or later or at intervals or anniversaries, in a variety of locales, while useful socially for commemorating the dead and paying tribute to their memories, lack an essential manifest and function: the disposition of the dead. In this sense, the option to dispose of the dead privately, through the agency of hirelings, however professional they might be, and however moving the memorial that follows may be, is an abdication of an essential undertaking and fundamental humanity.

A second essential, definitive element of a funeral is that there must be those to whom the death matters. A death happens to both the one who dies and to those who survive the death and are affected by it. If no one cares, if there is no one to mark the change that has happened, if there is no one to name and claim the loss and the memory of the dead, then the dead assume the status of Bishop Berkeley's tree falling noiselessly in the forest: if no one hears it, it did not fall, it never was. It is the same with humans. And like Bishop Berkeley, it may become for us the case for a God who sees and hears and claims everything in creation.

A third essential, definitive element of a funeral is that there must be some narrative, some effort toward an answer, however provisional, of those signature human questions about what death means for both the one who has died and those to whom it matters. Thus, an effort to broker some peace between the corpse and the mourners by describing the changed reality death occasions is part of the essential response to mortality. Very often this is a religious narrative. Often it is written in a book, the text of which is widely read. Or it might be philosophical, artistic, or intellectual—a poem in place of a psalm, a song in place of prayer—either way there must be some case to be made for what has happened to the dead and what the living might expect because of it. "Behold I show you a mystery," or words to that effect are often heard.

A fourth and final essential, definitive element of a funeral is that it must accomplish the disposition of the dead. They are not welcome, we know intuitively, to remain among us in the way they were while living. And while this disposition often involves the larger muscles and real work, it also enacts our essential narratives; assists in the process of our essential emotions, images, and intellection about the dead; and fixes their changed status in the landscape of our future and daily lives, whether the dead are buried, burned, entombed, enshrined, scattered, hoisted into the air, cast into the sea, or left out for the scavenging birds, our choice of their oblivion makes their disposition palatable, acceptable, maybe even holy, and our participation in it remedial, honorable, maybe even holy.

These four essential, definitive elements, then: the corpse, the caring survivors, some brokered change of status between them, and the disposition of the dead make a human funeral what it is.

Finally, once we can separate the essential elements from the accessories, the fundamental obligations from fashionable options, the substance from the stuff, the necessary from the knick-knacks, the core from the pulp, we might be able to assign relative measures of worth to what we do when one of our own kind dies. We might be able to figure not only the costs but the values. Thus, coffin and casket, mum plants and carnations, candles and pall, vaults and monuments, limousines and video tributes—all of them accessories, nonessentials. They may be a comfort but they are not essential. Same for funeral directors and rabbis, sextons and pastors, priests and clerks, florists and lawyers and hearse drivers—all of them are accessories who may, nonetheless, assist the essential purpose of a funeral. And when we do, when we endeavor to serve the living by caring for the dead, we are assisting in the essential, definitive work of the funeral and the species that devised this deeply human response to death.

There was a disciple whose name was Tabitha, which in Greek is Dorcas. She was devoted to good works and acts of charity. [37]At that time she became ill and died. When they had washed her, they laid her in a room upstairs. . . . [39]All the widows stood beside him, weeping and showing tunics and other clothing that Dorcas had made while she was with them.

Acts 9:36–37, 39b

Chapter 4

HABEAS CORPUS . . . *NOT*

Thomas G. Long

Habeas corpus, which means literally "you have the body," is a quaint Latin phrase that still lingers in our legal vocabulary. Tyrants and despots often get the idea that the way to solve political problems is to toss their opponents into prison and conveniently forget where they put the key. After all, it can be dangerous to behead one's foes; way too many martyrs have been created that way. But if you simply hide their bodies in the slammer forever, their memory and power will eventually fade. In a society of laws, though, citizens are supposed to be protected against such treatment, and that's where the idea of habeas corpus comes in. Whether it's the sheriff holding a DUI offender in the county tank or the queen shackling a rival in the castle dungeon, no authority has the right to imprison another without justification. So the court can order the authorities, "OK, we know you have the body of so-and-so in custody. Bring him physically to court and make your case." In the old courts, the opening

83

words of this order were dramatic: *habeas corpus . . . You* have the body.

Interesting phrase: "you have the body." Sometimes our language is a repository of truths only faintly remembered and values almost forgotten. Hidden in the words *habeas corpus* are profound social convictions, namely that human bodies matter, that selves and bodies are inextricably joined, that authorities do not have unlimited rights regarding people's bodies, and that society is just only when bodies are treated justly. No autocrat can get away with saying, "Well sure, we have Joe Doakes' *body* down here at the county lockup, but who cares? After all, his spirit is still free, right?" Now, Joe may indeed be the very model of a free spirit, whiling away the time in his cell composing romantic poetry, singing freedom songs, and allowing his imagination to wing him beyond the gray prison walls and into fantasy fields of wildflowers. But make no mistake: if Joe's body is in jail, *Joe* is in jail. If Joe's body is treated unjustly, *Joe* is the victim of injustice. Habeas corpus—You have Joe's body, and that means you have Joe.

Bodies matter, and a society is only as healthy as its concern for the safety and health of the physical bodies of its citizens. When Martin Luther King Jr. wrote his famous "Letter from Birmingham Jail," he wrote as one surely confident of his own dignity and convinced of his standing before God as a free man. None of this could be stolen away by some humanly imposed jail sentence. But, even so, King did not say, "My body may be in a Birmingham jail, but no matter. I'm free at last! Thank God Almighty, I'm free at last!" Instead he was quite aware of the embodied character of what was happening to him, and he said that the tribulation being inflicted on his body and the bodies of the others in the civil rights movement was not only a matter of injustice but also a form of testimony. He wrote, "We had no alternative except to prepare for direct action, whereby we would present *our very bodies* as a means of laying our case before the conscience of the local and the national community. . . . [W]e repeatedly asked ourselves: 'Are you able to accept blows without retaliating?' 'Are you able to endure the ordeal of jail?'"[1]

If King was to make a powerful testimony to the nation's conscience, he knew it would take more than speeches and good wishes. It would take bodies in action, bodies at risk—feet on the pavement, a refusal to move to the back seats of the bus, a resolute sitting on lunch counter stools. King went on to say in his famous letter from jail that the support that really counted from white clergy was not from the so-called moderates who had good intentions, nice thoughts, and soothing words, but rather from those who were willing to set their own feet in motion and to put their own bodies into harm's way:

> I am thankful to God that some noble souls from the ranks of organized religion have broken loose from the paralyzing chains of conformity and joined us as active partners in the struggle for freedom. They have left their secure congregations and walked the streets of Albany, Georgia, with us. They have gone down the highways of the south on torturous rides for freedom. Yes, they have gone to jail with us. Some have been kicked out of their churches, have lost the support of their bishops and fellow ministers. But they have acted in the faith that right defeated is stronger than evil triumphant. Their witness has been the spiritual salt that has preserved the true meaning of the gospel in these troubled times. They have carved a tunnel of hope through the dark mountain of disappointment.[2]

"The body does not lie." So goes the old saying. Indeed, if you want to know a person, really know the truth of a person's character, watch where her feet take her, what tasks she takes up with her hands, where she chooses to sit and stand, whom she embraces, what she speaks with her mouth. We human beings are the tapestry of a thousand embodiments, and the oldest blessing in the world, the one we still crave, is not a greeting card or a bouquet but hands placed on the head of another. A touching of bodies, a passing of power and good-will from one body to another.

THE BODY IN LIFE . . . AND IN DEATH

Habeas corpus—you have the body. Society knows . . . we know . . . that it matters what happens to bodies. This makes perfectly good sense when we are speaking of living bodies, of bodies that can feel and experience joy and pain. But what about the bodies of the dead? A quickened body with a beating heart is, to be sure, worthy of care and protection, but when a body is dead and cold, the person departed, and the flesh rapidly disintegrating into dust, what's the concern?

Surprisingly, though, we intuitively know better. Deep in our social and personal DNA lies the conviction that the body of one who has died is just as worthy of respect as the living body. Let an unblinking television camera hover over a body on a crime scene investigation show, and it feels invasive, voyeuristic. We know it's a TV fable, that the "corpse" will get up and go to lunch when the filming is done, but nonetheless, even a fictional gaze without love or care at the body of a stranger feels like an invasion of privacy, a violation of a sacred trust. Small-town funeral directors often report that local folk sometimes express anxiety that when they die the funeral director will "see me naked." Why should anyone care, unless there is an instinctive conviction that one's dead body is an even more vulnerable version of one's living self?

What happens, or doesn't happen, to the bodies of the dead tells us much about what we believe about life and death, what we think of ourselves as a society. A corpse is entrusted to the care of the living for only a matter of hours or a few days, but how we carry out our responsibilities to the bodies of the dead is a strong clue as to how we will treat the bodies of the living. A culture prepared to hide the bodies of the dead as if they were an embarrassment or an insult to the living or to throw the bodies of indigent dead into a common ditch is also a society prone to cast aside its elderly, neglect its sick, leave its poor without shelter, and deprive its young of proper care.

Karla Holloway, in *Passed On,* her book on African American funeral practices, underscores the connection between the care of the dead and the treatment of the living. She recalls a time a century ago when there were few black-owned funeral establishments. The bodies of black folk would be taken to white funeral homes for embalming, carried out of sight through back entrances and cellar doors. The question whispered in the black neighborhood then was, "Who's got the body?"—an echo of habeas corpus, an expression not only of curiosity but also of concern and even suspicion. As Holloway says, "whites were often as disrespectful to black bodies in death as they were in life."[3] When blacks began to open funeral homes, this was more than a business opportunity; it was a matter of reclaiming the cultural responsibility to treat people in death with the tenderness and respect they deserved in life. Holloway says, "Black families *knew* black morticians— they were our kin, our neighbors, our fellow congregants in Sunday church services."[4]

THE BODY AND RELIGIOUS WISDOM

The concern to treat the bodies of the dead with regard runs deep. It is not always visible from the surface, but the impulse to treat the human body with dignity rests on a religious foundation. "The bodiless God takes an insatiable interest in the doings of human bodies,"[5] said religion scholar Catherine Madsen, and this divine concern embraces the fullness of our days and deeds, from before birth to beyond death.

Here is a great religious truth: the very thing about us that seems so ordinary and routine, the ways we move our bodies—separately and together—from room to room, from bed to table, from desk to TV room, from bus stop to workplace, from handshake to eager embrace, indeed from cradle to grave—is, in fact, a dance performed in the presence of God, a silent confession of faith in bodily action. "Every dance," said the great choreographer Martha Graham, "is a kind of fever chart, a graph of the heart," and the ballet of everyday movement is, in fact, the one creed confessed by all, those who consider themselves religious and those who do not. As Madsen puts it,

> There is a faithfulness stronger than any vow; a faithfulness that can neither be promised nor abandoned; a faithfulness which is not even consciously undertaken, but informs consciousness more surely than any deliberate act. . . . This faithfulness is bodily, it enters not into your religious observances but into your synapses. It is not a social or personal obligation but something between a lifework and a fate. . . . It is steadier and more austere than any promise: you promise only to the things you have chosen, but you are faithful to the things that chose you.[6]

To rouse ourselves out of bed to face the day is not just an obligation, something we have to do. It is in its own way a profession of trust, a moving of our bodies toward something in life worth having, a receiving, however begrudgingly, of a holy gift. To give one's body in pleasure to another is an amalgam of love and lust, taking and yielding, but also a testimony that love is finally stronger than death. To slide a grilled cheese sandwich out of the pan onto the plate of a guest is not simply an everyday gesture but also a sign of care for others and even a leaning toward that great hoped-for feast where there is a place at the table for everyone. And this extends to death— to wash and dress the bodies of those who have died and to accompany them to the place of farewell is a confession of faith that something lies beyond this life and that these whom we cherished were not only treasures to us but precious in the sight of God.

The major religious traditions may disagree about many things, but on this one theme they all raise their hands in assent: we will learn wisdom about how to live when we care lovingly and reverently for the bodies of the dead. When Fumie Arai finally found the body of her mother, it was a heartbreaking discovery, but there was one small, deep comfort. Sadly, her mother had been swept away in the devastating Japanese tsunami of 2011, and, after a long and desperate search, Arai finally located her mother's mud-covered body in a vacant middle school that had been turned into a makeshift morgue in the devastated city of Kamaishi. But there was this one solace: someone had evidently cared for her mother's body, tenderly washing her face clean and setting the features. "I dreaded finding my mother's body, lying alone on the cold ground among strangers," Arai said. "When I saw her peaceful, clean face, I knew someone had taken care of her until I arrived. That saved me."[7]

The caregiver, unbeknownst to Arai, was Atsushi Chiba, a retired undertaker and a father of five who attended to the bodies of more than 1,000 tsunami victims. Why? Because of an awareness of the Buddhist tradition of caring for the dead. What Chiba had done was to remove the bodies, which were often twisted cruelly with faces frozen in agony, from the plastic sheeting in which they had been hastily wrapped. He would then speak to each of the bodies, expressing compassion and asking them for their help. "You must be so cold and lonely, but your family is going to come for you soon so you'd better think of what you're going to say to them when they arrive." He would then get on his knees and gently massage the bodies to relax them into a posture of peacefulness. Workers at the morgue, moved by Chiba's tenderness and reverence, responded by constructing a Buddhist altar out of old school desks. They lined up with heads bowed in prayerful respect each time a body was claimed by a family member.[8]

Atsushi Chiba, a Buddhist, had a kindred spirit many generations and many miles away in a pious Jew named Tobit, who also cared for the bodies of the abandoned dead. Tobit is the main character in an ancient Jewish folk tale, dating probably from the second or third century BCE. The story is told in the book of Tobit, which is now included in Catholic and Orthodox versions of the Christian Bible.

Himself a very righteous man, Tobit is among the citizens of Judah captured in an Assyrian invasion and taken to Nineveh, the enemy capital. Now in exile in this foreign land, Tobit is determined to maintain his Jewish faith, but he must practice it cautiously under the watchful eye of his captors. In the privacy of his home, he keeps a kosher table and refuses to eat the food of the heathen Assyrians. In public, Tobit practices the charity commanded in the Torah by generously sharing his food and clothing with the impoverished refugees who fill the streets of Nineveh.

Surprisingly, the one expression of Jewish charity that gets Tobit in deep trouble with the Assyrian authorities is that he becomes the unofficial undertaker for the forsaken refugees, reclaiming the bodies of the dead and giving them a decent burial. The Assyrians contemptuously threw the Jewish dead over the city wall, leaving them to decompose outside the city under the heat of the Mesopotamian sun. For the Assyrians, this was not only tossing out the "refuse" but also an act of tyranny, exposing the Jewish dead to shame and reminding the captives who held power. Tobit recovered these bodies, cared for them, and buried them decently. The point of the story is clear: what Tobit did was an act of charity, virtue, and religious faith. It was also a politically defiant statement of the worth of Jews to the human community and to God.

Jewish convictions about the holiness of caring for the dead were inherited by early Christians. Just as Tobit's caring for the dead arose out of his Jewish piety and offended his pagan Assyrian captors, the first Christians' views about bodies shocked the Roman society around them. To the Romans, a human body was exactly what wise Plato had taught, a corrupted vessel, a prison entrapping pure souls yearning for release from the flesh. But the strange Christians not only believed, as did their Jewish forebears, that God had created the human body and called it "very good," they were also persuaded of the almost unimaginable notion that in Jesus the very self of God had taken on flesh, and that, as one version of the New Testament puts it, "The word became flesh and blood and moved into the neighborhood."[9] When it came to regard for the human body, this settled it. Jesus had trumped Plato.

The aspect of this regard for the body that most perplexed the Romans was that these early Christians took upon themselves the role of undertaker, volunteering to bury the dead, not just their own dead but also the bodies of impoverished Romans, who would otherwise have been unceremoniously dumped into a common pit. As theologian Margaret R. Miles has said, "Corpses [in Roman society] were considered ill-omened," and the puzzling behavior of Christians in caring for dead bodies was thought of as "fleeing from the light," as something no intelligent, well-informed person would do. To the cultured Romans, the primitive Christians were misled by "a failure to understand that it is the mind that is to be honored and cultivated, while the human body must be ignored, disparaged, and 'scorned.'"[10]

Whenever Roman officials attempted to teach the Jesus sect a lesson by executing a few of them as public examples, the Christians baffled their tormentors all the more by treating their remains with reverence. Miles writes:

> Equally bewildering to their secular neighbors, Christians insisted on gathering the bones of those who had been executed for refusal to renounce the Christian sect. They put

these bones in a place of honor and described them as capable of possessing the sanctity of the living holy person. . . . [T]hey cared for living bodies and dead bodies because they understood that the Incarnation of Christ had once and for all settled the issue of the value of human bodies.[11]

Atshushi Chiba, Tobit, and the early Christians who cared for the dead out of faithful vision have a contemporary Islamic counterpart in Adil Imdad of St. Louis. When Imdad's cousin died of cancer in 2010, the family's grief was deepened by the reality that her body was not treated in the reverent way called for by their religious faith. There was no Imam to offer the proper ritual, no Muslim funeral director to supervise the traditional washing and shrouding of the body, no Muslim cemetery in which she could be buried. Distressed by this, Imdad, an environmental and geotechnical engineer, began taking night courses in a local mortuary school. His intention is to open Missouri's first Muslim funeral home, but his deeper goal is to care for the Muslim dead in a reverent manner consistent with the teachings of Islam, and at virtually no cost to the families. "Helping people satisfies something inside you," he says. "When they pray for you later, you know it comes from their inner heart."[12]

The trend is unmistakable. Religions east and west proclaim that caring for the bodies of the dead is both a humane thing to do and a sacred thing to do. When the dead are not treated with tenderness, life loses some of its mercy, holiness, and import. Astonishingly, when seen in the light of these religious convictions, undertaking turns out to be not merely a job, but an act of faith, as ancient as the priesthood. When society loses its soul and abandons or mistreats the dead, people of religious vision respond not simply by falling to their knees in prayer but also by rolling up their sleeves, digging graves, and burying the dead with reverence—prophets with fragrant oils, shrouds, and shovels.

This prophetic vision, shared by many religious traditions, of the human body as a sacred treasure, from beginning to life's end, acts as leaven in the loaf of social values. It works to form humane standards beyond the walls of temple, shrine, church, and mosque. For example, Marykate Connor, a San Francisco-based advocate for homeless people, drew on profound religious themes when she called for more reverent care for the bodies of the homeless who die on sidewalks and in abandoned buildings. There are sometimes memorial services for homeless people who die, she says, "but the wrenching image of a body lying cold and anonymous in the county morgue brings feelings of helplessness, and the specter of a terrible death alone to those of us who remain." This neglect of the bodies of the homeless, she states, creates a diminution of worth and a denial of a sense of place, and no mere memorial service can possibly make up for these losses.[13]

THE STRANGE DISAPPEARING CORPSE

So, our deepest ethical and spiritual wisdom calls us not only to watch vigilantly over the bodies of the living but also to care tenderly for the bodies of the dead. So why don't we do it? The sacred responsibility of caring for and accompanying the dead has weakened considerably, and not just for the homeless, the indigent, or the refugee. The bodies of the dead in general are being treated with casual disregard. Curiously, we are rapidly becoming the first society in the history of the world for whom the dead are no longer required—or desired—at their own funerals.

Ironically, this trend away from the presence of the body at funerals began with a religiously defined group, namely white, educated, urban, and suburban Protestant Christians, but it is taking hold now among other groups, religious and secular. Instead of a ritual in which the mourners accompany the body of the deceased to the place of disposition, a disembodied memorial service, or no ceremony whatsoever, is rapidly becoming the standard death practice for many Americans. Instead of habeas corpus—you have the body—our funeral slogan is frequently "Habeas corpus . . . not!" We don't have the body, and much of the time, we don't want to have the body.

At first glance, the fact that we now quite frequently observe our death rites without the dead person present is, like cutting down trees in the rain forest, a social practice that seems patently irrational and self-destructive. The New York physician and professor of medicine Siddhartha Mukherjee, remembers when he was a boy being taken by his father one night to see the cremation pyres on the River Ganges in the Indian city of Varanasi. The sight was unforgettable and haunting: row upon row of burning bodies, men carrying their dead down to the water to bathe the bodies before placing them on the fire, the Hindu priests shoveling the still smoldering ashes into the flowing river. He sees a man standing beside one of the funeral pyres with his arms still outstretched and taut, as if he were still holding the weight of the body of his loved one.

Years later, recalling his experience that night, Mukherjee questioned some of his medical students in the hospital about their experiences with death. How many of them, he wondered, had carried the body of a parent? How many had felt the weight of a dead body or bathed a body? The questions, he said, made them nervous. He writes, "Our experience of death has become disembodied. The corpus has vanished from the most corporeal of our rituals—and we are left standing with our hands outstretched and taut but with no counterweight to bear, like the man on the riverbank holding air."[14]

A funeral is, by definition, what we do with the body. It is about the weight of the body, its gravitas, and the bearing of that weight by others as they carry the dead to the place of disposition. It is not a sing-a-long, a prayer meeting, a therapy session, or a memory exercise. It may include elements of all these things, but funerals are about bodies and movement. Funerals are occasioned by a great human necessity, namely that the body of the deceased must be taken from among the living to a place among the dead. This movement of the corpse is the central and inescapable reality, the unavoidable fact at the center of all death rituals. We may accomplish it with a prayer, a psalm, a shout of rage, or somber silence. We may believe that we are carrying the dead to God, or we may walk to the place of farewell convinced that there is nothing beyond us and this world. That is a matter of custom, creed, and taste, but the fact that we must do this deed is not subject to whim or choice. We may do it in public or hidden from sight. We may do it in resignation, in despair, or in hope. But we will do it; we *must* do it. How odd, then, that we now so often hide this central event of the human death ritual, or simply hand the task to others. And, as a result, the central actor—the body of the deceased—has gone missing in action. Why?

Several explanations have been suggested. Some say that the root of the change is simply a quest for convenience. Dead bodies are, frankly, a hassle, an encumbrance. Preparing and transporting them is work that is sometimes grim and always laborious. So we no longer bear our dead to their funerals for the same reason that we no longer wash our clothes by pounding them out on river rocks. Our great-grandparents had no choice but to perform the labor that way, but we have now been relieved of that inconvenience.

Others argue that the disappearance of bodies from funerals has to do more with the location of cemeteries nowadays. Beginning in the nineteenth century, the "rural cemetery movement" started a trend toward placing graveyards away from towns in lovely park-like settings with willows and brooks. The goals were two: meditation and sanitation. Rural cemeteries were lovely, landscaped, and serene places where one could reflect quietly on death and life. They also allowed the living to keep their distance from the dead, preventing the alleged contaminations of decomposing bodies from defiling the air and ground water.

The fears about deadly pollution were misinformed, but the movement caught on nonetheless, and cemeteries are now often located off by themselves, away from the population. Once graves were only a few steps away, and funerals could move seamlessly from church to graveyard or from parlor to the family plot on the farm. But now the rhythm of a funeral is broken up by a drive of some miles to the burial ground. Add to this the rise in preference for cremation and it just seems to make sense to spare the mourners a trip and to handle the disposition of the body privately and in advance of any ceremony.

Still others point to the vastly different tone of death rituals today. Funerals have become increasingly joyful, more like celebrations of life than solemn observances of death, and nothing is more disruptive to these upbeat ceremonies than the morbid presence of a dead body. Dead bodies are not emotionally buoyant, and they place a drag on the light banter, jokes, laughter, and storytelling prized in contemporary services of memory.

Plausible reasons all, but a deeper truth lies beneath the surface. Why, in defiance of our best ethical and religious wisdom and against the grain of strong human instinct, do we loathe to bring the bodies of the dead to their own funerals. Or, perhaps more accurately, why do we memorialize the dead by banning them from our presence? Fashion, convenience, and mood are all in play, but the real reason has to do with a more profound shift in values, even in religious conviction. In a way, our culture has been experiencing a religious conversion over the last few generations, turning from the traditional faiths, with their emphasis on embodiment, and toward less embodied, more free-flowing forms of spirituality. If it was, in the first place, religion that prompted us to accompany our dead to the place of farewell, it is a shift in religion, at least of the civic variety, that allows us to leave the dead by the wayside.

It may seem odd to argue that religion is a major cause in the disappearance of the body in American funerals when not every American is, by any means, a religious believer. But historians of religion have long recognized that religions form societies, and then those societies retain their religious form, even if the organized specific practice of religion wanes. Rock-and-roll music still carries the DNA of its parents, blues and country. So, the kid on the subway rocking away to his iPod is being shaped by the whole history and ethos of rock, whether he knows it or not and even if he hates country music or blues. Likewise, even Americans who reject "organized religion" still swim in the stream of American culture and are thus affected by the religious impulses that continue to shape the culture.

Also, the term "religion" can be used in a broader sense than a specific creed or sect. Most people, even if they are not involved in a church, synagogue, or a mosque, still have a sense of ultimate truth, a set of treasured symbols that point toward that truth, and a way of making connection with that deep place in life. Sometimes this is called "civic religion." It is not traditional religion, certainly, but if we fly over it at 35,000 feet, it often looks and behaves much like its more conventional religious cousins. If the practitioners of civic religion are becoming "spiritual but not religious," well, so are Catholics, Episcopalians, and Jews. If American Methodists and Muslims are increasingly looking inward in their quest for spiritual truth, so are Americans generally.

Religion, in both its traditional and civic forms, is moving away from embodied expressions, like brick-and-mortar buildings, official creeds, communal membership, and binding vows, and toward free-form quests for personal meaning and "spiritual tinkering" to use Robert Wuthnow's apt phrase.[15] As a culture, we now bow in the temple of a god who reigns over the airiness of souls set loose but who disdains the gravity of bodies and concrete practices. Here in this new place of worship, floating above time and circumstance, no wonder the dead are viewed as an embodied form of blasphemy.

For the classical religious traditions, faith is an all-embracing reality. The phrase "spiritual but not religious" would be absurd, since to be spiritual *was* to be religious, and vice versa. What people believed not only prompted them to pray in temple or mosque or church but also shaped the way they raised their children, dealt with their neighbors, spent their money. You could tell much about people's faith by the way they farmed or ran the dry goods store: if the butcher made sure that the shop's scales were accurate, if the school teacher attended to the slow learner as well as the bright, if the rancher mended the fences for the livestock, if the banker watched over other people's money as if it were his own, it was more than a sense of decency. It was a manifestation of a faithful worldview, an understanding of the sacredness of all of life, and a display of gratitude for the goodness of creation.

Almost from the beginning, though, there has been another religious impulse coursing through American culture, namely that religion is not, in fact, about everything there is. Rather, it is about a small compartment of life, a spiritual zone cordoned off from all else, God's little acre. We can hear this impulse in such expressions as, "We are speaking here not of material things, but of spiritual things." Really? Judaism, Islam, Christianity never countenanced such a distinction. Material things *are* spiritual things; spiritual things find their expression in embodied and material life here on *terra firma*.

Indeed, classical religious traditions warn that there are

two ways to go off the rails here. The first is to think that material things aren't spiritual, just material. Travel that road very far and it will lead to Enron, Bernie Madoff, and Wall Street piracy. The second is the reverse, to get excited about things of the spirit, but to forget that spiritual things are inextricably entwined with the material. Go that way, and faith quickly becomes a helium balloon, floating free of everyday reality, getting smaller and smaller as we watch it rise. For the most part, it is this second misstep that has had an impact on the world of funerals.

Part of the reason why contemporary Americans have a religion that majors in spirituality and minors in materiality is the result of a crisis of faith and intellect. In the contemporary world, the truth claims of traditional religion have come under stress and have become, for many thoughtful people, increasingly difficult to maintain. In the last part of the nineteenth century, what had occurred to philosopher geniuses like Isaac Newton and Joseph Priestley a century before began to happen to ordinary folks: they started to see the world through scientific eyes. They didn't become scientists, not most of them, but they began to think in scientific ways. In the medieval world, for example, people would have talked about the weather, saying that it was "mighty hot" or "terribly cold." When people started thinking scientifically, they began saying things like "it's 92 degrees outside" or "the barometer is falling and there's a 40 percent chance of snow." As the whole culture began to be shaped by science, truth mostly came to mean "facts" and facts were things that science could observe, probe, and measure.

The world was clearly changing. Horses and wagons were being replaced by steam engines and horseless carriages. Messages were crackling with lightning speed along telegraph wires. Practical scientists like Thomas Edison and Alexander Graham Bell were revolutionizing society with inventions like the electric light bulb and the telephone. As the nineteenth century yielded to the twentieth, the trend was clear to all. Science was changing the world, and we human beings were using our own powers to harness the forces of nature and to become masters of the universe.

Inevitably, the religious view of life and the scientific view were thrown into conflict. It became increasingly difficult to talk of miracles, divine revelation, and the highest heavens in a cosmos probed by telescopes, governed by the "laws" of physics, and measured by empirical observation. What do you do with "God makes the sun rise on the evil and on the good and sends rain on the righteous and on the unrighteous" in a world where we know perfectly well that the earth orbits the sun and we also know how to track cold fronts, measure humidity, and ascertain the dew point?

At first it seemed like a clear battle: science versus religion, and religion appeared to be greatly disadvantaged. A dowager, upon being told that scientist Charles Darwin had shown that human beings were the evolutionary descendants of apes, famously gasped, "Oh my, I hope that's not true! But if it *is* true, I hope it won't become widely known." Indeed, some were quick to proclaim a knock-down victory for scientific rational thought. Twenty-first century atheists such as Christopher Hitchens and Richard Dawkins had their precursors. In the late nineteenth century, agnostic Robert G. Ingersoll, a spellbinding orator, provoked and titillated Chautauqua audiences with such statements as "An honest God is the noblest work of man" and "The inspiration of the Bible depends upon the ignorance of the gentleman who reads it." In the 1950s, Charles Templeton, who had once barnstormed the revival circuit with his friend Billy Graham, lost his faith under the withering glare of scientific scrutiny. He penned a memoir titled *Farewell to God: My Reasons for Rejecting the Christian Faith*, and spent his last years evangelizing for clear rational thought unclouded by the superstitions of faith.

Many religious people simply soldiered on, mostly untouched by these doubts. And those believers who were aware of the challenges were not without response. Some argued that the game was rigged against faith and that if scientists would just come clean about the full range of data, they would find evidence of a Creator and would have to admit that God is in the details after all. This is the view that propels Creationism and Intelligent Design. Others, more satisfactorily in my view, recognized that science and religion were two different perspectives on truth, almost like two different languages. Sometimes they overlap, and what is claimed by one can be translated into the other. But sometimes they see different aspects of the truth and measure reality according to differing standards and commitments. Each has something of value to offer to the quest for truth, both have blind spots, and a richer quest for truth comes when science and religion engage in civil conversation.

But there was a third option, one that turned out to be easier and much more popular than the first two, and it is this choice that has generated much of the mischief about bodies and funerals. This approach was not to engage in a religious battle with science and not even to forge a dialogue between the two, but to put a firewall between them. Instead of allowing the scientific and religious worldviews to engage each other, why not solve the problem by dividing the game into two separate playing fields? Science gets the universe; religion gets the soul. Science gets physics, religion gets metaphysics. Science gets to say what is true about black holes, sunspots, the speed of light, thermodynamics, and the growth of cells, and religion gets to say what is true about prayer, angels, affairs of the heart, and the inner spiritual life.

It is easy to see that this is a bad real estate deal for religion. Science inherits almost the whole spectrum of human

experience, while faith gets confined to a tiny band somewhere out in the nether limits past the gamma rays. Science
gets to speak about everything in the cosmos, except for a
nebulous little patch called "spirituality." White, educated,
Protestants were among the first attracted to this disembodied form of spirituality, but gradually it has become the religion of the masses. A great number of Americans live the
majority of their lives in a basically secular way with goals
and expectations tempered by the horizon of what is scientifically possible. But there is a small leftover place, a spiritual
center that hungers to be fed.

When it comes to meaning making, faith gets to talk for
the most part only when science has shut up and has nothing left to say. And that is precisely the case when someone
dies. The brute empirical facts are bleak. Someone is dead and
the process is scientifically irreversible. Science can describe
the physical cause of death and the expected rate of bodily
decomposition, perhaps, but after that, nothing. It has no
word of comfort or meaning. So, with science quieted, now is
the time for religion to step forward and offer its succor. But,
even now that it gets a chance to speak, religion is pressed to
obey the new rules and is obliged to stay on its own playing
field and off of the scientific turf. No sweeping declarations
about the full embodiments of life are permitted; no brash
unscientific claims of resurrection of the body or a life beyond
are allowed.

Faith is now most at home speaking only of inward spiritual things, sentiments confined to the tiny tableau of the soul
and psyche. It will not speak boldly of the embodied human
being who ate and drank and loved and sinned and hoped and
wept and whose life and very body are now carried forth as
an offering to God, but rather more meekly of "memories we
will always have," of "a loving spirit that will endure in our
hearts," of the "grief that may last for a night but vanishes in

the morning," of "the laughter she will leave with us forever" and "the inspiration of his life."

Add to this yet another complication. The classical religious traditions once gave people hope by proclaiming powerful visions of life as a journey toward God, a journey toward a joyful life beyond this one. The problem is that the only way we have to speak of the next world is through language borrowed from this one. So we spoke of "streets of gold" or "mansions on high" of "a shady grove across the river" of a "heavenly choir singing ceaseless praise." Religiously considered, these visions of human destiny are true, but they are framed the only way human beings can state them, metaphorically. These are poetic expressions, attempts to tease thought toward the unimaginable, to speak truths that are ineffable, to describe intimations of mystery. To imagine the dead, now in a land full of light and life and joy, wearing robes of glistening white, and singing doxologies before God's throne night and day is an extraordinarily fine act of the faithful imagination. To think in literalistic ways about this, to picture our late Uncle Sid actually standing on a cloud in the middle of a gaggle of choristers, wearing a choir robe, strumming a golden harp, and crooning "praise to the Lord" 24/7 is, by contrast, a fatal failure of imagination.

But a century and a half ago, many, if not most, religious people did think of these images of the afterlife quite literally. That meant that the more people adopted a scientific outlook, the more pressure was placed on literal views of heaven and the afterlife. The sacred canopy began to crack, plausibility structures gave way, and many finally abandoned literal pictures of the afterlife as unsustainable. Even those who did not abandon those views began to think of them less often and less confidently. When Cosmonaut Yuri Gagarin became the first human being to travel into outer space, Soviet leader Nikita Khrushchev crowed, "Gagarin flew into space, but didn't see any god there." Khrushchev's mistake, of course, was to confuse the religious and scientific ways of describing truth, as if God were simply another object, like a carbon molecule or a paramecium, available to scientific discovery and analysis. Religious claims are thistles; you can hold them confidently, but if you squeeze them, they begin to hurt.

Preachers and believers forgot the power of their own theological poetry. More and more they thought of images like "streets of gold" and "pearly gates" in the same way as they thought of water boiling at 100 degree centigrade, that is, as straight facts and not as metaphors. These profound beliefs became wooden literalisms, and scientific rationality bowled them over like tenpins. Once there was a time when people put down their plows, hammers, schoolbooks, and baking pans, and they lifted the coffins of their loved ones, carrying their bodies to the grave, confident that they were accompanying them on the last earthly mile of a great journey to be with God. But when they lost the poetry in this, the acids of doubt eroded their confidence, and all that was left for enchantment was a tiny spiritual place within. The dead were dead, traveling nowhere, except maybe into the ether of memory, and nothing was happening to the mourner, except for a thin salve of optimism and faux celebration superficially applied to the raging emotion of grief.

One could say that this is evidence that our culture has become more secular, and that would be true in its own way. Another way to think about it, though, is that people are as religious as they have ever been, but they have switched religions to one with more vapor and less body. Instead of a religion that cinches up the cords on all of life, that discovers the soulfulness in what we do in the flesh, the new religion is one of airy spirituality. It's a religion that feels trapped by solid things. It is allergic to institutions and buildings, creeds and structures. And it doesn't like bodies. The real stuff, after all, is spiritual, so the body, with its weighty encumbrances, its wrinkles, and its tendency to break down, is a hindrance to the living, and to the dead, the body is "just a shell." So, if the task of a memorial service is to become disembodied—to be inspired, to feel lifted above the sheer facts of death, to become spiritually centered, to have my memory activated and my grief soothed with laughter and upbeat sentiments—then, for God's sake, don't roll a heavy dead body onto the set. So, we stopped bringing our dead to funerals because they get in the way of our spiritual reverie, and we stopped accompanying the dead to the grave because, frankly, they have nowhere to go.

THE UNBEARABLE LIGHTNESS OF MEMORIAL SERVICES

What can funeral directors and pastors do about the strangely disembodied character of American death rituals, the "bodiless obsequies" as Thomas Lynch calls them? At one level we might simply shrug our shoulders and face up to the new reality. After all, we can adjust. Funeral directors can figure out how to maintain a business model around immediate interments, direct cremations, and celebrant emceed "celebrations of life." And as for clergy-led funerals, we pastors can still find a place in all this, moving people to tears and laughter with witty memoirs of the deceased, massaging their nostalgia with a few expected Scripture readings and inspiring them with a sentimental poem or two.

But to do so would be a tragic dereliction of responsibility. Funeral directors have business concerns and pastors have their sectarian constraints. But even deeper than these concerns and constraints is the welfare of the human beings we are summoned to serve. Our society has forgotten what to do with the dead and persuaded itself that this amnesia is a sign of health and freedom. But the truth is that a people who cannot care for the dead and accompany them to a place of farewell are a people with diminished ability to care for the living and to join with others in communities of trust and meaning. If we cannot walk with the dead in hope, it is because we have lost our bearings in life. We become afraid of death, smoothing over our wrinkles with creams and injecting our bodies with Botox to keep its reality at bay. (*The New York Times* obituary for Helen Gurley Brown, who restyled *Cosmopolitan* magazine into a slick rag for the sexual revolution and who wore fishnet stockings and miniskirts into her ninth decade, reported that at her death, "She was 90, though parts of her were considerably younger."[16])

Wise funeral directors and pastors can work together to help people remember what it means to be human in the face of death and what it means to do a human thing humanely. There will be resistance of course, and plays called in the huddle will have to be "audibled" on the field. But deep in the soul there is a sensibility about how to care for the dead and how to do a funeral with meaning and hope, and this means that every now and then a family will get it right and do this well. They will walk with their loved one to the place of farewell and, with tears and gratitude, will let them go. Such an act carries its own human and religious power, and nothing is more instructive to a community than a funeral well done. It's like a chorus right on pitch, a well-executed double play in baseball, a beautifully prepared meal with hospitality and just the right wine—*that's* the way to do it.

If funeral directors are to assist each other in helping people to remember their humanity at the time of death, we will need to start by stopping, by refusing to reinforce the disembodied, overly spiritualized impulses in our culture. For funeral directors, this will mean a "cease and desist" on all marketing ploys aimed at personalization and sentimentality rather than emphasizing that a funeral is what we do together for and with the dead. People can acquire personal meaning and sentiment all by themselves out in the woods, and increasingly that is exactly where they are going to get them.

For pastors it will mean emphasizing—in preaching, teaching, and guidance—the world-embracing character of the great faith traditions, the materiality of our spirituality. Jayber Crow, the protagonist in Wendell Berry's novel of the same name, is the barber and also the gravedigger in the small village of Port William, Kentucky. Although Jayber is a common man with an ordinary vocation, he is nevertheless a wise everyman philosopher and a teller of truth about the human condition. At one point in the novel, Jayber expresses bafflement over the preachers he hears in their local church who preach sermons denouncing the world and the flesh. He muses,

> This religion that scorned the beauty and goodness of this world was a puzzle to me. . . . While the wickedness of the flesh was preached from the pulpit, the young husbands and wives and young courting couples sat thigh to thigh, full of yearning and joy, and the old people thought of the beauty of the children. And when church was over they'd go home to Heavenly dinners of fried chicken, it might be, and creamed new peas and hot biscuits and butter and cherry pie and sweet milk and buttermilk. . . . [A]nd the preacher, having just foresworn on behalf of everybody the joys of the flesh, would eat with unconsecrated relish.[17]

When he was an old man, Saint Augustine, the renowned North African bishop, was asked a practical ministry question by another pastor.[18] It seems that a man had died in this other pastor's flock, and the dead man's grief-stricken mother, wanting to do right by him, desired that he be buried in a certain church building next to the grave of a saint. Augustine was a respected theologian, a wise pastor, and a seasoned bishop, and his colleague now wanted his opinion: would it be of any benefit to the deceased man to have his body laid next to a revered saint?

I suspect that most pastors today would scoff at such a question, at least privately. What possible advantage could it be to a dead man to be buried next to a saint? If he were buried in a flower garden, would he become a gladiola? Who cares how or where he's buried? Next question.

Augustine, however, gave a response that was more nuanced, and more astute. He acknowledged that his pastor friend had asked a good question and that behind the question there was a deep and accurate perception of the connection between bodies and holiness. Augustine said that caring for the bodies of the dead and being concerned with the manner of their physical burial was "an office of humanity."[19] If even the pagans know how to bear the bodies of their dead with dignity, he said, how much more should believers do this humane act in a holy way as a "testimony of . . . the faith"[20]?

Having said this, though, Augustine rejected magical views of what was happening to dead bodies. No, being buried three feet away from a saint did not make one holy by spiritual osmosis. His reasons for saying this are important. First, the kind of burial one has doesn't change one's relationship to God. The bishop pointed out that the bodies of many faithful Christians had been desecrated by persecutors, thrown to lions, and dismembered by the sword. The blood of Christians, Augustine said, flowed "like water round about Jerusalem, and there was no man to bury them." Even though they were not buried in a decent and holy way, they were still "precious in the sight of the Lord." The rich man in Jesus' parable had undoubtedly had a fine funeral, said Augustine, but it was Lazarus, the beggar whose body was covered with sores, who was carried by the angels to the bosom of Abraham.[21]

Second, the thought that it would be of merit to a dead person to be buried next to a holy person was actually an undermining of the embodied character of the faith. You can't borrow embodied holiness. To bury someone is to acknowledge the sacredness of *that* person's body, to lift up in memory and to God the actions of *his* body, to make as an offering the way of life *that* body followed—not the body of the other guy in the cemetery, even if he was a saint.

So, if a good burial can't make a dead person more holy and a bad burial can't break the protection of God, then why be concerned about burial at all? Again, Augustine advances two well-crafted reasons. First, caring tenderly for the dead benefits the living. It increases their faith and provides meaning, comfort, and hope to them. Second, those who bury the dead are performing a piece of theater in which they act out the deepest truths they know about life and death. When a father dies, Augustine said, the children prize his robe and ring because they love their father and holding those things he put on is a way of acting out their affection toward him. How much more, then, do we prize the bodies of the departed, said Augustine, even more so because the body is not a garment or an ornament, but bound "to the very nature of a human being." We should care for the bodies of the dead, Augustine said, in the same way that the followers of Jesus took his body from the cross and laid it reverently in the tomb.[22] They did this not because dead bodies have feelings but because they were acting out in their human care what they believed God was doing, divinely caring for Jesus' body as God cares for the bodies of all the dead.

Augustine got it just right. In our funeral rites we are performing a piece of community theater, one which enriches our own lives, in which we announce our deepest convictions, and one in which we act out the drama of what we believe to be happening in this world and beyond. This allows us to take bodies seriously, even sacredly, but not ultimately. It allows us to embrace and anoint the dead tenderly, but also to let them go where they need to go. It allows us to weep and laugh, to remember and to tell the truth, to grieve over and to celebrate what was done in the body on this earth even as we send the dead toward that land to which they are traveling. It allows us to love this world, even as we hope for the next one.

As John Ames, the aging Congregationalist minister in Marilyn Robinson's novel *Gilead*, says,

> I know this [world] is all mere apparition compared to what awaits us, but it is only lovelier for that. There is a human beauty in it. And I can't believe that, when we have all been changed and put on incorruptibility, we will forget our fantastic condition of mortality and impermanence, the great bright dream of procreating and perishing that meant the whole world to us. In eternity this world will be Troy, I believe, and all that has passed here will be the epic of the universe, the ballad they sing in the streets. Because I don't imagine any reality putting this one in the shade entirely, and I think piety forbids me to try.[23]

Funeral Directors and Clergy

Dirge without Music

I am not resigned to the shutting away of loving hearts in the hard ground.
So it is, and so it will be, for so it has been, time out of mind:
Into the darkness they go, the wise and the lovely. Crowned
With lilies and with laurel they go; but I am not resigned.

Lovers and thinkers, into the earth with you.
Be one with the dull, the indiscriminate dust.
A fragment of what you felt, of what you knew,
A formula, a phrase remains,—but the best is lost.

The answers quick and keen, the honest look, the laughter, the love,—
They are gone. They are gone to feed the roses. Elegant and curled
Is the blossom. Fragrant is the blossom. I know. But I do not approve.
More precious was the light in your eyes than all the roses in the world.

Down, down, down into the darkness of the grave
Gently they go, the beautiful, the tender, the kind;
Quietly they go, the intelligent, the witty, the brave.
I know. But I do not approve. And I am not resigned.

Edna St. Vincent Millay

Chapter 5

OUR OWN WORST ENEMIES

Thomas Lynch

IN *THE AMERICAN LANGUAGE,* HIS CLASSIC STUDY OF THE POWER of words, H. L. Mencken quotes an article in the January 1932 edition of *Editor and Publisher*, to wit: "'The decree goes forth,'" announced the (Chicago) Tribune, 'not for lack of sympathy with the ambition of undertakers to be well regarded, but because of it. If they haven't the sense to save themselves from their own lexicographers, we shall not be guilty of abetting them in their folly.'"[1] Of course, "the ambition of undertakers to be well regarded" is hardly different from the ambitions of farmers or freemasons, candidates for public office, revenue agents, or the reverend clergy. We all want to be trusted and admired. Mencken was lampooning the tendency to become the enemies of our best intention. In this case he was remarking on the evolution of "undertakers" during the mid-nineteenth century, to "funeral directors" soon after the Civil War, and then to "morticians" early in the twentieth century.

His efforts to keep the undertakers of that gilded age from shooting themselves in the same foot that they would eventually put into their mouths proved, predictably, unsuccessful. Then, as now, we were our own worst enemies. Our mortuary forbears, wanting to be taken seriously, were trading a serviceable and quietly sublime occupational title—undertaker—for a contrivance. To undertake meant to bind oneself to a particular task or enterprise, to pledge or promise to get it done, to take on something others would not rise to. The word bore its share of gravity and purpose and was well known to the public at large: you have a crisis that produces a corpse, you call an undertaker. It occupied a respected place on the Main Street of occupations. Based on a clear understanding of what it is one does—an understanding shared by the public at large—it kept one from going too far astray. Of course, then as now, the undertaker might have a sideline or two—a furniture store or livery stable, a flower shop or saloon—but everyone knew what an undertaker undertook: to serve the living by caring for the dead.

Elmer Davis's article, "The Mortician," had already appeared in the pages of *The American Mercury*, which Mencken edited:

> It is a cause of much grief to morticians and funeral directors—there are no undertakers any more, or if there are, they are men of so little vision as not to be worth considering—that the public is inclined to regard their profession with levity. They argue, quite reasonably, that the disposal of the dead is a function that has to be performed, and one, moreover, which the surviving relatives usually feel must be performed with a certain amount of ceremony and parade. The mortician provides the refined and decorous display which the customer demands—and then the customer roars about the size of the bill and regards him, ever after, with a compound of resentment and derision which would get on any man's nerves.[2]

It was ever thus: the comingling of mortality and money, death and dollars, sadness and sales, is a tricky business. Like the editors of the *Chicago Tribune* and Elmer Davis, Mencken was trying to save us from ourselves—we undertakers, funeral directors, morticians—and from our persistent failure to discern what the public wants from us, what it will pay us for, and what it won't.

Nearly a century later, the cover story of the August 2012 edition of *The Director* magazine, which circulates to the 8,500 members of the National Funeral Directors Association, is called "Listening to Your Customers" and offers as evidence, "Results of the 2012 NFDA Consumer Awareness and Preferences Survey." It occupies, between text and graphics and pie charts, as well as the considerable ad copy throughout, nearly seventeen pages of the magazine's hundred or so monthly pages and is coauthored by Deana Gillespie, NFDA's research specialist and Ed Defort, editor of *The Director*, who also pens an editorial called "Survey Says . . . Opportunities Await to Educate Consumers."

The range of questions is impressive, from "What Are the Most Important Qualities You Look(ed) for When Choosing a Funeral Director?" to "Are You Aware of an Alternative to Burial and Cremation Called 'Alkaline Hydrolysis?'" Seven percent answered "yes" to that. And there are comprehensive sections on cremation, prearrangement, religious identity, age, and ethnicity. In all, the survey is designed to give the reader of the magazine—members of NFDA and their staffs—a finger on the pulse of consumer preferences, the better to design a model of service that delivers what the customer wants.

Mixed throughout the pages of the article are ads for bronze sculptures and urns, rose petal rosaries, retirement plans, commemorative video production companies, brass keepsake necklace pendants, a mortuary school, a bank that has loan programs for funeral homes. The top banner on the front cover promises "2012 NFDA Charlotte Expo Preview," which lists the vendors who will be displaying at the upcoming convention in Charlotte, North Carolina. That "preview" occupies another seventeen pages of alphabetical listing of exhibiting companies, a detail of Platinum, Gold, Silver, and Bronze sponsors, each with their logo and thumbnail company history well displayed, and a centerfold of the exhibit floor with booths numbered, bars and concessions detailed. Again there are ads—a full-pager for a half-ton body lift, quarter- and half-pagers for finance companies, urns and hearses, shipping services and architects. So, seventeen pages on consumer surveys and seventeen pages on the suppliers to the trade—the August *Director*, like the convention itself, is an odd proximation of the often juxtaposed and competing interests within the mortuary marketplace. One presses toward better services, the other toward better sales.

This tension between the provision of services and the selling of stuff is at the center of many enterprises. In my experience, funeral directors lose public trust when interests of consumers are superseded by the interests of vendors; and when those who ought to be listening to their customers, begin, rather, to pay too much attention to the suppliers to the trade. Think of the doctor who spends more time with pharmaceutical sales reps than with patients.

When I went into mortuary school forty years ago, the casket companies held the most sway. More money and energy and space were dedicated to the sale of boxes—coffins and vaults—than anything else. Our classes included mock display rooms and students were taught how to describe the differences between one casket and another. It was training for their future in which "product knowledge" provided by casket companies masqueraded as continuing education. Batesville Casket Company, the largest manufacturer in the country, would fly funeral directors down to their compound in southern Indiana for a couple of days of plant tours and training, then send them back home with new sales pitches that, back in those days, revolved around the concept of "protection." Batesville had managed, around midcentury, to engineer a casket with a rubber gasket that "sealed," according to the marketing bromides, "against air and moisture." They made the "Monoseal" and "Monogard" in dozens of different colors and models in various gauges or thickness of steel as well as the "precious" metals of copper and bronze and stainless steel. Some models were made, furthermore, with "cathodic protection"—a magnesium bar that was clipped to the bottom of the casket to prevent rusting or corrosion should the casket be scratched. They had crepe and velvet interiors with embroidered scenes of pine trees and praying hands. They had "keys" to seal and unseal the things. Often, after sealing the casket, we'd proffer the "key" to the next of kin.

I remember my father walking me through our casket display pronouncing the words of the script he had learned from his Batesville Casket rep—an elegant, likable man who visited every other week to show my father new products and sales aids. Lifting the velvet overlay of the casket he would display the edge and its rubber seal. "Some caskets are what we call 'sealed' or 'protective' caskets," he would begin. "To some people this is very important. To others it means nothing at all." It was at this point the bereaved buyer would, if the salesman was correct, naturally associate the dead persons worth with "very important," or "nothing at all," and be moved accordingly to the suitable purchase.

Let me make something perfectly clear: I'm all for caskets. I think they remain among the few things surrounding a death in the family about which we actually have some control, some choices, some say in the matter. I remember standing out in my parents' garage with my brothers discussing what type of casket we'd get for our mother who was dying upstairs where our sisters were tending to her, every bit as helpless as their brothers out in the garage and our father keeping his vigil with her. Having some say about the casket was a tiny compensation, but compensation all the same for having no say about our mother's cancer. And I'm all for the way caskets make moving the dead from one place to the next that much handier. I like the way they let us get a "handle" on that. What's more, I'm unopposed to wholesale and retail and profit on sales for the casket manufacturer and their end-market provisioners. It's just that I think so many of my colleagues in funeral service spend so much time considering caskets that they come to believe that caskets are their product and profit center. The public has come to that conclusion too—that mostly we are interested in the sale of boxes and that we associate a good funeral with a good casket in the way some might mistake a good diamond for a good marriage.

It's easy to understand how Batesville got on to selling "protection." These were the years after World War II and Korea; years when Vietnam and the Cold War were raging and the country moved from crisis to crisis. Protection and permanence were concepts that had great resonance, whether selling bomb shelters or life insurance, diamond rings or underarm deodorants, tampons or vaccinations or Batesville caskets. We inhabited a dangerous world where invasion, inundation, leakage, and wreckage lurked among the contingencies. In such a world, an eighteen-gauge, cathodically protected steel casket with a seal that was warranted for fifty years seemed as sensible as good homeowners coverage, even if the worst that could happen had, by nature of the transaction, already happened.

Still, I remember attending one of Batesville's regional seminars—an evening where funeral directors gathered for cocktails and dinner, all paid for by the casket maker in trade for enduring an hour or two of what they considered continuing education. The presenter was making the case that a room full of Batesvilles was the best way to achieve "Optimal Return on Investment," and that the higher the "wholesale investment" the greater the return. This seemed at odds with the "buy low, sell high" doctrines of retail that governed other markets. Furthermore, he was saying, the only difference between one casket and another, so far as the customer was concerned, was whether it was sealed or unsealed, which was to say, those that were "protective" and those that were "non-protective" caskets.

This did not make too much sense to me and I raised my hand to tell him so. "What if a family has their heart set on a blue casket?" I asked him. To which he responded that the company made dozens of models in dozens of shades of blue. In which case, I said to him, the only difference among caskets for that family would be those that are blue and the ones that aren't, regardless of whether or not they were sealed. He did not seem enthused at my suggestion. "Or what if," I continued, "the dead person always said they wanted an oak casket or a pine box or the cheapest available or the priciest? Wouldn't the only difference between caskets for them be the oaks or the pines or how much or how little they cost?" "Well," he said, "people don't always know what the most important things are. That's why it's our job to let them know."

At some level, of course, I agreed with him. People get little practice at these contingencies, and someone with reliable information can be of great help to the family in need. I just didn't think it had much to do with caskets. And yet, the effort of the casket manufacturers to turn the nation's funeral directors and their facilities into well-staffed and well-maintained casket stores is understandable, even while it must be resisted. Casket makers want to sell caskets. Funeral directors want to provide funerals. One is not the same as the other. All the same, suppliers trying to turn funeral directors into their agents and sales reps is nothing new, nor is it limited to the mortuary marketplace. Doctors become peddlers of the latest drugs and tests, procedures and surgeries, some of which might not be entirely necessary.

The response to decades of sales pitches about "protection" was one among many factors that lead, from the 1960s, to five decades of shifting consumer preference about the way in which we dispose of our dead. From a near 100 percent preference to earth burial in 1960 to a cremation rate now in the mid-forty percent range, the concentration of cost and energy and attention on caskets has become a point of imbalance between consumer preference and vendor interests. In response to the increasing consumer preference for cremation, Batesville Casket Company bought up smaller manufacturers of wooden caskets and began to market what they called "options" to the ever-expanding cremation market, coincidentally about the same time that the notion of "choice" began to replace permanence and protection in the national conversation and sensibilities. Of course, wooden caskets were every bit as costly at wholesale and retail, and the options consumers were left with at first did not include caskets priced below the typical range of metal caskets. In order to have a funeral with the body present, a casket had to be purchased. Even in those instances where funeral homes would rent caskets, at a typical charge of one quarter of retail and a typical rental being of higher-end wooden caskets, the actual savings to families was minimal. The reliance of funeral firms on casket sales as the principle profit center of their business lead to the public perception that there was a "box tax" that had to be paid in order to have a meaningful funeral. Thus, the public began to think in terms of choices between a funeral and a cremation. If you wanted the body embalmed for preservation and buried in a sealed casket, it might be worth it to spend considerable funds on a sealed casket and sealed burial vault. But if protection and permanence made no sense when applied to the case of a dead human body, and there were few choices that did not require spending on a casket if the body was to be present for the service, a more popular option became doing without the body and its boxes. Thus the memorial service, as an alternative to a funeral with the body and box, became the convenient, cost-efficient, and sensible choice. The failure of casket manufacturers to produce a lower-priced option and the failure of funeral directors to require an inexpensive and yet aesthetically acceptable alternative container that would have allowed families electing to cremate their dead to have a funeral with the body present without having to spend considerable funds on a casket were among the prime movers of the culture towards dismissing the corpse from the funeral. It was the first of many examples of listening to vendors, when listening to customers might have made all the difference.

Another version of the same miscalculation occurred when the advance selling of funeral goods and services became all the rage. Preneed, as it was called, was coincident with and correlated to the merger and acquisition of funeral homes by large conglomerates, which began in the mid-1980s. Ray Loewen of Manitoba, Frank Stewart Jr. of Louisiana, and Robert Waltrip of Texas, each took family held regional conglomerates and built them into larger, sometimes multinational, publicly traded companies. Apart from the capital raised by selling stock, the cash flow from day-to-day operations of funeral homes and cemeteries was augmented by the aggressive preselling of funeral and cemetery goods and services, most of it done by commissioned salespeople. As with the marketplace's failure to discern what the consumer wanted in boxes, the failure to discern what the consumer wanted in planning options has done irreparable damage to the public image of funeral directors and created an environment of abuse and scandal from which funeral service may find it impossible to recover.

The merger, acquisition, and consolidation frenzy of the 1980s fueled a seismic expansion of preneed sales. If one can't expand the market, expand the market share. Of course, the "death care" conglomerates were following the leads of burger joints and booksellers and other expandable markets that created new synergies between supply and distribution and retail outlets. Bertelsmann buys Random House then Barnes & Noble Online, whilst Barnes & Noble attempts to buy wholesaler Ingram while the bookstore on the corner disappears. Service Corporation International, the nation's largest mortuary conglomerate, does a deal with Batesville Casket for deep discounts and another with the Catholic Church—the original merger and acquisition firm—for management of its mortuary details through its Christian Funeral Services (CFS) subsidiary. The church, finding the traffic in souls a little off, reckons the traffic in bodies might do better. The bishops read the same demographics as the multinational conglomerates. Everyone wants to be ready for the bang and whimper of the baby boom, that last hurrah expected between 2010 and 2040 when the annual deaths in the United States will reach three million (compared to 2.5 million these days). And what funds the acquisitions and promises their future market share is the presale of funeral services and merchandise.

At the same time, traditional funeral directors, frightened that someone might sell the families in their towns something in advance that they have been waiting to sell when someone dies, scrambled to establish their own preneed sales programs. They mortgaged their brick-and-mortar to fund telemarketing schemes to fight telemarketing schemes, junk mail to fend off junk mail, door-to-door solicitors to beat other door-to-door solicitors to the punch. Their national associations, state and federal regulators, famous for nothing so much as doing nothing, do nothing. Their trade press is full of warnings and woe. After a few years of trying to compete locally with a multinational corporation, jumping through the compliance hoops of OSHA and the FTC, and watching the perennial hidden-camera "Mortuary-Cam" exposés on the network news, more and more second and third generation ma and pa funeral homes every year sold their good names to the conglomerates, took their cash and stock options and called it a day. This is how the preneed bubble inflated in the funeral marketplace in the last two decades of the twentieth century, a bubble that began to leak and finally burst in the first decade of the new millennium.

⚬✖⚬

Let me make another thing perfectly clear: I'm all for planning ahead and being prepared.

The pre*arrangement* of funerals has been around since the species first noticed that mortality was part of the human condition. Portal graves and pyramids, passage tombs and ossuaries, church yards and catacombs dot the landscapes of our planet. Knowing they were going to die drove our ancestors to plan accordingly. No less did they provide pre*funding* for their funerals. Since the beginning we've put aside something to pay for the disposition of our "remains"—a bit of insurance, money stuffed in a mattress, the sexton's fee and preacher's stipend. But the aggressive pre*selling* of funeral wares is a late-twentieth-century invention, driven entirely by vendor interests and the cash hunger of consolidators within what is now called "the death-care industry."

Advance planning for funerals is in no small way based on Mitford's advice that arrangements made ahead of death are more sensible, less risky, more likely to be minimalist. Furthermore, she figured, the mortician would be less abusive to the dispassionate advance shopper than to the recently bereaved. Since she saw funeral directors as eager to prey on fresh grief, she preferred a shopping experience unencumbered by feelings.

And people like to be prepared. Thus the aging consumer's sensible impulse to plan ahead, an existential concern that is met in the marketplace by a variety of essentially retail experiences—a Certified Preplanning Consultant (a hybrid of insurance and mortuary salesperson) or Memorial Counselor (read commissioned salesperson) who is eager to peddle, in advance, anything and everything but the commemorative kitchen-sink. Traditional, community-based funeral directors with mortgages on their brick-and-mortar, and longstanding reputations to keep intact have been driven by local patronage if not high morals to heed the undertakerly charge to serve the living by caring for the dead. Because their future business depends on it, the new "death-care professionals"—accountable to a corporate up-line that leads to corporate headquarters in another state, and having little more than a briefcase and a prospects list invested in the transaction—are schooled to do what must be done to close the deal.

They always called in the middle of dinner. And they were always from places that sounded folksy and green—Willow Park, Heritage Creek, Oakland Hills, Forest Lawn. And it was never quite clear just what they were selling—golf club memberships or time-share condos, new age religion or nursing home care—the names always sounded genially nondescript. Maybe they're selling all of the above. "Protection . . . inevitable . . . eventual reality." There's a flurry of meaningful concept words.

Eight times out of ten it was the cemetery ten miles east off the interstate calling to sell me my "memorial estate." There'd be a silky voice giving the sales pitch involving "Millennium Discounts" and "End of the Century Savings" on what she was calling my "final expenses."

I always told them I'm a funeral director and thus had my own caskets and vaults and urns—at wholesale. But this never seemed to put them off. They'd be halfway through the first page of script, earnestly inserting my name in the blanks.

"So much better to do this when heads are cool, Mr. Lynch, before the need arises. Before your family is vulnerable to someone who might take advantage of their grief. Our counselor will be happy to come to your home!"

While a death in the family does, in fact, place the consumer in a bad bargaining position—they have, after all, a corpse to deal with—the folks they call for help in times of trouble are either honest, or they are not, before, during, and after the fact.

"Preplanning is something you can do for your family. They'll always remember that you cared enough to take care of these difficult decisions. You can be sure everything is done the way you want it."

There'd be this hint in her voice that my kids wouldn't do me properly—they might spend too little and blame it on me ("Dad would come back to haunt us if we put him in that casket!"). Or they'd spend too much—wasting the money on caskets and sentimentals that I wanted spent on my future grandchildren's college tuition. Either way, they'd never get it right. The fashionable flash of generational mistrust and the basic narcissism of the age were somewhere in the subtext of her soft contralto. That I could run my affairs literally into the ground was meant to be a kind of comfort. "Have it your way" she seemed to be saying, like Burger King or Frank Sinatra.

My father directed funerals all his life and whenever we'd ask him what he'd like for himself he'd only say, "You'll know what to do."

We did, of course.

We wept and laughed and waked him, took him to church then buried him in the ground next to our mother, who had died two years before him. We kept their names alive in the talk of their people and kept it on the signs that keep us all accountable to the communities we serve.

"We have many, many options to choose from. Dozens of different payment plans."

She was pushing the right buttons for us boomers now: planning, choices. We love these things. Planned parenthood, prenuptials, prearranged funerals—always this hopeful notion that we might pre-feel the feelings, the untidy, potentially embarrassing dynamics of birth and love and grief; the blubbering and baby talk; the sense that these unpredictable, existential events might be turned into manageable retail experiences with numbers and prices and a bottom line that always adds up. The notion of choice in the contemplation of our own mortality—that part of our nature about which we have no choice—was especially comforting.

"You don't want to be a burden to your children, do you?"

This was always the telemarketer's coup de grace, reaching deep into the parental psyche to tap the wellspring of guilt over not taking them to Disney World or the therapist or dermatologist enough, for never spending enough quality time with them, for not buying them a pony or a new car, or for not sending them to a private school. Here was the chance to make it all up to them by prearranging my own funeral, saving them from all the difficult decisions that they will eventually have to live with.

I see them now—my darling sons, my fierce daughter—heartsore and vulnerable at the news of my untimely and possibly heroic death. I think of them with their cell phones and gold cards and higher educations and inheritance. And it occurs to me: Why shouldn't I be a burden to my children?

My children have been a burden to me. Lovely burdens, every one of them. Taking care of their earaches and heartaches and broken bones and disappointments, paying for their college and dance classes and car insurance—they've been a burden. I think they were supposed to be. Over the years I've had to explain the death of their grandparents, the suicides of classmates, the divorce of their mother and father, the misbehavior of our political leaders, and how love hurts and life isn't fair. I've done car pools and made bag lunches and answered overwhelming questions; I've tended broken hearts, been involved in little league and PTA, discussed with them difficult choices and the facts of life. Sometimes it got really heavy. Sometimes I had to tell them I don't know.

And bearing these burdens of love and grief has made me feel alive and involved in ways I never thought I would be; it's made me feel needed and necessary and part of the family. It has made me feel "called" to be a parent. And if it has left me bald and near broke and fairly bewildered, it has likewise left me wondrous, blessed, and thankful. After everything, being their father has brought more meaning to my life than any other thing I've ever done or been.

And when I die, bearing the burden of burying me or burning me or blasting me into cyberspace should be theirs to do. My funeral will belong to them and they will be paying for it emotionally, financially, actually. Since they have to live with the decisions, why shouldn't they make them? If I've done my job, they'll know what to do. If the burden of my death, borne honorably, makes them feel as capable as bearing the sweet burden of their births has made me feel, I can do them the favor of leaving well enough alone.

When I tell the disembodied telemarketer on the other end of the line these things, she goes silent. It is not in the script. She hangs up. We return to what's left of our lives and times.

All the same, for funeral directors, it has seemed like a list of bad choices, between selling hard, selling out, or watching one's business be raided by presellers working for the conglomerates or the competition. Firms that had built their businesses on reliable service and fair dealings with their clientele began to fear that their hard-earned reputations for excellence were not enough. The conglomerates based their growth strategies on the notion that the money in the bank is better than the public trust when it comes to holding future market share. The "buy now, die later" brand of package deal has meant a lost connection between the sale of funerals and the delivery of them, and with it the loss of face-to-face accountability between buyer and seller that used to provide reliable consumer protection. Now the recipient of services (the bereaved) and the provider of same (the funeral director) are both perilously out of the loop of the original transaction: a deal often brokered years before, between a commissioned salesperson and the now newly deceased. In such an environment there can be little real accountability.

Just as casket makers sought to turn funeral directors into casket peddlers, the finance and insurance industries sought to turn them into insurance and finance agents. Funeral types were well-dressed, locally trusted, and highly motivated to protect their market share, and the vast majority of them have traded in their readiness and willingness to serve for an anxious, eagerness to sell. The "first call," formerly made by the next of kin to alert the funeral director that someone has died is now more often made by the funeral home's "certified preplanning consultant" who is commissioned to sell whatever they can in advance. Likewise, the pool of money that accumulates for services and merchandise that do not have to be provided for months or years to come present, to cash-strapped and undercapitalized enterprises, an often irresistible occasion for consumer abuse and criminal conduct, examples of which are all too frequently reported in the general media.

Again, it is important to distinguish the vendor-driven interest in preselling funerals from the consumer's interests in prearranging a funeral and those few instances—almost always having to do with a spenddown of assets for Medicare purposes—when it might be wise to pre-fund a funeral with a funeral home.

In the decades on either side of the turn of this century, the aggressive preselling of caskets, graves, funeral home and cemetery services became the junk bonds of the mortuary marketplace and became the source of scandals and abuses that were reported in local, regional, and national media. For all the damage done to funeral directors and to funeral consumers, it remains remarkable that it was so enthusiastically embraced by funeral directors, their associations, and conglomerations. An examination of how this happened might provide some prevention if not a cure for our inclination to become our own worst enemies.

Plan Ahead, Pay in Advance, Buy This, Sign Here. Everything gets taken care of exactly as you want it. Such bromides became the approved message on preneed adopted by the marketplace. Everyone agreed. Everyone approved. The funeral trade associations approved because it attracted the insurance companies and marketing firms to their conventions. They sponsored convention speakers, bought full-page ads in the trade press, and often provided a commission on sales to the association itself. The merger and acquisition firms approved because preneed sales, along with some creative accounting, propped up the illusion maintained for Wall Street that expanding market activity meant an expanding market.

I remember one investment guru calling me in the late 1990s to ask my best counsel on the relative worth of the "death-care portfolio"—those publicly traded companies that were buying up the local firms across the country, and the few casket makers that were publicly traded. He was very bullish on this sector, it was evident, because, as he told me with enthusiasm, "*Everybody* is gonna die once!" To which I suggested that he say the same thing slowly again, letting the emphasis fall where it might fall, thus: "Everybody is going to die *once."* Ours, I told him, is an un-expandable market, which is to say that nothing in the marketplace could change the fact that there would only be one death per customer and most were neither eager nor enthused about even the one. A funeral home on every corner, free parking, big discounts, a reputation for excellence—these might change the market share but not the market itself, which would remain stubbornly yoked to the way of things, made clear in Hebrews 9:27, to wit "it is appointed unto men once to die" (KJV).

Nonetheless, the sense that more market activity might, in some way, widen the actual market created a frenzy of preneed sales. The casket makers and insurance companies approve because they were poised to become to funeral service what the pharmaceutical companies and HMOs had become to medicine: the tail of finance and manufacturing that wags the dog of professional care and service. Just as health care is increasingly dominated by the pill makers and insurers, death care is increasingly dominated by the box makers and insurers. And just as some factotum with a list of approved procedures calls from Blue Cross to tell the doctor what treatment is covered and what is not, the day may not be far off when someone will call to say whether visitation is "covered" or the procession is "approved" or the presence of the body at the funeral is "fully funded."

And there were all those preneed "counselors" to train to become a kind of death-care professional or funeral-director-lite, without all the bother of college or apprenticeship, testing or licensure. The associations, for a price, can do it in a day—they even give you letters you can use after your name. A "CPC" or "Certified Preplanning Consultant," is the mortuary marketplace's commissioned seller.

The effort to turn funeral directors into insurance agents and casket sellers has had the effect, of course, of making anyone who sells caskets or insurance seem like, well, a funeral director.

Everyone agreed: funeral associations, the multinational merger and acquisition firms, casket manufacturers and financial services, the trade press and media and the experts that write for them and provide the training and continuing education—the approved message on preneed became *Plan Ahead, Pay in Advance, Buy This, Sign Here. Everything is taken care of.* Any message to the contrary was silenced, censored, marginalized, or ignored.

This is how funeral service, like many specialized occupational sorts, creates its own bubble of reality, its own echo chamber where everyone is mostly talking to each other, mostly on topics they agree about, and word from the world at large is seldom heard.

When *Modern Maturity*, the AARP magazine, published in its March–April 2000 edition an article unambiguously titled "RIP Off," that told its several million readers that prepaid funerals were fraught with abuse, the funeral associations blamed the AARP and wrote letters of protest.

When, that same spring, the Senate of the United States held two days of public televised hearings on funerals and burials and preneed abuses, and the testimony was manifestly at odds with their approved message on preneed, the associations blamed the senators and wrote a letter of protest.

When ABC News, in February 2001, broadcast a segment called, predictably, "The High Cost of Dying: Funeral Homes Accused of High-Pressure Sales Tactics, Fraud, and Abuse" on the evening news, it opened with a local funeral director giving the industry's approved message on preneed: "I've just had so many families mention to me, 'I'm so glad that we did this years and years ago, because everything was taken care of exactly as we wanted it to be done.'"[3]

The rest of the segment was spent making the case for why paying a funeral director in advance for goods and services that may not be provided for years would be among the worst decisions any consumer might make. Of course, the funeral director looked more than a little silly, as did the trade associations he represented, which dutifully wrote a letter of protest.

The uninterrupted litany of press accounts of scandals and the attendant decline in public trust wrought by preneed sales schemes did little to slow the frenzy for preneed within funeral service. Insurance companies, trust fund companies, consultants who would train new sellers to sell an array of commemorative package deals to aging consumers, provided fodder for the trade press, and exhibit income to state and national conventions. "Thought leaders"—often connected to trust and insurance companies—provided programming for association meetings and filler for their trade magazines and newsletters. Of course many state associations, as administrators of preneed trusts, covered most of their operating expenses and executive bonuses with money earned from commissions on sales. Everybody stood to take a piece of the action.

The pie of funeral expenses and revenues, formerly distributed among providers of goods and services, rarely provided more than single digit profits. Now the slices were many more and accordingly narrower—a commission for the contract seller, a piece for the referral and finder's fees, something for marketing and management of the preneed account, and, of course, a profit for the financier, whether trust account or insurance company. These "transactional expenses," which paid neither for mortuary services or merchandise, came out before the funeral director and clergy, the florist and newspapers, the soloist and cemetery, stood in line for theirs. It was money spent on the shuffling of paper. Likewise the falling of interest rates made the guarantee of future services in exchange for the interest that might accrue to the account a drag on the market. This "freezing" of expenditures to current day prices was among the most powerful marketing inducements for paying for a funeral years in advance. It was seen as the illusive win-win situation for both buyer and seller. No few funeral directors would find that a policy sold years before had lost cash value by the time it was needed. Guarantees that "everything has been taken care of," came back to haunt more than a few operators who found their preneed funerals being subsidized by at-need sales—just the reverse of what was intended. Many funeral homes, under whose aegis the preneed packages were sold found themselves taking the shortfall from an underperforming policy or trust account. They were also finding that the commission they took and spent years prior produced a revenue shortfall at the time a death occurred. More often, as the financial markets declined and the recession progressed, the portfolio of prepaid funerals that a funeral home kept in its files seemed like a liability rather than an asset. Of course the very same analysts, consultants, and gurus who formerly advised aggressive preneed sales programs, now began to caution about the actuarial facts of the matter: that buy now and die later produced more often a lose-lose situation for the bereaved and for the funeral provider.

Direct mail and telemarketing companies sold their services to funeral homes on the notion that out of every so many thousand mailers or cold calls, so many hundred consumers might respond, out of which so many dozen might schedule an appointment, out of which ten or twenty might actually pay in advance for their funeral. This was the moment that generated a sale and commission. But what these preneed gurus never reported was the number of people out of every thousand who might respond to the junk mail or cold call as they might to someone offering to sell them some chemotherapy in advance, or a future heart bypass or radiation. A funeral, it seemed never to occur to the death-care professionals, is closer to such contingencies than it is to, say, a trip to Disneyland or the Poconos. And yet the performance reviews always made much of the half a dozen "sales" and nothing of the several thousand permanently offended consumers.

To have done so might have modified the message and brought the marketplace sooner to the admission, still not evident to many, that the junk-mailed, telemarketed, bargain-in-the-briefcase brand of presold funeral service that has turned every sadness into a sales-op and every funeral into a retail event has not been good for the funeral, the funeral consumer, or the funeral director. Nor has it been good for their associations. There has always been a difference between the ones who call in the middle of dinner to sell you a bill of goods and the ones who are called in the middle of the night when there's been a death in the family. The failure of funeral directors and their associations to affirm those differences has made us our own worst enemies.

Furthermore, the frequent incidents of malfeasance and criminal conduct associated with the advance sale of funeral and cemetery goods and services has done irreparable damage to the public trust and public image of all funeral directors. Local and regional scandals, most often involving a funeral director who, rather than depositing funds with an insurance company or third party trust, used money from advance sales to cover current costs of operation, or to finance a more lavish lifestyle than funeral service typically affords, or to pay for a drug or gambling habit, soon gave way to larger and more lucrative thefts and subterfuges. One need only Google "Menorah Gardens" or "Clayton Smart" or "NPL Preneed Scandal" to get a sense of the scope of such crimes that involved tens of millions of dollars. The latter often left honest brokers and honorable funeral directors holding the bag for services they'd undertaken to perform while the funds for same had long gone missing.

State legislatures, which varied widely on trusting requirements, allowable commissions, portability, cancellation policies and other aspects of the transaction, were slow to react to the quickly changing market in preneed sales. The frequent scandals, some involving state funeral directors' associations (many of whom operated on the commissions earned by holding trust accounts or insurance pools), further undermined the public trust in local funeral directors.

The effort in some states to remove sales commissions from the preneed transaction—an effort supported by enlightened funeral directors' associations and the consumers' lobby—has been guided by the principles that there ought be no profit in preneed transactions, and that once the carrot of sales commissions is removed from the transaction, the incentive to sell hard is removed and preplanning returns to the public utility and professional accommodation that it ought to be, whereby only consumer interests drive the market. Whether it is to "spend down" assets to qualify for health-care benefits, to sequester funds from a larger estate, to make known to survivors what is and is not important to the future deceased, or some sought after "peace of mind," the buyer, not the seller, should initiate the transaction.

⟡

The hard-sell, buy-now-die-later schemes that have been peddled across the country through the 1980s and 1990s, and that treated every potential sadness as a sales-op had, by the turn of the century, created such a record of abuse and scandal that even the thought leaders, analysts, and convention gurus who formerly promoted their own paradigms of preneed, began to rethink their enthusiasm for it.

Around the turn of the century the Federal Trade Commission, the General Accounting Office, the Senate Special Committee on Aging, Consumers Union, the New York City Department of Consumer Affairs, and a variety of media sources—everyone from *Episcopal Life* to *Consumer Reports*—had investigated and reported on the abusive preneed sales practices and various "take the money and run" schemes of mortuaries and cemeteries. At the same time, the National Funeral Directors Association, sensing there might be a reality at odds with the one they built policy around, staged what they called their "Preneed Prize Fight," at which pros and cons on the subject were debated for the first time. The International Cemetery, Cremation, and Funeral Association (ICCFA) held their own preneed debate at their convention the following spring. These were the first indications that organized funeral service was willing to hear contrarian views on preneed, though such cautions had been given many years before.

Howard C. Raether, the executive director of the National Funeral Directors Association from 1948 until 1983, who debated Jessica Mitford during the decade following the publication of *The American Way of Death*, was arguably the nation's most knowledgeable commentator on and advocate for funeral service. He wrote and advised the association until his death in 1999, and authored several books on funeral management and ethical practice. It was Jessica Mitford, previously a great proponent of prearranged funerals, who quoted Raether's remarks to a funeral directors' convention in the early 1980s: "If funeral directors insist on soliciting preneed funerals, they are in fact prearranging the funeral of their profession."[4] Two decades before this, in testimony before Congress in 1964, on the subject of preneed funerals, Mr. Raether had made known his opinion that the occasions for fraud and abuse and outright scamming were so prevalent that states should be encouraged to pass legislative safeguards to protect its citizenry:

> Before getting into some of the many examples of how people are being fleeced (in supplementation of the testimony of Messrs. Bell and Carpenter), it must be stated that unless a person knows when, where, and under what circumstances he is going to die and who will be responsible for his funeral,

arrangements made in advance of death create problems
instead of avoiding them. The opportunities the prefinancing
of funerals offers promoters for a fast profit has resulted in a
number of "consultants," "exchanges," and other individuals
and groups being setup to hit a community, milk it as fast as
they can and go on to other areas.[5]

Raether, a lawyer, scholar, and fierce advocate for funeral
service, understood that preneed would become the junk food
of funeral service, shifting the transaction from one made
between bereaved family and a funeral director eager to please,
to one made between a commissioned sales person and the
contingently deceased. Agreements and contracts that bound
the present and the living to terms cut between the dead and
absent, were, Raether understood, fraught with peril and possible abuse.

Sadly, Raether's good counsel was ignored.

In the face of growing national scandals and after years
of doing nothing at all or too little too late or courting
irrelevance in the name of "risk aversion," NFDA's policy
board adopted a resolution that said funeral arrangements
should be made by funeral directors and only funeral directors,
whether before or after a death. This is about as exceptional as
saying that only lawyers should do lawyering or accountants
do accountancy or proctologists practice proctology, but the
hue and cry from the preneed lobby was loud and labored and
immediate. Licensed funeral directors, after all, are educated,
tested, regulated, licensed, and overseen by state and national
boards and commissions. They come with scrutiny and something to lose.

The newly adopted policy nonetheless widened the divide
between funeral directors wary of preneed selling and those
who were eager to expand the market. The trade journals and
newsletters were full of contentions between those who felt the
future belonged to those with huge preneed folios and those
who believed it would eventually cost funeral service whatever

trust they maintained at the local level. Those in the former camp were eager to quote the conservative columnist George F. Will, who devoted a column in *Newsweek* to the issue of rent seeking and how it pertained to the funeral marketplace.

"If licensed funeral directors are the only qualified sellers of preneed," Will asked rhetorically, "does it follow that physicians are the only qualified sellers of health insurance?"[6]

The answer to Mr. Will's question is self-evident. The answer to the preneeder's is not, turning as it does on the widely variant practice and understanding of preneed. To paraphrase a former president: "It depends on what the meaning of preneed is." If preneed were only an insurance policy purchased on the prospect of our mortality, then anyone with a briefcase, an actuary, and an underwriter could do the job. The blurring of these roles is evident in the shift from what we used to call these people—insurance agents—to what we now call them: deathcare professionals. Mencken is no doubt chuckling in his grave. But preneed is more than an insurance policy. It ties the decisions about what will be done to the decisions about how it will be funded and, as earlier noted, separates the transaction from the provision of the funeral.

Perhaps the more instructive rhetorical might be: Would you trust your heart-valve replacement to the agent who sold you your health-care coverage? Ought the one who writes your dental plan do your root canal? Or would you let your auto insurance sales person fix the brakes on your Buick? Or should your liability underwriter also be your lawyer when you get sued? Or ought the one who insures your home advise about its architecture or construction? Or, to frame it for Mr. Will's consumption: ought the fellow who sold you your wingtips remove your bunions and treat your tendonitis too?

A death in the family is more than a retail event, and more than an actuarial one.

When we tie the decisions about a funeral to the merchandise or funding instruments, we are moving the profession and the consumer in the same problematic direction that health care has moved in the past two decades. Too often now, the nineteen-year-old reading off the codes and coverages makes the decisions about appropriate medical care over the phone at the insurance headquarters. Or the decisions are made with the cost of the pills in mind. We have seen the costs of health care rise while the professional status of physicians declines, the number of lawsuits increase and the quality of health care becomes marginalized to the profits of the insurance companies. Medicine is more than the pills and the coverage.

A funeral is more than the box and the bill.

Of course, the casket manufacturers and insurance moguls and publicly traded multinationals who have tried to redefine the role of the funeral director have been largely successful. They have used licensed funeral directors as an articulate, well-dressed, locally trusted, and optimally positioned sales team for their products, whether caskets or insurance. Too often good marketing has wrapped itself in the garb of good counsel. But the consumer—the bereaved survivor—is not better served; they have only been better sold. There is a difference.

In addition to the damage to consumers and funeral directors, preneed has damaged the funeral itself as an effective familial and community response to death. Whether it is coincident with, correlated to, or caused by the widespread preselling of funerals over the past thirty years, the slow disappearance of the funeral as the purposeful disposition of the dead is steadily disappearing from our religious and community landscapes. In short, the harder the funeral is sold in advance, the fewer funerals we seem to have. Decisions formerly made by family and friends, most often in concert with community or religious practice, have been replaced by largely narcissistic choices. The question about what we should do when one of our kind dies has given way to a question about what do I want done with me when I'm dead. The elderly and sick are pressured to make their arrangements in advance to spare any of their people the burden of having to make decisions about the disposition of the dead. More and more people, sensing the intergenerational estrangement implicit in such pressure, have decided to do as little as possible. Why pay for a gathering one will not be around for? Possibly this is what Howard Raether intuited all those years ago when he counseled against working the marketplace for planning and payment in advance. He understood the essentially responsive nature of funeral practices—that while death and grief were inevitable, we cannot pre-feel our feelings, regardless of our efforts to plan ahead. He knew that caring people would make more careful decisions than careless ones, and who cares less than the recently dead?

The eager embrace of preneed—the high pressure selling of mortuary wares in advance—by funeral directors, their suppliers, their "thought leaders," and their associations represents the most serious and largely self-inflicted wound to the mortuary marketplace in the century and a half since funeral directors emerged as a distinct occupational group. We lost, as H. L. Mencken figured we might, our essential mission and purpose. Neither Mitford, federal or state government oversight, the trend toward cremation, nor shifting social or religious norms has done as much to damage the repute of funeral professionals or the place of the funeral in our cultural landscape, as we have, alas, ourselves. Likewise, preneed has become the "ground zero" of consumer abuse related to a death in the family. Mencken and Raether, it turns out, were right: we have been our own worst enemies.

After "protective" caskets and preneed sales lost their luster in the marketplace, the concept of personalization emerged as the next new thing. Changes in technology—desktop publishing, graphic design programs, video and photographic advances—made customizing everything suddenly easier. Convention speakers decried "cookie-cutter" funerals and the mass-produced, systematic sameness of everything from caskets to eulogies; we entered the age of the funeral as performance art, where everyone was encouraged to do their one and only thing. What my colleague Thomas Long had called "sacred community theater"—the ritual enactment of social and religious metaphors around the disposition of the dead—devolved into a kind of theater of the smarmy and absurd. The souvenir shop was crossed with karaoke to produce a commemorative event heavy on knickknacks and light on last things. The sacred was replaced by the silly, eschatology by easy listening: "My Way" became the most requested song at such events. Theology has been replaced by themed events heavy on hobbies and sports metaphors. Heaven becomes a kind of nineteenth hole where, if you've kept an honest score, not taken too many mulligans, and raked out the sand traps of your life and times, the bar is open, all of your friends gather, and your trophies are at long last presented to you. Not incidentally, this was about the time, early in the new century, when the pig-in-the-python generation of the postwar baby boom had reached the age when they'd be making more funeral arrangements for their dying parents and rehearsing their own distant obsequies, each of which they would certainly want to be an entirely bespoke, one-of-a-kind event. The mortuary market place was eager to oblige. Thus the casket catalogues were filled with interchangeable corner hardware—tackle boxes, gardening tools, golf bags, black bass, personal memory drawers, and camouflage crepe interiors. Bagpipers and dove releases became de rigueur, as

did a eulogist who did a little comedy club standup before
the burial.

Here again Batesville Casket lead the way. Their catalog
"Accessories" includes suggested "visitation vignettes"—the
stage arranged around neither Cross nor Crescent nor Star
of David, but around one of Batesville's "life symbols" caskets featuring interchangeable corner hardware. One "life
symbol" looks like a rainbow trout jumping from the corners of the hardwood casket, and for dearly departed garden-
ers, there is one with little plastic potted mums. There is the
"sports dad" vignette done up like a garage with beer logos,
team pennants, hoops, and hockey skates, and of course a
casket that looks a little like a jock locker gone horizontal.
There's one for motorcyclists and the much-publicized "Big
Mama's Kitchen" with its faux stove, kitchen table, and apple
pie for the mourners to share with those who call. Instead of
Methodists or Muslims, lapsed or devout, we are golfers, gar-
deners, bikers, and bowlers. The bereaved are not so much
family or friends or coreligionists as they are fellow hobbyists
and enthusiasts. And the funeral director has become more
the memorial caddy of sorts, getting the dead quietly out of
the way and the living assembled within a theater that is neither sacred nor secular but increasingly silly—a triumph of
accessories over essentials, of stuff over substance, gimmicks
over the genuine. The dead are downsized or disappeared or
turned into knickknacks and doodads in a kind of memorial
miniaturization.

Let me, as before, endeavor to make something perfectly
clear. I am all for very personal funerals, ones that engage and
involve the actual persons most affected, which is to say the
recently deceased and the recently bereaved. But "personalization," like other initiatives of the mortuary marketplace,
is based on the notion that something you buy—this casket,
this vault, this urn, this video, this printing package, these

party favors—renders the event somehow "one of a kind." Of course, each of these things is not one of a kind, but rather they are one of a sort. Which is why, even though they might "fit" the personal circumstance of the deceased—"he loved to golf," "her favorite color was peach," "they always loved Bette Midler tunes," "he always wanted us to have a party"—the fit is more like the rental tux he wore to the prom or her first gown and hairdo and pair of high heels, lovely but a little clumsy, awkward but otherwise correct. What makes a funeral one of a kind is the irreplaceable person who is dead and people to whom that death most matters. And the funeral has the ability to get the living and the dead through this maze of changing statuses. The present becomes the passed away, the formerly here becomes the gone, the wife becomes the widow, and son and daughter suddenly orphaned.

I am thinking of the family of an infant boy I buried who came in to talk some months before he died to get some sense of what might be done. At the end of a discussion that included questions about burial and cremation, wakes and requiems, I asked the young couple about their parents, the grandparents to the dying child. They told me that the grandmothers were helping with the cooking and cleaning and the grandfathers kept looking for home improvements to do. This is how we act out our helplessness, our wretchedness in the face of death. I told the young father to tell his father that we'd be needing a box for the baby's burial or cremation, something to lay him out in and take him to church in and take him to his final disposition. He could call me with any questions if he had any. Some days before the child died, the grandfather, a man near enough my age, came to the funeral home with the tiny coffin, perfectly built and painted a pearl-white enamel with a gilded cross on the coffin lid that matched the tiny gold handle rails. The interior was a multicolored quilt of squares sewn together of embroidery made by the grandmothers and aunts and the mother's women friends. And this man said he could never thank me enough for suggesting this job, the doing of which felt like a gift he was giving his son and his grandson. It made him feel necessary and needed and useful. "Powerless," he said, "but useful."

This then is the difference between a personal service and a service that has been personalized. The first is the genuine article; the second is a poor but often pricey substitute. The one is real, the other virtual. The former is a gift, the latter a purchase.

The one-off, "monogramed" bespoke funeral is based on the notion that each of us is *the only one* of a kind. "There'll never be another like Aunt Pat!" So we make much of her recipe for banana bread, her knack for canasta, her ways with begonias and church bazaars, all the habits and pastimes, foibles and fondnesses that made her unlike anyone else. But we are also, especially in social, scientific, and religious terms, only one of a *kind*. At some level we are all versions of beloved and familiar "characters" that cross cultures and geographies and time. Thus, does a family's intention to observe the death of their one-and-only mother or father sometimes run at cross-purposes with the church's intention to place us all in son or daughterly kinship with God? The pall we cover coffins with, much like the baptismal garment we dress our babies in, obscures inevitably individual differences, the better to make plain their manifest status as one of our own—humans, believers, Christians, Lutherans, Missouri Synod, and so forth. Same for flags, which proclaim the citizen, the war, the country, and the causes, all while covering over the personal identities. The stones at Gettysburg and Arlington suggest this uniformity and mute the individual voices long since stilled. This is why the ancient sameness of familiar liturgies, military honors, and tribal and family custom surround the dead, known and unknown to us, because we are all both *one* of a kind and one of a *kind*.

The Three P's, I call them—Protection, Preneed, and Personalization—are each part of the diversion du jour, the new new thing sold to funeral directors so that they can sell them to their communities; the fools gold, junk food, and flash in the pan that have marked my four decades in funeral service. Each has tried in its own way to make a death in the family something it is not: a retail experience, a preplanned event, a bit of performance art. And each has, in its own way, made the funeral directors peddling them look ridiculous, greedy, abusive, or strange.

The next new thing has to do with pets. Always on the lookout for something to augment the revenue stream lost to overeager pursuit of the former new thing, some morticians have landed on cocker spaniels, parakeets, and cats. Something for everything: every sadness a sales-op, never considering how steep the downside to such border crossings might be.

A report in the *Washington Post*[7] uncovered that the U.S. military had cremated the remains of some American service members killed in Iraq, Afghanistan, and elsewhere at a facility that also cremated pets. Despite the fact that the human remains were cremated in a separate crematory from pets, the site was labeled Friends Forever Pet Cremation Service. After the news reached the press and Congress, the military announced a change. The Pentagon no longer permits crematories not located with funeral homes to handle the remains of U.S. troops.

Even the suggestion of impropriety with cremations touched a raw nerve at the Pentagon. Military culture instills that showing respect for the fallen is an extremely important and solemn duty. Funerary rituals such as removing flags from military caskets and presenting them to the deceased's family are carried out meticulously, while other demonstrations of respect include personally delivering news of the loss of a loved one to the next of kin.

"Take care of the service," our father was fond of reminding us, "and the sales will take care of themselves." His faith in the families he served proceeded from the trust they placed in him. Each of these market initiatives is an effort to take care of the sales first and leave the service to take care of itself. The inability to resist the temptation of the next new thing has, over the course of half a decade, estranged the living from the dead, downsized the human response to a death in the family and denatured the funeral and the disposition of the dead. If we had spent as much time in the past half century helping people do something rather than pressing them to buy something, we might still be having funerals. Our job was never to sell, but to embolden, to assist folks with the corporal works of mercy—what the bodies of the living owe the bodies of the dead: this last courtesy, this prudential grace, this decent disposition.

If we are ever to redeem the funeral from the vacuous and fatuous end it is working its way to, we must first admit our part in its devolution. Funeral directors who mistake merchandise for real value, prepayment for a job well done, and accessories for essential elements have sold the consumer and themselves a bill of goods. Clergy who found it easier to preach to the living without a corpse on hand to challenge the faithful in their grief or who banished the dead from their own funerals in the name of ease and convenience or who let the dead go to their final dispositions without the witness or testimony of their family of faith, have had a hand in the funeral's devaluation. Hospice workers who have, with the best of intentions, counseled the bereaved to have their dead disposed of without witness or rubric while the living join a "grief recovery" group, or plan a memorial event to provide some "closure," are trafficking in user-friendly obsequies-lite at the expense of the deeply human duty those who survive owe to those who don't. This separation of the dead body from the living's response to a death is at the core of the commemorative silliness we see too much of now. And if we are ever to recover a semblance of purpose it will begin by communities of family and friendship, acquaintance and faith, along with the frontline professionals they most often deal with at the end of life—health care and hospice, ministerial and mortuary—all encouraging the bereaved to get their dead to the edge of whatever disposition is assigned to them: the grave, the tomb, the fire, the sea. At graveside and fireside is where the verities about death and loss, love and grief, mystery and memory are best proclaimed and enacted. This is where the corporal works are best articulated between bodies in motion and at rest. And yet the cemeteries—especially the larger, corporately owned and operated urban and suburban cemeteries—have followed procedures that make burial seem almost surreal. "Chapel" and roadside committals, "false" setups and the overuse of machinery and heavy equipment for work that could be better done by family and friends has made the earth burial of the dead an exercise in excavation rather than in humanity. Some cemeteries argue that the living ought be kept distant from an actual grave, citing "liability" as the all-purpose excuse du jour, forgetting that a culture that can insure against the downside contingencies of bungee jumping ought to be able to handle the worst case scenarios involved with a graveside service. Here is where the Christian clergy and the funeral directors they work with have been especially timid about insisting on their place around the grave of their "saints." Among Jews, the burial of the dead is a hands-on and holy chore, to which the community of faith is unambiguously summoned:

> Most rabbis gently try to dissuade mourners from leaving before the coffin is lowered, for both religious and psychological reasons. The idea of leaving the mitzvah of burial entirely

in the hands of paid strangers deprives the family of its last act of kevod ha-met, respect for the dead. Even more important, helping to fill the grave means you have left nothing undone. After you have emptied a shovel onto a loved one's casket, there is no denying death—which makes it possible for healing to begin.[8]

Green or "natural" burial movements on both sides of the Atlantic seek to address these issues of the actual and emotional environment. With gasoline topping four dollars a gallon, the planet in peril from climate change, and urban and exurban sprawl turning farm fields into malls and housing tracts, the notions of nature preserves and land conservancy, recycling and green living have found fertile ground in the current culture. Once the province of "tree huggers and environmentalists," going green, both in theory and practice, now informs choices made by consumers and policy makers on everything from architecture to medicine, transportation to education, finance to foodstuffs and, of course, funerals and final disposition.

How the mortuary marketplace adapts to changing consumer preferences is, of course, another matter. If history is instructive we can make some predictions. Some will decry the shift from "traditional" practices and insist there's something un-American or irreligious or about it all. This sort digs in their heels or hides their head in the sand and insists that change is never for the best. Others will insist their communities are not interested in such "fads" and will likely remain outside the loop of new services and products that will emerge to meet demands. Their customers will go elsewhere for what they need. As always, the most successful will combine continuing professional education with a commitment to best practices and a willingness to meet people wherever they are on the continuum of "green" or "natural" funeral and cemetery practices. Not all bereaved consumers are alike and the best professionals are those who have tuned their responses to a range of consumer preferences.

There are as many motivating factors in green burial as there are variations on the practice itself. Just as four decades of increasing cremation rates can be traced to economic, social, and religious changes, so too with green burial. Not everyone who burns their dead is fond of fire or opposed to funerals or put off by the prospect of ground burial. Not everyone who wants to bury without embalming or a sealed casket or cement vault is into land conservancy or recycling or especially concerned over global warming.

Still, funeral directors and cemetery operators would be mistaken not to notice that among the motivating principles behind cremation and green burial is an eagerness to return to elemental practices and customs organized around issues more meaningful than product choices.

Consider, for example, Shannon Merton's experience. When her mother died in 2006, Shannon took the train from her home in Northeast England down to London to catch a plane back to the country she still called "home," though she'd been living in the UK since her college days. It was a long journey back to Kansas, and when she arrived at the mortuary, she asked to see her mother's body. The funeral director said she'd have to wait until the preparation was complete. She was shown some photos of caskets and vaults, customized thank you cards and floral sprays. She chose one of each and was told to come back the following day for "visitation."

After a viewing at the funeral home, the body was taken to the church where the priest told Shannon that the brief eulogy she'd written on the plane could not be shared during the service because church policy forbade the inclusion of such remarks in the liturgy. Perhaps at the cemetery, the priest suggested. The cemetery was half an hour away in a suburb off the interstate. Shannon followed behind the hearse in her rental car with some nieces and nephews. The final prayers for Shannon's mother were not said over her grave, but rather, under a metal tent just off the roadside where her mother's casket had been placed at some distance from her actual grave. After the brief words of committal, all in attendance were invited to join the family at a local eatery and everyone was directed to return to their cars.

Shannon thought there must be some mistake. She had come a long way to see her mother into the ground and she wondered now why everyone was leaving with the job undone. The priest got in the hearse with the funeral director and they drove away, their duties apparently finished. When she inquired of the cemetery official, he assured her that "the actual burial" was done after everyone was gone. "We'll take care of everything," he said. When she asked why the graveside service wasn't held at the grave, the man from the cemetery said, "liabilities." When Shannon assured the man that she would not be leaving until everything was done, she was told to stand in the road at a safe distance. "Our insurance won't cover you," is what he said.

Then a small armada of heavy equipment appeared: a backhoe and, swinging from its bucket, a large grey cement box. There was a dump truck laden with dirt, a brace of green-clad workers. Four of the latter now lifted Shannon's mother's casket from the "pretend" grave the pallbearers had placed it on—a lowering device on some green Astroturf set at roadside. In some states this is called a "false setup," in others they call it a "dummy setup," neither with any sense of irony. The workmen lowered the body in the shiny box into the grey cement box with straps and, after placing the lid on the latter box, it was hoisted by a harness hooked to a chain hooked to the bucket of the backhoe and driven upland over to the hole in the ground that was her mother's grave. Whereupon the whole lash-up was lowered into its final position in time for the memorial dump truck to back up and do what dump trucks do. "Earth to earth, ashes to ashes, dump to dump" Shannon thought to herself and wished she had put a handful of dirt in first. After the workmen left, she read the little eulogy aloud over the grave then said a prayer and left.

From the time Shannon Merton's mother died until the time the ground was leveled over her, no member of her family was encouraged to do much but stand and watch, as various professionals handled things for her—the funeral home, the church, the cemetery. Each had their services and facilities and staff, each had their best intentions and their reasonable charges, each had their professional standards and protocols. And each, in their own way, kept Shannon at an arm's length from dealing hands-on with her mother's death. Even the simple human acts of witness were often discouraged in favor of convenience, cost-efficiency, safety, or procedurals that limited liability and participation. She had been given abundant choices of what to buy—caskets, vaults, videos, flowers, headstones, and monuments—but very few options of things to do.

Such experiences are the driving force behind green burial and its not-too-distant cousin, the "do-it-yourself" or "home funeral" trends. The yearning to "return to nature" owes to the systematic denaturing of final disposition in many parts of the country. The marketplace has, albeit inadvertently, distanced the living from the dead in ways that make them eager to return to former ways, closer to the earth, nearer to nature, less obstructed by even the most capable of professionals. And like cremation half a century ago, the popularity of green burial and do-it-yourself funerals will expand in direct relationship to the general failure of funeral and cemetery directors to understand the difference between assisting and obstructing, between help and heavy-handedness, between essentials and accessories.

Too often we confuse a concept, a set of values and organizing principles, with a set of product offerings. Just as "personalization" is about more than casket hardware, videos, and monogrammed urns, green burial is about more than wicker caskets, biodegradables, and nature preserves. Funerals have always been about what humans do rather than about what they buy when someone they love dies.

If funeral service rises to this occasion in ways that intersect with consumers' desires for more meaningful, natural, family-centered, hands-on, participatory services, funeral and cemetery professionals will thrive in the changing, greening marketplace.

If we have denatured burial, we have entirely obscured cremation. Across most of the mortuary geography, the crematory is as distant and unknown to the vast majority of mourners as the delivery room was to expectant fathers in the 1950s. Too few funeral directors invite and encourage the living to accompany their dead to the retort, and seldom, if ever, do the reverend clergy, who routinely go to the grave to bury the dead, insist on going when fire is the final disposition. Thus the cremation process is industrial, efficient, and secret, rather than familial, honorific, and open. Where the open grave is given the commemorative surround of natural and scenic beauty and calm, the open retort is housed in a factory setting more than a ceremonial one. It is more a furnace than a holy fire. Without someone to watch—family or friend, pastor or undertaker—the dead are dropped off, left alone to wait their turn in the retort like planes on the tarmac at O'Hare. Their remains are processed and returned in greatly reduced versions of their former selves. There is a "don't ask, don't tell" detachment observed by those on all sides of the procedure. North Americans are among the only cultures that practice cremation without a clue about where it is done, by whom, or how, thereby missing all of the ancient and remedial comforts our species has long associated with fire, including warmth and illumination, spiritual presence and purification.

We could learn from others who have long known how to do it better:

> The body is dressed in fresh clothes, and verses are chanted reminding the dead person to give up the old clothes and remember good deeds that were done. The hair, beard and nails are trimmed, and the thumbs are tied together and bound to the funeral bed. Then the body must be carried to the cremation ground. Ancient ritual prescribed a cart drawn by two bulls, but in modern times blood relations carry the body on the funeral bier themselves, with the eldest son in the lead carrying a torch lit from the home fire.
>
> The cremation is understood as a sacrifice to the gods, and mantras invoke the blessings of heaven. The god Pushan is asked to accept the sacrifice and guide the soul of the dead, and the god of fire, Agni, is asked to consume the physical body but create its essence again in heaven.
>
> The funeral party then proceeds home, extinguishes the old family fire, kindles a new one and celebrates the end of the period of impurity with a funerary feast.[9]

We might also take to heart the cautionary tales from cultures where cremation has been the norm much longer than it has been here.

> In Britain today cremation is the normal rite; it is the destination of 72 percent of the population, having reached what may be an upper limit after a century of rapid acceptance. More recent justifications of cremation include the saving of land from becoming worthlessly cluttered by graves, its simplicity and lack of fuss and the creation of greater choice in depositing the remains. Such "pragmatic" concerns belie complex changes in attitudes to the corpse, to the significance of the dead, and to religious beliefs.
>
> The uniformity of urns, niches and plaques, the scattering

of ashes into anonymous gardens of remembrance . . . all contribute to the dislocation and anonymity of the dead . . . and a growing sense of privacy in bereavement, in which the immediate family and friends were not to be intruded upon in their grief.[10]

This "dislocation" and "anonymity of the dead" were at the narrative center of the 2006 British film *The Queen*, directed by Stephen Frears, written by Peter Morgan, and starring Helen Mirren as Queen Elizabeth II. It depicted the events in August of 1997, the drama focusing on the differing views between the British public and royals on how to deal with Princess Diana's death. The Queen wants quiet and privacy while her son, Prince Charles, speaking for his sons and the nation-at-large, presses, along with the recently elected Tony Blair, for a more fulsome show of respect.

Bereft of royalty, on this side of the Atlantic, our dislocation from our actual dead begat a raft of books and films about the "living dead." Twilight and zombie films have become all the rage for a generation of Americans who might easily live into their forties without ever having to confront an actual corpse. Alan Ball, the filmmaker who brought us *Six Feet Under* took on his own vampire project called *True Blood*.

To humanize burial and cremation, we must be emboldened to inhabit these spaces, much as we learned to humanize sickness and dying by adding to "intensive care," the presence of humans who really cared. Bringing the dying home to occupy their familiar spaces offers access and participation by family and friends. In the same way, emboldening the living to tend to their dead, to participate in their requiems and dispositions, inures to the benefit of the individual and the species.

Presence—the showing up, the being there—is very often

all we can do. Often as not, it is enough. Each of us is called to find our place on the continuum of care to the dying, the dead, and the bereaved. Some of us dig graves or carry flowers, others make casseroles or caskets, still others pray or sing or lend their voices to the silence and the lamentations with which the living will surround their dead. Some lift and carry, some bear and uphold. All who show up pay their dues in the association of humanity . . . and in their presence become the gifts we ought to be to one another.

Joseph of Arimathea . . . asked Pilate to let him take away the body of Jesus. Pilate gave him permission; so he came and removed his body. [39]Nicodemus, who had at first come to Jesus by night, also came, bringing a mixture of myrrh and aloes, weighing about a hundred pounds. [40]They took the body of Jesus and wrapped it with the spices in linen cloths, according to the burial custom of the Jews. [41]Now there was a garden in the place where he was crucified, and in the garden there was a new tomb in which no one had ever been laid. [42]And so, because it was the Jewish day of Preparation, and the tomb was nearby, they laid Jesus there.

John 19:38-42

Chapter 6

FUNERAL DIRECTORS . . . WHO NEEDS THEM?

Thomas G. Long

The pollution of the dead is . . . the reason why, in so many places of the world, grave-digging and the handling of the corpse are carried out by a specialized, ritually avoided and generally despised class. . . . In many places in the world undertakers are confined in special neighborhoods outside the walls of the city lest they pollute the rest of the community.

—Pascal Boyer, *Religion Explained*

AFTER INTERVIEWING ME, ALONG WITH TWO OTHER CLERGY, about contemporary funeral trends, the host of a public radio show opened up the phone lines for the listeners. We had been talking for nearly an hour about what we considered to be the high impact issues: the curious downsizing of funeral rituals, the often unbearable thinness of contemporary "celebration of life" ceremonies, the dramatic rise in cremation, the cultural view of dead bodies as "pornographic," the increasing number of people who specify "no service" to mark their deaths, the growing interest in green funerals, and more. Electric stuff, we thought.

The callers, however, did not rise to our bait. They brushed aside every one of our topics and went straight for the jugular and to their own hot-button issue: rage toward funeral directors. They were nearly unanimous. Funerals directors, fumed caller after caller, were rapacious, unctuous, willing to feign compassion for a profit, ready to take advantage of people in their most vulnerable moments, and eager to shill for unnecessary goods and services—in short, funeral directors were, not to put too fine a point on it, dissembling and greed-ridden bottom feeders.

My first reaction to this, beyond being slightly bruised that the callers had leapfrogged over our agenda on the way to their own, was a nod of recognition. I'd heard these complaints before, and not just about funeral directors. Indeed, the charges the callers were slinging at funeral professionals were the same familiar complaints that have been hurled at clergy for centuries, indeed long before there was such a thing as funeral directors. Smarmy? Willing to act compassionate but always interested in the offering plate? Ready to impose their own agenda on the vulnerable? Check, check, check.

For example, part of what precipitated the Reformation was that priests in the sixteenth century, perhaps like funeral professionals today, had managed to lodge themselves in the public imagination as greedy, insincere, and quite willing to exploit the defenseless by hawking sacred things, such as indulgences, for the right price. Still today, the hypocritical and mendacious minister, eager to proffer the sacred for a buck, is a stock pop-culture character, such as the legendary radio evangelist who was notorious for praying at the close of every broadcast, "And O God, touch the hearts of many to make generous offerings, and lead them, O Lord, to send them to Post Office Box 313, Pasadena, California." Such caricatures of sticky-fingered ministers have much in common with the stereotypical black-suited mortician with the Cadillac limousine and the gold-handled walking stick.

Those who earn their livelihood caring for vulnerable people in times of trouble stand on a precarious ledge. If they stumble and lose public confidence, the fall can be precipitous. When the medieval priests lost widespread trust, the public, who had no radio talk shows on which to vent, extracted consequences far more dramatic. Luther bolted into action with his ninety-five theses, the Catholic Church was split into pieces, bloody religious wars lasting more than a century were touched off, the face of Europe was reshaped, and refugees fled across the perilous Atlantic in search of surcease and religious freedom in the New World. Small wonder, then, that the broadband rage of the public against funeral directors today keeps the public relations directors of funeral professional societies awake through many a fretful night.

But when the radio callers peppered us with their grievances, what was the true source of their anger? Had they been swindled by an unscrupulous funeral director? Had they been emotionally abused by the staff of a funeral home? No, they claimed none of this. Such offenses have happened here and there, of course, but these callers were not talking specifics. Instead, it was the very *idea* of funeral homes and funeral directors that had them riled, not specific experiences. It's a curiosity, and people who study these sorts of things have noted it, that folks are often quite negative about the whole lot of funeral directors *except* for the ones they actually know and have worked with. "Funeral directors are a bunch of sharks, but Charlie Baxter down at Smith and Sons, now he's a great guy, different from the rest of 'em." Being enraged about the funeral business, like being enraged over Washington politics, big oil, lawyers, institutional religion, or the IRS, is a largely unfocused cultural reflex, something we are entitled to feel, have been schooled to feel.

In fact, whether they knew it or not, the callers to that talk show were mimicking both the heat and the arguments of an influential muckraking book published four decades earlier, a book that altered the way we think and speak about funerals, namely Jessica Mitford's famous takedown of the funeral industry, *The American Way of Death,* about which Thomas

Lynch has had much to say in previous chapters. Mitford's ideas and her umbrage have seeped into the popular vocabulary and shaped mainstream attitudes so much that her reproach of funeral directors is now the orthodox view. Even if the callers had neither heard of Jessica Mitford nor read a single page of her book, they were nevertheless swayed by the book's ripple effect and were still using Mitford's arguments and making her complaints.

As cultural historian Gary Laderman has pointed out, Mitford's book was largely a recycling of accusations made toward funeral directors that had been around for decades, but her blistering prose style, savage wit, and striking examples caught fire among readers and generated a widespread outcry against funeral directors. "Mitford," writes Laderman, "singlehandedly revolutionized many critical details of the American funeral industry. Her book, in fact, permanently changed the public face of death in America."[1] Perhaps those talk show callers imagined themselves to be generating their own freshly minted indignation against funeral directors, but they were actually channeling Jessica Mitford.

CASHING IN ON DEATH

When *The American Way of Death* was first published in 1963, some thought that Mitford's targets were the rotten apples in the funeral business, the small percentage of unscrupulous funeral directors who spoil the image of a whole profession. But, no, Mitford was far more ambitious. From the first paragraph of her book, she made it clear that it was her intent to indict the whole lot of funeral directors, good and bad, and the entire ecology of the funeral business:

> This would normally be the place to say (as critics of the American funeral trade invariably do), "I am not, of course, speaking of the vast majority of ethical undertakers." But the

vast majority of ethical undertakers is precisely the subject of this book. To be "ethical" merely means to adhere to a prevailing code of morality, in this case one devised over the years by the undertakers themselves for their own purposes. The outlook of the average undertaker, who does adhere to the code of his calling, is to me more significant than that of his shadier colleagues, who are merely small-time crooks such as may be found in any sphere of business.[2]

Mitford's criticisms of the funeral industry basically branched off in two directions: money and mythmaking. On the money side, Mitford laid out all the usual denunciations. Funeral directors, she said, extort people with outrageous markups on caskets, urns, vaults, clothing, jewelry, and other merchandise. Plus they charge people for unnecessary and sometimes silly services, like embalming, flowers, and "comfortable footwear" for the deceased.

So, was she right? What about money and funeral homes? The matter is complex. On the one hand, there is reason to be grateful to Jessica Mitford on this score. Because of her book, the general public has a much higher level of consumer awareness about funerals and there are important consumer protections in place. For example, the Federal Trade Commission now requires funeral homes to give customers an itemized price list when discussing funeral arrangements and to provide a casket price list before customers view any caskets. Funeral consumer advocacy groups argue that this is too little, too late and that much work remains to be done before full transparency and competitive pricing are achieved, but the fact that the feds regularly send undercover agents into funeral homes to ferret out rule-breakers, and then file lawsuits against them, tends to put teeth into the regulations.

We can also be grateful that Jessica Mitford called us to vigilance, not because funeral homes are corrupt, but because they are, after all, businesses that sell things and buyers do well to beware, regardless of the merchant. One recently introduced product in the funeral business merits particular caution, namely, the rapidly growing practice of prepaid funerals, or "preneed arrangements," as this is sometimes called. It seems like a good idea at first. Go ahead and plan your funeral now and pay for it in advance, This way, your final wishes are clear, you are protected from inflation, and, since your funeral is already paid for, your family is spared any high-pressure sales and the sudden and unexpected expense a death often brings.

But, as *Smart Money* magazine warns, prepaid funerals are usually a better deal for the funeral home than for the consumer.[3] Preneed contracts are often insurance policies with inflated premiums or escrow arrangements with disadvantageous trust provisions. There is currently very little regulation or oversight of preneed sales and practices, and buyers who later change their minds about their desires, move to another area, or purchase a prepaid funeral from a funeral home that goes out of business are sometimes out of luck. Charges of outright fraud have occurred in some cases. The National Funeral Directors Association (NFDA) publishes a detailed "Bill of Rights for Funeral Preplanning,"[4] complete with a list of protections wise consumers should demand as their due. But the fact that the NFDA feels the need to post this "Bill of Rights" on its Web site is not only a display of good business will; it is, if we squint a bit between the lines, also a red flag warning that the ice can be thin in this part of the lake.

Mitford reminded us, then, that whatever else it may be, the funeral transaction is a business deal, and all the usual chariness and prudence should be in place. On the other hand, there is a good bit of evidence that the storm Mitford stirred up over funeral home profiteering is overblown. In 2011, *Businessweek* magazine compared the average profit margins of various types of enterprises and found that businesses in the category "death-care services" (which includes

funeral homes, crematories, and the like) yields an indus-
try-wide profit margin of 11.87 percent (a bit lower for the
smaller, family-owned funeral homes). This figure is close to
the norm for small businesses generally and is about the same
for veterinarians (11.55 percent); slightly ahead of day-care
centers (10.43 percent); and well behind financial investment
firms (16.11 percent), chiropractors (16.14 percent), and
dentists (17.04 percent).[5] In other words, people may not like
thinking of funeral homes as businesses, but as commercial
enterprises, their profits fall somewhere in the normal range.

Normal perhaps, but are funeral home profits fair and
moral? Only God can finally say, I suppose. Much depends on
whether funeral homes are providing services and goods we
really want and need, and that taps into Mitford's second area
of criticism. Before we look in that direction, though, it should
be noted that not all the rage people spill over funeral directors and money is irritation over sales tactics, profit margins,
and markups. At the deepest level, the anger about money and
funerals can mask a fury about death itself.

At a dinner party we talk of children and jobs, movies
and books, the new restaurant in town, and the prospects of
the local sports team. We may even venture into politics, sex,
and neighborhood gossip. But no one will dare ask the host,
"So, Ralph, how much money do you make nowadays?" or
"Say Gladys, you're no spring chicken anymore. How do
you feel as you contemplate your impending death?" It's not
just that these matters are simply impolite or too personal
for table talk. The prohibition is stronger. Death and money
are as close as our freewheeling society gets to taboo topics.
Both lie close to the bone of our identity, and the explora-
tion of them exposes the precariousness of the self. In their
own ways, death and money represent dire threats to our
self-understanding, our self-regard, our status as humans,
our very existence, and to raise them in a pointed way is to

transgress a sacred boundary. Sometimes even intimacy cannot break the code of silence. Note this letter, sent to the "Dear Abby" newspaper column:

> I am a twenty-three-year-old liberated woman who has been on the pill for two years. It's getting pretty expensive and I think my boyfriend should share half the cost, but I don't know him well enough to discuss money with him.[6]

We can perhaps go a lifetime avoiding money talk, keeping our financial affairs secret. But death is different. Death works hard to publicly humiliate us all, exposing our mortality to full public glare. Death observes no courtesies, keeps no secrets, obeys no vows, heeds no sanctions, transgresses all boundaries, imposes the reality of itself with random disregard and malevolence, and violates us all with abandon. When it inflicts itself on us, it seems futile to rail out at death itself. After all, death is a faceless, anonymous force whose cold hand grips all of us eventually. But the funeral director's invoice, the wages of death, now that's a different matter. It angers us because . . . why? Because we had no choice, we didn't plan on it, it came without proper warning or justification, we were taken advantage of when we were defenseless, it violated us and robbed us of something dear, it fell on us so callously and heartlessly—which are, of course, the very spoils of death itself.

To experience the death of someone we love and then to be expected to pay for it with our purse as well as our grief only deepens the feelings of helplessness, victimization, and impotence death spreads in its wake. We more calmly pay for our family weddings, even though they now typically cost over three times more than funerals, and one would hardly call a radio show to fulminate about wedding consultants, florists, and bridal shops. Weddings, after all, are about freedom, choice, love, the future, and joy—the very treasures death steals from us. When it comes to death, the funeral director may mail the invoice, but it is death itself that writes the bill.

SLEEPING BEAUTY: THE MYTH OF DEATH

When people recall Jessica Mitford's book today, they usually remember the parts about money and greed. The more serious side of Mitford's critique, however, had to do with the cluster of myths, sentimental images, euphemisms, and "half-digested psychiatric theories" she saw morticians fabricating as they reinvented the American way of death. After all, the money part of Mitford's critique could be fixed. If it's true that funeral homes overcharge for their services, well, consumer advocacy can see to it that stronger regulations are established and that the competitive forces of the marketplace are unleashed, bringing prices in line. But when Mitford claimed that funeral directors were merchants of myths, this was far more devastating. She was not merely saying that funeral homes charge too much for what they do. She was saying that what they do isn't worth doing, that funeral directors and what they sell are unnecessary and harmful. This was more than a flesh wound; this was a dagger to the heart of the funeral business.

With a few florid stokes of the pen, Mitford carped, undertakers had cleaned up their dismal trader act and splashed perfume over the stench of their business. They became "funeral directors," corpses became "loved ones," embalming rooms morphed into "full-service funeral homes," coffins became jewel-box "caskets," cremation ash and bone became "cremains," and flowers became "floral tributes." This all allowed for a critical mass of euphemisms, a sickly sweet funeral porridge. When someone "passes away," the "funeral director" comes in as "coach" to take the "loved one" to the "funeral home." The "loved one" is "prepared," dressed (warm, comfortable slippers and special bras "for post-mortem form restoration" are available), and placed in a walnut "casket" with a satin lining and an innerspring mattress so that the family can view the cosmetically prepared "loved one" and retain a "beautiful memory picture." The casket is then closed, activating the permanent-seal gasket, and the casketed "loved one" is then placed in an "everlasting vault," and the "resting place" is marked by an "eternal monument."[7]

So what's the problem with speaking positively, even euphemistically, about funerals? After all, don't we do the same about other important life passages? Weddings, for example. There, too, a luxury coach ferries the loved ones to their destination. There, too, the loved ones are prepared cosmetically, dressed in their finest, arranged under a canopy of floral tributes for beautiful memory pictures, and then bid farewell for their life ever after. Talk about sentiment—one popular wedding spot, Disney World in Florida, lays down euphemisms as if they were aces in a poker game: "Create the perfect fairy tale beginning for your life together at one of Disney's magical locales. Complete with Victorian charm and royal refinement, these enchanting places set the stage for your dreams to come true. Pixie dust is guaranteed."[8]

Sprinkling pixie dust over a wedding couple may be a welcome touch of romance, but, as Mitford revealed, trying to spread it over the grim face of death comes across as duplicitous. When Mitford gathered all the funeral industry pixie dust into one pile, it was worthy of ridicule. She managed with wit and scorn to mock funeral directors as cartoon characters, purveyors of the most mawkish form of sentimentality. Funeral directors were not just greedy to Mitford's eye; they were downright silly, intellectually and culturally bankrupt, peddlers of fatuous myths. Funeral directors were blindsided by Mitford's critique and left trembling with rage. "These dames that write these books—they don't want to hear anything good," sputtered one New York mortician. "If you

kill sentiment you're a dead pigeon. The world runs on sentiment."[9]

And that was part of the problem. It was the world of the
1950s that ran on the kind of sentiment funeral homes were
pushing. Mitford's book connected with a rising new and rebel-
lious generation. It appeared in 1963 just as the military run
up in Vietnam was gaining speed, the year John F. Kennedy
was assassinated, and only months before the Beatles invaded
America as the harbingers of a cultural revolution. The times,
they were a-changin'. Funeral directors were not the only ones
who failed to anticipate the social convulsions of the 1960s,
but Mitford caught the funeral business flat-footed, presenting
a message that was already passé for a generation intent on
overthrowing authority, convention, and pretense. It was the
age of the Rolling Stones, hippies, lunch counter sit-ins, and
"tell it like it is, man." Funeral directors and their mythologies
were still all Dinah Shore, the Lucky Strike "Hit Parade," hula
hoops, and "when you wish upon a star."

Funeral marketing soon caught up to the new social trends,
rebellions, and anxieties, of course. Thomas Lynch wrote of
how his father, also a funeral director, sold caskets in his day,
emphasizing "protection" and "permanence" to the children
of the Depression and two global wars. He writes:

> In the years that have passed since my father taught me cas-
> kets, I have sold my share of them. We don't push protection
> anymore. "'Choice'" is the buzzword. Everything is custom-
> ized. The generation now in the market for mortuary wares
> is redefining death in much the same way that, three decades
> back, it redefined sex and gender.[10]

Here, by the way, is yet another place where funeral directors and the clergy stand on common ground. If funeral directors constantly scramble to match their pitch to the changing
tides of culture, so do clergy. We, too, used to talk of funerals and life after death in terms of eternity and permanence,

but now we are all aquiver with messages about personalization and choice. It is a long way from the colonial American preachers who spoke in their funeral sermons almost impersonally of "that excellent person now departed from us."[11] So today's pastors, eagerly soliciting the bereaved to name "what your mother would have wished for in her service," are setting up display tables of the deceased's personal mementos and leading the congregation in stanzas of "The Wind Beneath My Wings," because it was "mother's favorite song."

Puritan minister Cotton Mather would never have dreamed of asking his flock at Old North Church in Boston what they would like to have done in their funerals. The question would have been preposterous, the very idea that someone could own "*my* funeral" would have struck them as vain. It would be as if Mather had asked, "What would you like your weather to be today?" or "Would you prefer that your sun rise in the east or the west?" Funerals in the past were not vehicles of personal choice. They were what people had learned over time to do when there was a death. Funerals were like farm-to-market roads—born of necessity, carved out and maintained by the community, designed to get people where they needed to go when the time came to go, and traveled by everyone. But today, ministers and funeral directors conspire as interior decorators to help consumers fashion improvised, throwaway ceremonies of self-expression.

Herein lies my deepest complaint against funeral directors, a grievance I also have with my fellow reverends. Having lost sight of the main purposes of a funeral, we have replaced those purposes with half-baked ideas of choice, personalization, and hyped emotion, thus offering people a confused tangle of myths about death and memorials, a mess of pottage instead of the birthright to which they are entitled.

If this sounds like I am agreeing with Jessica Mitford, I am . . . in part. She was right that we have swallowed dreamy, sentimental, superficial, and finally injurious myths about death and funerals. But Mitford was also wrong, wrong in ways that matter, wrong in ways that inflict damage to the human prospect. First, she was wrong to place the full weight of blame for funeral mythmaking on funeral professionals. Funeral directors perhaps had all manner of incentives to romanticize funerals, but they had plenty of help from the rest of us in doing so. They could market death myths only because our society generally is confused about the meaning of death and the place of funerals. Funeral directors may have spread weeds, but they planted them in a badly neglected garden.

Second, Mitford's attack on American funerals scored some hits, but it ultimately rested on a deficient understanding of the character of human death and life. Mitford laughed at funeral directors when they claimed their methods were "scientific" and "hygienic," but Mitford was a pseudo-scientist herself. She fancied herself as the true practitioner of rationality and mental hygiene, but she was simply an acolyte for the superstition that truth reveals itself to a cold, bloodless rationalism. She decried the sentimentality of American funerals, but her real target was any emotion at all over death. She poked fun at the way funeral directors cosmetically treat bodies, but her real disdain was for the embodied character of human life generally—the way that life is defined by the places our feet take us, by what we do with our hands, speak with our mouths, and embrace with our arms, and the ways, therefore, that the bodies of the dead are sacred temples, worthy of our respect and tenderness.

Mitford, a Brit by birth, was something of an Edwardian snob, ready to sneer at the foolish stories Americans tell in the face of death, but the sneer covered up the sad fact that she had herself no story worth telling, no full-bodied grief to express even in her own losses. Strangely, she wrote the most influential book about death in our time, but the book scarcely mentions death at all, not real death. She was caustic, smart, and had an eye for pretense, but in probing how human beings respond to death's mystery, she was way out of her depth. She made good sport attacking our silly ways of death. What she lacked was a grasp of the truly human vision people were yearning for beneath the myths and how profoundly the ways of death are connected to the ways of life.

BACK TO THE NECESSITIES

A good way to figure out the proper role of funeral directors—and clergy for that matter—is to imagine what funerals would be like without them. This is not difficult to do. Not all that long ago, indeed still within the memory of many, funerals were essentially home and family affairs. When someone died, the body was washed and dressed at home. Neighbors came to visit, to comfort, to pay their respects, and to fill the family table with dishes of food. A coffin was made, a grave dug, and within a day or two the deceased was carried to be buried.

Sometimes a minister accompanied the procession to the grave, offering prayers and saying a few words, but not always. Sometimes the local hardware or furniture store, with a sideline in funeral merchandise, would sell the family some brass handles or a readymade coffin, or if the grave was in town and not on the family farm, charge a small fee for transporting the deceased in a horse-drawn, glass-walled funeral carriage. But none of this was indispensable. The dead could be prepared and prayed over, carried to the grave and buried just fine by family and neighbors.

When we pare away the nonessentials of death, then, what do we see? Two things: an act of human necessity and a local folk drama saturated with meaning. As for the human necessity, when someone dies, the body must be moved from the place of death to somewhere else—the grave, the pit, the sea, the fire. The bodies of the dead are never left among the living but are always carried by the living to a place of disposition. Moving the body from here to there is not an option; it's a necessity.

But when we remember our humanity, this act of necessity is never done in a perfunctory way, as if the dead were of no consequence, as if the living did not have before them yet again the never-ending task of discovering and proclaiming meaning in this and all deaths. The actions are simple—caring tenderly for the one who is dead, washing and dressing the body, placing the body with care into a coffin, gathering with family and neighbors, walking with the deceased to the place of farewell, reciting words that say what is happening here. But these simple actions are not discrete events, like beads without a string. Taken together they form an enacted narrative, a script for a piece of community theater infused with powerful meanings. When people perform this script, when they accomplish these ancient actions, over and again on the occasion of each new death, they announce, in a language deeper than mere words and broader than a single creed, that the dead are of great worth and that we are accompanying them as they travel from one place to another.

We know in our DNA that this is the human thing to do. We do not throw the dead onto trash heaps. We treat the bodies of the dead with reverence. We search for them diligently when they are lost. We wash them, anoint them with fragrances, set their features lovingly, dress them with honor, and stay awake with them and guard them through the night. And then we accompany them to the place of farewell. There is embrace and there is release. We gather those we love into our arms, and then we yield to the truth that we must eventually let them go. Taking the dead to the place of disposition is not simply a trip across the graveyard; it is a journey, a crossing from here to there. By walking with the dead on this last passage, we are reminding ourselves and telling all who will listen that life is a story with beginnings, middles, and ends, and that our lives will be markedly different at the end of the day than they were at first light.

What do funeral directors and ministers add to this act of necessity and to this drama of meaning? At one level, nothing . . . absolutely nothing. When someone dies, people already know what must be done and how to do it. When people keep sensibilities intact, the necessary human drama around death is a part of our repertoire as human beings. Everything needed is already present, and people hold all the wisdom necessary to perform these essential human actions.

The sooner funeral directors and clergy acknowledge the fact that we are not essential to the funeral process, the better. To admit our dispensability will keep us from imposing false meanings and actions on the funeral and will prevent us from stepping between people and the very human deeds they know they need to perform.

When George Foy lost his one-month-old baby boy, he buried his son's ashes himself under a cypress tree on a hill overlooking Nantucket Sound. Foy did not use the services of a funeral home, choosing to build the cremation coffin, take his son's body to the crematory, and to dig the grave single-handedly. "I'm not saying that they're bad people, or even most of them are," he said of funeral directors. "But a lot of them do now belong to big chains and they do have this kind of institutionalized separation between them and the family and the deceased. And I think it's that separation that might be the point. That's what I reacted against. And what I reacted toward was to be able to stay in touch with this boy, who was still alive inside me and in the lives of my family. And the only way I could do that was by taking care of him myself."[12]

Actually, things are not quite that simple or pure in a complex urban society. The picture of a father taking matters into his own hands and burying his son's ashes under a cypress tree is lovely and idyllic, but it soon becomes chaotic and culturally problematic if we imagine millions people burying their dead wherever they choose—under home plate at Yankee Stadium, in their front yards and in library gardens, in public parks, golf course greens, and freeway medians. The point is not unregulated burial anarchy; the point is that caring for and praying over the dead is not neurosurgery requiring esoteric knowledge and the skills of experts. People have the social savvy and wisdom to do these things themselves, and centuries of our forebears managed to accomplish them without benefit of clergy or mortician.

When funeral directors and clergy realize that people can perform these actions quite adequately without us, ironically a window of understanding opens through which we can see what our proper roles might be and how it is that people can do this better *with* us. And what is this proper role? To put it succinctly, the task of both funeral professionals and clergy is to help people do this very human thing more humanely.

This is why, when it comes to funeral professionals, the old title of "undertaker" is so apt. People do not need to have their funerals "directed," any more than they need their lovemaking, birthing, bathing, eating, laboring, and going about the trials and obligations of everyday living directed. Women in labor don't need a birth director; they need a midwife. In the same way, people caring for and burying their dead don't need a funeral "director"; they need people who will undertake to help them accomplish these human tasks well.

People want to care tenderly for the bodies of their dead. They need the eyes and mouths of the dead to be closed and their features to be set. They don't want the dead to look asleep or still alive; rather, they want them to look like the treasures, the saints, they are. Often, because the funeral events will happen over several days, people need the bodies of the dead to be embalmed. People also need coffins, they need places for the community to gather and to pay respects to the dead, and they need the means to transport the dead to the place of disposition. They need graves dug, crematory arrangements made, places to sit and coverings when it rains, and death certificates filed. When people have their wits about them, they know what they need, and sometimes they do these things for themselves. Often, however, they need or desire help. And the best funeral directors are undertakers, those who undertake these helping tasks.

The same goes for the clergy; we are "undertakers," too, people who agree to undertake the helping tasks, or, to put it more theologically, we are servants of God and God's people. Ministers who think that their job is to make the funeral "sacred" badly miss the point. Human death rituals are already sacred. We need clergy who will serve as a midwife to this truth, who will undertake the task of allowing the sacredness that is already present in this great drama to be seen and magnified. The essential human act of caring for the dead takes on even deeper significance when it is set down into a larger religious narrative. In my own Christian faith, the deceased is not just a loved one, but a baptized saint, the path to the grave is not only the passageway to death but also the gateway to resurrection. The journey we travel is not simply from home to the grave but a baptismal journey from this home to our home with God, from the family table and the communion table to the heavenly banquet. Christians believe that telling this narrative at the time of death is not simply a way to be more religious; it is a way to be more fully human. The task of the Christian pastor is to help people perform this human act more humanely by undertaking the task of reciting this gospel story and pointing out, as we journey toward the grave, holy milestones along the pilgrim way.

But here is a major challenge that undertakers—both funereal and pastoral—face: the amnesia of our culture regarding death. People have forgotten how to do funerals, have erased the memory of what is called for at the time of death, have repressed at the surface what we truly know at the core. For so long now, other people have prepared the bodies of our dead and buried them that we have lost track of the fact that caring for the dead is an essential part of our humanity. Caring for the dead is not a chore like cobbling our own shoes, something we once did for ourselves but is now best left to others. It is, instead, an essential labor of humanity. We cannot be fully alive, fully humane, if we do not tend to the dead. Likewise, for so long now others have recited the prayers and preached the homilies that people have forgotten that it is also an essential mark of humanity to call on God and to recite the sacred narratives as we accompany the dead on their final pilgrimage. It is difficult to be faithful undertakers, to help people do a human thing more humanely, when people no longer have the desire to do the human thing at all.

What shall we do when people no longer remember what funerals are for, when people no longer see their humanity bound up in the care of the dead? The fatal mistake funeral directors make is to fabricate and to advertise some current, more fashionable definition of a funeral. "OK, don't worry about the body," the funeral director implies. "That's our job, not yours. We'll pick it up, embalm it, burn it, donate it, whatever. Your job is to view it or to gaze upon a lovely urn so that you can have a peaceful and beautiful last memory, or to sit in a chapel memorializing your loved one in such a way that you can achieve 'closure,' or to put on a 'celebration of life' so that you will always laugh and love and remember the funny and wonderful traits of your loved one, or to plan a farewell festival that expresses your loved one's final and fondest wishes. We can do this for you because we have professionalism, compassion, integrity, trustworthiness, dignity, personal service, dedication, a well-trained staff, a history of five generations of service, and so forth."

The problems with this are twofold. First, much of this is pure hogwash. For example, the deepest rituals of death make it clear that "closure" is neither achievable nor desirable. Death causes a wound that may scar over, but it does not fully heal. The human drama of a funeral does not come to a place where we who have accompanied the dead finally wipe the dirt off our hands and say, "Well, that's over and done with." Rather, the community theater that is a funeral takes us to a place of meaning, a place where we can let the dead go on ahead of us into a future of our unknowing and where we can manage the human task of putting one foot in front of another without them. Also, despite several spurious studies purporting otherwise, simply viewing the body of a deceased person is of little value. Instead, caring tenderly for the bodies of the dead, accompanying them along the last mile of their journey, understanding the dead to be gathered up into a drama of movement and meaning, these are the true ways of human worth.

Second, all of these fashion statements of death are disconnected from human necessity. It is necessary to move dead bodies from here to there and to do so in ways that speak our deepest understandings of life and death. Celebrating life, expressing daddy's wishes, sitting quietly and conjuring up memories—these may be things we want to do, but they are not essential and are disconnected from the hard core requisites of death. Our deepest life ceremonies rest on necessities—eating, washing, propagating, promising—and the rest are whims and fashions.

Much hinges on a tension that runs through the whole of human experience between external and internal meaning. The most profound wisdom, I am persuaded, is that human beings are ultimately incarnate and social creatures. We are not people who happen to have bodies; we are, rather, *embodied* beings. There is, therefore, an intimate connection between what we think and feel inside and what we enact and perform on the outside. "The body," as some philosophers remind us, "does not lie." If you want to know who people are, watch their bodies. They are, finally, where their feet take them; what they do with their hands; the blessings and curses they utter from their mouths; the ways they chose to touch, embrace, and lie with other bodies. If something springs forth within us, it becomes fully meaningful only when it comes to expression in our bodies, and what we perform with our bodies works its way into our inner beings.

A certain kind of popular wisdom, however, takes a radically different view. What truly matters, many say, is the inner life. The rest is merely external. What counts is the spirit; the body is the lesser part, merely a shell. The more people believe this, the more tempted they are to retreat to the privacy of their inner chapels and interior meditations to discover truth and wisdom.

In the world of religion, we clergy have often undermined our own faith by pandering to this philosophy of inwardness. "Yes," we have said, "you are right. True meaning is to be found within, not without. Mosque, temple, church—these are but institutions, material structures trying to contain spiritual realities, we admit it. But if you will attend services, you will find yourself inspired, your spirit uplifted, your inner life renewed." But, of course, people soon discover that they can be inspired, uplifted, and renewed far more effectively hiking in the woods, reading Wordsworth, or meditating on a beach than they can hassling with the quirky people who show up in houses of worship and making the commitments and compromises that communal expressions of religion require. Soon enough, they define themselves as "spiritual but not religious," and we never hear from them again.

Just so, funeral homes can sing all day long about their dignity and integrity, and they can advertise themselves as houses of compassion where people can make their personal choices and express their grief and affirm their wishes and find comfort and celebrate memories and have their spirits renewed and uplifted. For a while, people will continue to show up at the funeral home to conduct their memorial services and to conduct their thin celebration of life ceremonies. But people will quickly realize—and they already have—that all of these virtues can be found just as well, if not better, in a meadow of wildflowers or in the quietness of their own inner reflections. Finally nobody needs a funeral home—or a church—to bow before the altar of inwardness.

But if true wisdom is to be found in where we put our bodies; if profound truth about life and death is to be gained in caring for the dead and walking with them to the place of departure; if, indeed, we have a God who has decided to be present in flesh and blood, in human community, and in our living and our dying, then the healing and meaning we all desire cannot be gained by retreating to private sanctuaries and inner feelings. We have to get up on the public stage and recite the script and play out the roles in the great community theater that our ancestors have enacted so long and so well. If our society has forgotten the script and lost sight of these roles, then clergy and funeral directors will have to team up to refresh the cultural memory, to teach our fellow human beings how to perform a funeral. It's not a matter of saving our respective institutions. Much more is at stake, namely being human. It is the deepest form of undertaking to help fellow human beings to do this human thing in a humane way.

The Funeral

Our revels now are ended. These our actors,
As I foretold you, were all spirits and
Are melted into air, into thin air;
And, like the baseless fabric of this vision,
The cloud-capp'd towers, the gorgeous palaces,
The solemn temples, the great globe itself,
Yea, all which it inherit, shall dissolve
And, like this insubstantial pageant faded,
Leave not a rack behind. We are such stuff
As dreams are made on, and our little life
Is rounded with a sleep.

William Shakespeare, The Tempest

Chapter 7

THE THEORY AND PRACTICE OF CREMATION

Thomas Lynch

"WHEN I'M GONE JUST CREMATE ME," HUGHEY MACSWIGGAN told his third and final wife as she stood at his bedside while the hospice nurse fiddled with the morphine drip that hadn't kept his pain at bay. The operative word in his directive was "just." He wasn't especially fond of fire. He hadn't picked out a favorite urn. He saw burning not so much as an alternative to burial as an alternative to bother. He hadn't the strength to force the moment to its crisis. He didn't know if he was coming or going. He just wanted it all to be over—the cancer, the second guessing, the wondering whether he'd done irreparable harm, what with the years of drinking, the divorces, all of that carrying on.

It's not that he lacked faith. On the contrary, after long years of sobriety in the fellowship of Alcoholics Anonymous, he had sought through prayer and meditation to improve his conscious contact with God as he understood Him, praying only for knowledge of His will for him and the power to carry that out. He was, in extremis, ready and willing, grateful and gracious. He'd had enough. He just wanted whatever was going to happen to happen.

Loosened from his own ethnic and religious traditions, which were lost in the shuffle of postmodernity, he hadn't any particular sense of "the done thing" when it came to funerals. He just didn't want to be a burden to anyone, least of all the ones he loved. So when pressed by his family for some direction, "just cremate me" is what he told them all. And so they did.

They dispensed with the presbyters and processions, with casket, graveside, and monument. "Never mind the marines," they said, when I told them that his service during World War II, from Cape Gloucester to Peleliu to Okinawa, entitled him to military honors. "Daddy wouldn't want any of that." Neither flag nor flowers, hymns or limousines, obits or an open bar. His son-in-law put the charges on a credit card, which earned him frequent flier miles.

And Hughey was just cremated, which is to say his body was placed on a plywood pallet, covered with a cardboard carapace and, after the paperwork and permits were secured, loaded into the hearse and driven to a site toward the back of an industrial park where a company that makes burial vaults operates a crematory on the side. The line of boxes along the wall—a couple dozen of them—contained the bodies of other pilgrims, dropped off by discount cremation services and other mortuaries. They were waiting, like planes on the tarmac, for a clear runway, an open retort.

Because our funeral home's protocols require us to see the dead all the way into the fire, just as we see the dead who are buried all the way into the ground, the crematory operator lets us jump the line. We arrange this by appointment, same as for burials. It seems the last if not least that we can do.

When I invited—as is also our policy—any and all of his

family to come with us to the crematory, or to designate one among them to come along, "just to see that everything is done properly," they winced and shook their heads as if I'd invited them to a root canal or public stoning: a necessary but noxious procedure, the less talked about the better, thank you.

So it was one of the crematory staff who helped me roll Hughey out of the hearse and onto the hydraulic lift and stood by wordlessly while I recited the Lord's Prayer, which Hughey would have heard at AA meetings, and set the little numbered metal disk atop the cardboard box and helped me push it into the retort, closed the door and pushed the red button that started the fire that turned Hughey MacSwiggan's corpse into his ashes. Three hours later, after everything had cooled, the remnants of his larger bone structures were "processed" into a finer substance and all of it placed in a plastic bag inside a plastic box with a label that bore his name, the date, and the logo of the crematory. This greatly reduced version of Hughey was given to me to take back to the funeral home to await a decision from his family about what would be done with what remained.

"In a funeral we are carrying the body of a saint to the place of farewell," writes Thomas G. Long in his study of American funeral practice, *Accompany Them with Singing—The Christian Funeral*.[1] In short, we are carrying a loved one to the edge of mystery, and people should be encouraged to stick around to the end, to book passage all the way. If the body is to be buried, go to the grave and stay there until the body is in the ground. If the body is to be burned, go to the crematorium and witness the burning.

Ask any gathering of your fellow Americans—students at university, clergy or hospice workers, medical or mortuary sorts—how many have ever been to a graveside or watched a burial, and 95 out of every 100 raise a hand. The hillside and headstones, the opened grave and black-clad mourners are fixtures in our commemorative consciousness. If not in real life, then on TV, we've seen enough burials to know the drill. Next ask how many have been to a retort or crematory or witnessed a cremation and roughly the reverse is true: less than 5 percent have been there, done that.

Forty or fifty years ago, when the cremation rate in the U.S. was still in the low single digits, this would have made perfect sense. But today, when the national rate is over 40 percent and is predicted to be over 50 percent before another decade turns, it represents a kind of disconnect. How is it that so many people claim a preference for cremation but so few have any interest in knowing more about it? As a people we have thoroughly embraced the notion of cremation as an exercise in simplicity and cost-efficiency. But we remain thoroughly distanced from the fire itself and all its metaphors and meaning, its religious and ritual significance as a station in our pilgrimage of faith. For Christians, in particular—who, along with secular humanists, account for most of the nation's increase in cremations—this disconnect is even more telling.

In *Accompany Them with Singing,* Long documents a troublesome shift in religious practice. In the place of funerals—the full-bodied, full gospel, faith-fit-for-the-long-haul and heavy lifting of grief events our elders were accustomed to—what has evolved, especially among white suburban Protestants, is a downsized, "personalized," user-friendly, Hallmarky soiree: the customized, emotively neutral and religiously ambiguous memorial service to which everyone is invited but the one who has died. The dead have been made more or less to disappear, cremated as a matter of pure function and notably outside the context of faith. The living gather at their convenience to "celebrate the life" in a kind of obsequy-lite at which therapy is dispensed, closure proclaimed, biography enshrined, and spirits are, it is supposed, uplifted. If not made to disappear entirely, the presence of the dead at such services is minimized, inurned, denatured, virtualized, made manageable and unrecognizable by cremation. The "idea" of the deceased is feted for possessing a great golf swing or good humor, a beautiful garden or well-hosted parties, while the thing itself—the corpse—has been dispensed with in private, dispatched without witness or rubric.

Even when the cremation follows a wake or visitation and a public service in the church or elsewhere, we rarely process to the crematory, not least because the retort is often housed in an industrial park, not a memorial park. This disinclination to deal with the dead we burn has something to do with our conflicted notions about fire, which Western sensibilities and Western religious traditions still often associate with punishment and wastefulness.

⚬✿⚬

"If there is a problem with cremation in regard to a funeral," says Long, "it is that the cremated remains are required to stand in for the whole body of the deceased, which at its worst could be like asking Ralph Fiennes's hat to play Hamlet."[2]

This minimization of what Long calls a "worshipful drama" suggests more than a shift in religious fashion. The issue is not cremation or burial but rather the gospel, the sacred text of death and resurrection, suffering and salvation, redemption and grace—the mystery that a Christian funeral ought to call us to behold the mystery of life's difficult journey and the faithful pilgrim's triumphant homegoing. The memorial service, by avoiding the embodied dead, the shovel and shoulder work, the divisions of labor and difficult journey to the grave or pyre, too often replaces theology with therapy, conviction with convenience, the full-throated assurances of faith with a sort of memorial karaoke where "everyone gets to share a memory."

Thence to the fellowship hall for "tea and cakes and ices," having dodged once again those facts of death that, as T. S. Eliot famously says, "force the moment to its crisis."[3]

"The fact is," writes Long, "that many educated Christians in the late nineteenth century, the forebears of today's white Protestants, lost their eschatological nerve and their vibrant faith in the afterlife, and we are their theological and liturgical heirs."[4] Long is citing not a change of fashions but a lapse of faith in the promise of eternal life: a core principle of Christianity.

The crisis presented by a death in the family has not changed since the first human mourners looked into the pit or cave or flames they'd just consigned their dead to and posed the signature questions of our species: Is that all there is? Why did it happen? Will it happen to me? Are we alone? What comes next? The corpse, the grave, the tomb, and the fire became fixtures in the life of faith's most teachable moment. We learned to deal with death by dealing with our dead; to process mortality by processing mortals from one station to the next in the journey of grief. The bodiless obsequies that have become the standard practice in many mainstream Protestant churches represent not only a shift of mortuary fashions from custom and tradition toward convenience, but also a fundamental uncertainty about eternal life. They lack an essential task and manifest—to assist all pilgrims, living and dead, in making their way back home to God.

Abject grief, spiritual despair, anger at God, and serious doubt are common responses to suffering and loss. And while doubt is unexceptional in the life of faith, and most certainly attends a death in the family, the role of pastor, priest, minister, and congregation, indeed the raison d'être of the Christian community, is to uphold and embolden believers, shaken in their bereavement, with the promise of the gospel. This is how the faithful bear both death in the abstract and the dead in the flesh. It is by bearing our dead from one station to the other—

deathbed to parlor, parlor to altar, altar to the edge of eternal life—that we learn to bear death itself. By going the distance with them we learn to walk upright in the faith that God will take care of God's own, living and dead.

But how, Long asks, should the living take seriously a church from which the dead have been gradually banished, as if not seeing were believing? If dead Christians are redeemed saints bound for heaven, oughtn't we accompany them with singing? Oughtn't we bring them to church and go the distance with them, proclaiming the gospel on the way to the grave or tomb or fire, and there commend our dead to God?

To the extent that cremation has become an accomplice in the out-of-sight and out-of-mind nature of memorial services, it is at cross-purposes with the life of faith and the mission of the church. Of course, the problem is not with cremation, which is an ancient and honorable, efficient and effective means of disposing of our dead. Nor is the fire to burn our dead any less an elemental gift of God than is the ground to bury them in. The problem is not that we cremate our dead, but how ritually denatured, spiritually vacant, religiously timid, and impoverished we have allowed the practice to become. It is not *that* we do it, but *how* we do it that must be reconsidered.

It was back in the Gilded Age that the first modern cremation in America took place. In Washington, Pennsylvania, in 1876, the corpse of Baron De Palm was burned in a retort built by a local doctor. A hundred years later, cremation remained very much the exception to the general rule—still less than 7.5 percent.[5] But the past thirty years has seen a steadily growing acceptance of cremation. Across the nation, more than a third of all deaths are now followed by cremation. Among Protestant Christians the numbers are even higher if we consider that Jews, Muslims, and Orthodox Christians almost never cremate their dead and that Catholics still bury the large majority of theirs.

The reasons for this change are manifold. For our ancestors in the nineteenth and early twentieth centuries, the land remained foundational. Borders, boundaries, beliefs were all fixed and settled. But modern American culture seems in constant transit and flux. We are more mobile, more modular, less grounded than our grandparents. Our ethnic, religious, and family ties do not bind so tightly as in former times. We multitask and travel light through lives that seem to be in constant states of revision. Careers are a series of five-year plans. Communities have become virtual entities— social networks—as home pages replace home places as a key to identity. Marriages and families have been reconfigured. Cremation seems to suit many of us better—making us more portable, divisible, and easier to scatter. But while technology has made the process odorless, smokeless, and highly efficient, the culture remains ritually adrift when it comes to fire, consigning it most often to private, industrial venues rather than public, ceremonial ones.

In cultures where cremation is practiced in public, among Hindus and Buddhists in India and Japan, its powerful metaphorical values—purification, release, elemental beauty, and unity—add to the religious narratives the bereaved embrace. The public pyres of Bali and Calcutta, where the firstborn brings fire from the home fire to kindle the fire that will consume a parent's body, are surrounded by liturgical and civic traditions. Elsewhere, however, cremation is practiced in private, the fire kept purposefully behind closed doors. Whereas the traditional funeral transports the corpse and mourners from parlor to altar, then to place of disposition, cremation, as it is practiced in the U.S., often routes around, not through, such stations in the pilgrimage. We miss most if not all of the journey, the drama, and the metaphor.

Of course, some of this has to do with consumer dissatisfaction with a mortuary marketplace interested more in sales than in service, inclined more toward the stuff than the substance, and geared more toward Hallmark sentiments than real meaning. Still, a death in the family is not a retail event; rather it is an existential one. It involves core values rather than commodities; a marketplace that spends more time and energy cataloging the possible purchases and their price points instead of the ways to engage and participate in this first among the human rubrics is of little lasting value.

For persons of faith, the essential elements of a good funeral remain few and familiar: the dead pilgrim, the living to whom the death matters, and someone to broker the mystery between them and enunciate the new status of the soul. Last but not least among the essentials is the task at hand: to get the dead and the living where they need to be. For the former that means the tomb or fire or grave or sea. For the latter it means to the edge of the life they will be living without the deceased, whose blessed body is consigned to the elements and whose soul is commended to God. Everything else is accessory. Coffins and flowers, obits and eulogies, bagpipers and dove releases, organ music and stained-glass windows, funeral homes and funeral directors—all accessories; though helpful certainly, comforting sometimes, maybe even edifying, whether costly or bargain priced, they are but accessories. Corpse and mourners, gospel and transport: these are the requisites. Everything else is incidental. To Christianize cremation requires only that Christians—clergy and laypeople— treat it as an alternative to burial, rather than an alternative to bothering. The fireside, like the graveside, is made holy by the death of saints, the witness of faithful pilgrims, and the religious context in which the living take leave of their dead.

Long writes:

> Resistance to going the full distance with the dead will occasionally be encountered from some crematoriums, which are not accustomed to people who want to stay for the firing up

of the retort, and some cemeteries, which view trudging to
the grave as an inefficient use of employee time or don't like
the idea of families being present for the dirt being placed
on the coffin in the grave. These cemeteries much prefer for
funeral processions to end not at graveside but in some plastic pseudo chapel where the ceremonies can be peremptorily
put to an end and the worshipers dispatched without delay,
thus freeing up the burial crew to get on with their business
unimpeded. These so-called chapels—why mince words?—
are Chapels of Convenience and Cathedrals of Funeralia
Interruptus. Tell the cemetery owner or crematorium man-
ager, kindly of course, to step out of the way, that they are
impeding the flow of traffic. You have been walking with
this saint since the day of baptism; the least you can do is go
all the way to the grave, to the end, with this child of God.
They may refuse, but if enough clergy demand to be able
to go the last few yards with the dead, change will happen.[6]

So much of what I know of final things I have learned from
the reverend clergy. These men and women of God drop what
they're doing and come on the run when there is trouble. These
are the local heroes who show up, armed only with faith, who
respond to calls in the middle of the night, the middle of dinner, the middle of already busy days to bedsides and roadsides,
intensive care and emergency rooms, nursing homes and hospice wards and family homes, to try and make some sense of
senseless things. They are on the front lines, holy corpsmen in
the flesh-and-blood combat between hope and fear. Their faith
is contagious and emboldening. Their presence is balm and
anointing. The Lutheran pastor who always sang the common
doxology at graveside: "Praise God from Whom All Blessings
Flow," his hymn sung into the open maw of unspeakable sadness, startling in its comfort and assurance. The priest who
would intone the Gregorian chant and tribal Latin of the "In
Paradisum" while leading the pallbearers to the grave, counting on the raised voice and ancient language to invoke the
heavenly and earthly hosts. The young Baptist preacher who,

at a loss for words, pulled out his harmonica and played the mournful and familiar notes of "Just as I Am" over the coffin of one of our town's most famous sinners. "Between the stirrup and the ground," he quietly promised the heartsore family and upbraided the too eagerly righteous, "mercy sought and mercy found."

❧

My friend Jake Andrews, an Episcopal priest, now dead for years but still remembered, apart from serving his little local parish, was chaplain to the fire and police departments and became the default minister, the go-to guy for the churchless and lapsed among our local citizenry. Father Andrews always rode in the hearse with me, whether the graveyard was minutes or hours away, in clement and inclement weather, and whether there were hundreds or dozens or only the two of us to hear, he would stand and read the holy script such as it had been given him to do. When cremation became, as it did elsewhere, the norm among his townspeople and congregants, he would leave the living to the tea and cakes and ices in the parish hall and ride with me and the dead to the crematory. There he would perform his priestly offices with the sure faith and deep humanity that seems to me an imitation of Christ.

It was Jake Andrews's belief that pastoral care included care of the saints he was called on to bury and cremate. Baptisms and weddings were, he said, "easy duties," whereas funerals are "the deep end of the pool." I think he had, as we all do, his dark nights of the soul, his wrestling with angels, his reasonable doubts. His favorite studies were on the book of Job. But still, he believed the dead to be alive in Christ. He met the mourners at the door and pressed the heavens with their lamentations. It was Jake who taught me the power of presence, the work of mercy in the showing up, pitching in, bearing

our share of whatever burden, and going the distance with the
living and the dead. He taught me that a living faith founded
on a risen corpse and empty tomb ought not be estranged from
death's rudiments and duties.

In the end Hughey MacSwiggan was scattered in Scotland.
"He never made the trip but always wanted to go" is what his
family told me. They knew my writerly duties often took me
to the British Isles. "Take him with you the next time you go,"
his third wife said. And so I did. I'd been invited to launch a
book at the Edinburgh Festival.

When the X-ray at the airport showed "some dense pack-
aging" in my carry-on, I told the security guard it was Hughey
MacSwiggan's cremated remains and asked if she'd like to
inspect them further. She shook her head and let me pass. I did
not declare Hughey at customs in Heathrow and kept my own
counsel on the train ride north and checking in at the Chan-
nings Hotel. I considered the gardens off Princess Street or
maybe some corner of the castle grounds, but the mid-August
crowds made those sites impossible. I toyed with the notion of
leaving him in a pub near Waverley Station on the theory that
heaven for Hughey might mean that he could drink again.

But it was the view from Dean Bridge, the deep valley,
the "dene" that names the place, the river working its way
below under the generous overhang of trees—the valley of the
shadow of death, I thought—that beckoned me further in my
search. I worked my way down into Belgrave Crescent where
I found an open, unlocked gate to the private gardens there.
But it was a little too perfect, a little too rose-gardenish and
manicured, and I was drawn by the sound of falling water. So
I went out and around past the Dean Parish Church and the
graveyard there.

I made my way down to the water by the footpath, and working back in the direction of the bridge I found a wee waterfall, apparently the site of an old mill. Kneeling to my duties, I poured Hughey's ashes out—some into the curling top waters and the rest into the circling pool below. I remember the quick pearlescent cloud, the puff of white it made in the rush of current, almost like what you'd see when salmon spawn. And watching what remained of him disappear downstream, what I thought of was the thing they said whenever the masked man rode off at the end of the cowboy show I watched as a boy: "A fiery horse with the speed of light, a cloud of dust, and a hearty 'Hi-yo, Silver!' . . . The Lone Ranger!"

There goes Hughey now, I thought—hi-yo, Silver, away. The little bone fragments, bits and pieces of him, glistened in the gravel bed of the Waters of Leith while his cloud of dust quickly worked its way in the current downstream to the eventual river mouth and out, I supposed, into the Firth of Forth and the North Sea and the diasporic waters of the world. One with all the elements now—the earth and wind and fire and water—Hughey was like the Holy Spirit of God: everywhere or nowhere, in everything that lives or in nothing at all, endlessly with us or always alone; blessed and blissful nonetheless I prayed, at his first glimpse of whatever is or isn't.

When [the church] buries a man, that action concerns me: all mankind is of one author, and is one volume; when one man dies, one chapter is not torn out of the book, but translated into a better language; and every chapter must be so translated; God employs several translators; some pieces are translated by age, some by sickness, some by war, some by justice; but God's hand is in every translation, and his hand shall bind up all our scattered leaves again for that library where every book shall lie open to one another. As therefore the bell that rings to a sermon calls not upon the preacher only, but upon the congregation to come, so this bell calls us all. . . . No man is an island, entire of itself; every man is a piece of the continent, a part of the main. If a clod be washed away by the sea, Europe is the less, as well as if a promontory were, as well as if a manor of thy friend's or of thine own were: any man's death diminishes me, because I am involved in mankind, and therefore never send to know for whom the bell tolls; it tolls for thee.

John Donne, Meditation XVII

Chapter 8

A SENSE OF MOVEMENT, A SENSE OF MEANING, A SENSE OF HOPE

The Good Funeral

Thomas G. Long

When I was in my early twenties, I remember going to the therapist Ernst Schachtel and talking and talking and talking, and one day he said to me, "But what is it you want, Mister Broyard? What is it you want?" And I said, "I want to be transfigured."

—Anatole Broyard, *Intoxicated by My Illness and Other Writings on Life and Death*

CLOSE ENCOUNTERS OF THE BEWILDERING KIND

If a traveler from Mars, interested in studying the ways of earthlings, were to spy on a typical American funeral, he would probably be thoroughly confused by the experience. What would he observe? First, if he happened to set down his spacecraft in a fairly ordinary, white, suburban neighborhood, he would probably observe not a funeral at all, not in the traditional sense, but a memorial service. That is, a service about memories because the deceased—let's call her "Elizabeth"—would not be present for the occasion, her body already having been privately cremated or buried or donated beforehand. People, our Martian would see, would be gathering somewhere—in a church, a funeral home, an auditorium—taking their seats, sitting quietly, and waiting. Perhaps a pianist, an organist, a chamber ensemble, or a digital recording would be providing gathering music. What would follow would likely be an assortment of gestures, speeches, symbols, and mini rituals. Our Martian might see a video screen with flashing images—baby pictures, wedding photos, vacation shots—all of Elizabeth. There could well be a table display at the entrance to the room, showcasing objects from Elizabeth's life, maybe her golf clubs, some favorite recipes, a club medallion, a sports pennant, or items of clothing she had crocheted.

As the service proceeded, our interplanetary guest might well observe several people coming to a microphone to speak about Elizabeth, some of them telling wry stories, some cracking jokes, some reading handwritten comments with trembling hands and barely muted sobs. If he listened carefully, our Martian would learn that Elizabeth had died on Tuesday at Community Hospital, but that, according to the speakers, she had now become something other than what she was before—an "eternal memory, never to be forgotten" or "a light in the sky, like a twinkling star," or perhaps even "an angel watching over us and still protecting her children." Elizabeth, the Martian would no doubt hear, was a person who "loved laughter and fun" and who "wouldn't want us to be sad today." Even the people who were sobbing would say so.

Poems would be read, perhaps a passage of Scripture or the lyrics of a song, maybe a moving quotation, all chosen because they were "Elizabeth's favorites." Candles would be lit, music played. Presiding over this occasion, perhaps, would be a religious leader or a member of the family, but if our Martian visitor happened in on a service led by a "Celebrant," one of the newer breed of ritual presiders, he might even hear something like this:

Elizabeth's free spirit came through in music. Henry has put together a wonderful CD with all of her favorite songs. I hope you enjoy it and think of her and dance and get down to Elvis, the Beetles, and Fleetwood Mac. Okay everyone, at the count of three, I want everyone to say . . . "Let me take you to Funky town!!!" One, two, three . . . .[1]

What could all of this mean? Our undercover Martian would surely be baffled. Partly this would be because complex human ceremonies, such death rituals, are simply difficult for outsiders to figure out, regardless of whether they hail from Mars or Minneapolis or Mozambique. These events are saturated with insider codes that only the initiated can crack. In the same way that a German tourist attending a New York Yankees game for the first time might catch on to hits, runs, and even errors but would need many more games before grasping the mysteries of the double steal, the sacrifice bunt, and the seventh inning stretch, it is also with death rites. They are a complicated and intricate mixture of gesture and myth, emotion and thought, memory and anticipation, and their meaning can be deeply plumbed only by the experienced.

But it would not be complexity alone that would mystify our Martian. He would also be confused by Elizabeth's service because, quite frankly, like many similar services today, it was a bewildering mess. Even when they are crafted by caring people who are full of good will, these services often lack coherence. At their worst they are formless and aimless, without tradition or structure, sail or rudder. They can so easily slip into random odds and ends thrown together like a high school talent show, a potpourri of made-up pageantries and sentimental gestures combined with a few leftover religious rites that have broken loose from their moorings and floated downstream. Many have become a form of improvisational theater with upbeat emcees.

What to make of Elizabeth's service? Where was the structure to hold it together? Broadway plays have a structured sequence of acts; NFL football games move logically from kickoff to the two-minute warning; court trials progress logically from opening arguments to verdict. All of these public events are all built on narrative plots, and they tell stories—boy meets girl, the Bears were down early but came back to win, the jilted lover was guilty after all. But, by comparison, the rhythm and flow of Elizabeth's memorial service seems arbitrary and unstructured. It would be hard for anyone—space traveler, cultural anthropologist, or even a family member—to fathom exactly what story this ceremony tells. Even those who planned this service were probably simply following fashion trends and were not certain themselves what narrative they wished to follow, what deeper meaning they wished to convey. Except, of course, that they desired to stage some kind of celebration of the life and memory of Elizabeth.

What actually comes through in this service, though—and here is one of the problems—is not Elizabeth, but a vague, vaporous, and somewhat sanitized version of her. She was not present, not the embodied human being or the Elizabeth who really lived, whose life was a fabric of daily commitments and who is now really dead. The Elizabeth of this service was the cheerful but absent Elizabeth, the episodic Elizabeth, who in our wishful imaginations desires to be recalled but not fully remembered, noticed but not chronicled, missed but not truly lamented, the Elizabeth who, like the Cheshire Cat, has disappeared except for the smile. And as for the ceremony itself—candles, jokes, videos, pop music, familiar symbols drawn from civic religion and gauzy spirituality—it lacks narrative flow. It is a less a story of what Elizabeth's life and death mean and more a pot of ritual spaghetti thrown against the wall in hopes that something will stick, that something will evoke the positive feelings we desire.

THE NECESSARY GROUND SENSE

We can imagine several possible responses to the above critique of Elizabeth's memorial service. The first is, So what? OK, perhaps this ceremony was indeed a patchwork quilt of poems and anecdotes, reminiscences and tributes, witty stories and pop tunes. What's the problem? Who's to say that coherence is a virtue? After all, it was done in sincere appreciation for Elizabeth and performed for the benefit of those who loved her, and isn't it true that a collection of tributes and actions all devoted to her memory and to the positive feelings of her family and friends is exactly what is called for on this occasion? People who have suffered a loss do what they want and need to do in the face of death. The result may not have been smooth or professional, but it was heartfelt, and it allowed people to celebrate Elizabeth's life. Isn't that what a "good" death rite is all about?

A second response to our criticism is, Well yes, it's true that there wasn't much meaning to be found in Elizabeth's ceremony, beyond her family and friends doing some whistling in the dark. If it made them feel better, fine; we don't begrudge that. But the reason why there was no deeper meaning in this memorial service is simple. There *are* no deeper meanings to be found.

An increasing number of people in our society who feel precisely this way are choosing the "no service" option, deciding not to have any ceremony whatsoever for the dead. They have concluded that funerals and memorial services are at best unnecessary and at worst even harmful, in the sense that they are built on illusions and wishful thinking. Death, they say, is an expected event, a biological inevitability, no more and no less, and it must simply be bravely faced. Beyond this, there are no profound cultural, social, or religious meanings to be extracted.

When a woman becomes pregnant, the argument goes, we do not gather at a church or a synagogue or a hospital maternity ward to recite poems, sing songs, and tell stories. A sperm cell has simply fertilized an egg to form a zygote; that's all. It happens, and this biological fact is its own meaning, joyful or otherwise. Just so for the end of life. When a person dies, that biological fact is also its own meaning. So why gather to sing and recite poetry over it? Death may cause us to feel sad, but whatever responses of memory and mourning result, these are personal, inward, and fleeting experiences, and thus they can best be handled privately, without the charade of a public ceremony.

There is, however, a third response, and one that I believe carries more wisdom than the others. When Elizabeth died, her death was not just a biological occurrence nor was it merely a private event. Rather, Elizabeth's death, any human being's death, is a tear in the social fabric, and it evokes two great needs, both of them very public: first, the body must be cared for and given disposition. Second, the community needs to tell once more the story of the life of the one who has died and the larger, more ancient, and treasured story about how we understand death and life as a people. These two needs, the caring for the body and the telling of the story, are not separable; they are two sides of the same coin. Caring for the body is part of how we tell the great story and the great story of the meaning of life and death shapes how we care for the body.

A sixty-five-year-old New Orleans woman named Vera Smith was killed by a hit-and-run driver in the chaotic days after Hurricane Katrina devastated the city in 2005. The police, overwhelmed by more pressing matters such as life-threatening emergencies and widespread looting, had no time for someone who was already dead, and they ignored repeated calls from Vera's neighbors to retrieve her body. She lay unclaimed on the roadside for five days, and when a photo of her neglected body appeared in newspapers across the country, she became an icon of the annihilation of Katrina and the helplessness of the city.

Finally, Vera's neighbors concluded that something must be done and that no help would be coming from the outside. So they took charge themselves and did what human beings need to do when one among them has died. Gathering soil, rocks, and bricks from a nearby plot of land, they covered Vera's body and made for her a proper, if temporary grave, which they named "Vera's Corner." As they worked to cover her body, they told each other the story of Vera, how she was born in Mexico and moved to New Orleans with her husband Max, how she wore colorful clothing and bold costume jewelry, and how she had a ready and infectious laugh. They told how she was devoted to her two small dogs and was a regular at mass at the local Catholic church. "That's Miss Vera right there," a neighbor said, pointing to her grave. "We know her."

Eventually, Vera's body was cremated and her ashes were scattered near her parents' graves in Texas. But until Vera's family was able to provide this more dignified disposition, her neighbors had carried out as best they could, and under extreme circumstances, the two great necessities: they cared for her body and they told her story. They placed two red hibiscus blossoms on either side of Vera's grave, and on the sidewalk next to her grave they wrote, "Here lies Vera. God help us."[2]

The story of Vera Smith's burial is but one more indication that as human beings we instinctively know what to do in the face of death. Like Vera's New Orleans neighbors, our first impulse may be to leave things to the authorities, to hand the responsibility for caring for the dead to others. But when we are left to our own resources, we know intuitively what must be done. We also know, even when the circumstances are less extreme and there are thankfully people around to help us perform the necessities of death—funeral directors, pastors, cemetery workers, and others—that the responsibility for doing these human tasks ultimately rests upon us as human beings.

In his poem "Tract," William Carlos Williams says, "I will teach you my townspeople how to perform a funeral . . . you have the ground sense necessary."[3] We do have the "ground sense necessary," the social memory required to perform wisely in the face of death. The problem is that many of our current death practices have lost touch with this ground sense, have forgotten what is required of us, and the result is that we have wandered to a place where we think we have to make everything up as if we have never walked this path before. Thus we improvise for ourselves death activities that seem wise but in fact obscure and trivialize the realities of death, grief, and hope.

THE POSSIBILITY OF A GOOD FUNERAL

It may seem strange, perhaps even somewhat disrespectful of the dead, to speak of a "good funeral." How could a funeral, which is, after all, occasioned by loss and grief, be "good"? To call a funeral "good," however, doesn't mean that it somehow masks the pain of loss or that it was enjoyable—a "good time"—in the sense of entertainment. It does not even mean that it was artistically excellent with only the very best music and the finest poetry. A funeral can be called "good," rather, when it accomplishes its proper purposes, when it does the work a funeral is supposed to do. "A good funeral," says Thomas Lynch cogently, "is one that gets the dead where they need to go and the living where they need to be."

Many years ago, my wife and I had tickets for a Lincoln Center performance of Mendelssohn's *Elijah* by the New York Philharmonic Orchestra and the Westminster Choir. It was to be the final appearance for the legendary Leonard Bernstein as conductor of the Philharmonic. But, sadly and unexpectedly, Bernstein died of complications from cancer only weeks before the concert. Kurt Masur, who was soon to join the Philharmonic as principal conductor, was hastily brought from Europe to substitute for Bernstein. With only a short time to prepare, Masur poured himself wholeheartedly into the task, spending hours each day painstakingly studying the score and rehearsing with the musicians.

On the night of the performance, he rose to the occasion. He was alive with urgent energy. He did far more than conduct; his body in excitement arced toward the musicians, his baton was charged with electricity, summoning every measure of effort and excellence from the chorus and orchestra. Masur's achievement was both ethereal and muscular, the resulting music sublime, and, at the close of the performance, Masur was soaked in perspiration. As the audience stood in a rapturous ovation, he spread his hands, like a priest giving a blessing, first over the soloists and then over all the musicians. Because of his efforts, we had been given a gift—not merely the gift of a superb orchestra or of a fine choir or even of the talents of Kurt Masur. All of these things contributed to the fulfilling of the larger purpose of the concert: the gift of Mendelssohn's *Elijah*.

Just so, what makes for a good funeral is not so much that the speeches are good, or the mood positive, or the music fitting, but rather that all of these things, and more, work together to perform the essential music of a funeral, that is to bring to fruition the two primary purposes of a funeral: to accompany the body of the deceased to the place of farewell and to tell well the story of what this life and this death mean. When we keep these two purposes in view, we can identify some marks of a "good funeral":

A Sense of Movement. A good funeral is not static. The first great necessity of death, as we have said, is to move the body of the deceased from *here* to *there,* that is, from the place of death to the place of final disposition. In most places around the world, and throughout most of human history, carrying the body of the deceased to the grave or the fire or the mountain, weeping and singing, mourning and praying along the way, is not done *before* the funeral or *after* the funeral—it *is* the funeral.

We know that the body must be moved; there is no choice about that. However, we do have a choice about *how* the body is moved and what significance we give to that action. The contemporary trend is to move the body privately, out of sight and out of mind. Elizabeth will be taken to be cremated or buried or to be donated to medical science with only a few of the closest members of her family present. Or perhaps even they will be absent and only the funeral director or the excavator operator at the cemetery or the furnace technician at the crematory will attend to the disposition of Elizabeth's body.

To do this privately, however, involves two questionable decisions. First, it assumes that the presence of Elizabeth's body is somehow a deterrent to what we hope to accomplish, or even worse, an embarrassment sullying the upbeat mood we desire. But Elizabeth's body is the sign and token of Elizabeth herself and her life. Elizabeth did not e-mail or fax in her love for her husband, her care for her children, her labors as an elementary school teacher, or her compassion as a friend, saying, "You know I'm with you in spirit." Instead, the substance of her life is in its embodiments. She put her arms around her husband, touched her children with blessing, stood physically and lovingly in the presence of her students, set her feet along the path to be with her friends. Elizabeth was an embodied person, and she was defined by where her body was and what her body did. We know that Elizabeth's dead body is not all that was Elizabeth, but it is her sacred remains, the tangible and physical token of her life, and how we care for her body is an expression of our regard for her. If we wish to honor Elizabeth, then we must honor her body.

The second questionable decision in a private disposition is that nothing is at stake here in the larger community, that what happens to Elizabeth's body is of concern only to the small circle of the family and those who were intimately connected with Elizabeth. But as we saw in the case of Vera Smith, what happens to one person's body discloses how, as a society, we value human life more generally. People who have learned how to care tenderly for the bodies of the dead are almost surely people who also know how to show mercy to the bodies of the living.

In a few parts of the country, an older tradition still prevails. When a funeral procession passes on the highway, other motorists pull off of the road to show respect, and pedestrians stand in reverent silence as the hearse goes by. This points to a more general truth, which endures even in places where the custom itself is no longer observed, that one person's death represents a breech for the whole community and an occasion not only to bow in respect toward the deceased by also to remind ourselves of the transience of life and the meaning of life and death. Obviously, Elizabeth's death has greater impact on those who were closest to her, but her death is nonetheless a loss for the whole society and an emblem of human mortality.

In this way, a funeral shares at least one trait with a wedding. In a marriage service, those to be married walk in to the ceremony alone, and they walk out together. It is a piece of community theater that enacts the transition that marriage produces, both for the couple and for the community around them. The couple starts this day officially single; they end this day officially joined together as one, and the rest of us must now think of them differently, act toward them differently, alter the community narrative to account for their marriage.

So with a funeral. We enact once again the drama of a person's passing from here to there. One who lived among us as an embodied presence is now moving to a place where they are no longer among us in that way. We carry them tenderly to that place, and we let them go. We process our understanding of death by walking in procession with the dead, not only caring for this one dead body but also bringing vividly to mind all of those who have already passed this way and that we too will travel this path. To do this out of sight and out of mind is not only to hide our faces from the truth of what is happening, it is also, and perhaps more sadly, to deprive ourselves and others of the wisdom and healing to be gained by accompanying the dead on the last mile of the way. A good funeral, then, not only honors the body of the deceased, it also makes it clear, in an active sense, that the one who has died is moving from here to there and that the rest of us are accompanying the deceased along the way.

When my mother died several years ago, I had to make a persuasive case precisely on this point to the funeral director we worked with. This funeral director was most comfortable with the choreography supported by the architecture of his funeral home, a pattern that makes for an efficient funeral, perhaps, but, in terms of dramatic action, is ambiguous and finally misleading. The usual procedure at this funeral home is to seat everyone attending the funeral in the funeral home chapel, then to roll the coffin in from stage left and to place it on display at the center in the front of the mourners. Then the service, whatever it might be, is conducted, and at the conclusion of the service, the casket is moved again, this time stage right, out a door to a porte cochere, where a hearse is waiting for the trip to the cemetery.

But what could this movement, stage left to right, possibly signify? A bird flying through a barn? And why would the coffin be placed on exhibition at the front, sideways, like a sofa in a furniture store window? What this kind of staging conveys is that a funeral is simply a brief and mainly motionless time of reflection about the deceased. The mourners are in their seats, the coffin is brought front and center to signal the beginning of this contemplation, and then the coffin is whisked away at the end to mark its conclusion. Coffin in, let the meditating begin; coffin out, funeral over. If this is, in fact, what a funeral is about, then the current widespread practice of leaving the body of the deceased out of the equation altogether makes a certain kind of sense. People can reflect on the life of the deceased just as well, or perhaps better, without all the folderol of rolling a casket across the front of the room. Moreover, leaving out the casket, in part, has the additional advantage of eliminating any avaricious speculation about the price of the box or the lavishness of the floral displays.

But a good funeral is not a stationary experience; it is movement, a processional. We desired, therefore, an alternative choreography at my mother's funeral. We wanted to express that we were accompanying her as she journeyed from the place of her death to the place of farewell. What we were doing in that chapel was only a part of the funeral, a brief pausing along the path in order to pray, sing, and worship. When the chapel service was concluded, we would resume the procession to that place where she would be buried, where we would say farewell, and we would give her into the hand of God.

Consider this funeral rubric from a nineteenth-century edition of the Anglican *Book of Common Prayer*:

> The Priest and the Clerks, meeting the Corpse at the entrance of the Church-yard, and going before it, either into the Church, or towards the grave, shall sing or say, "I am the resurrection and the life . . . ."[4]

Notice the assumption here. The funeral is not a quiet, still gathering; it's a processional. The priest meets the "corpse" on the way to the grave. The funeral actually begins not when a funeral director gives a hand signal to the presider that all is in place but instead at the moment the coffin is lifted up and the journey to the grave commences. People carry the body of the deceased, usually from the home of the deceased, to the grave. The clergy go out to join the procession, already underway.

When the procession arrives at the churchyard, it travels to the grave. Now, in some cases it may wind its way into the church building for a brief season of prayer and song, but this is but an interlude like a rest in music, a momentary pause before the procession picks up its feet again and makes its way inexorably to the grave. There, while "the earth shall be cast upon the Body by some standing by," the priest commits the body to the ground, "earth to earth, ashes to ashes, dust to dust."

So, we decided to make this clear in my mother's funeral. She was on a journey, and we were traveling along with her. We brought her into the chapel not through a side entrance but through the same door used by all of the other worshipers at the funeral. We walked with her, accompanying her coffin down the same center aisle others had used. She was coming at that point in the journey to the place of worship, and we were accompanying her. When the service in the chapel was concluded, we turned her coffin around and accompanied her back down the center aisle, the same path all of the other worshipers would take, and remained at her side all the way along the path to the cemetery, where we buried her. In other words, we were attempting to allow the choreography of her funeral to make plain what was actually happening that day: she was traveling from here to there and we were accompanying her along the way.

A good funeral, then, shows the movement that is really happening, and its choreography displays for all to see—rather than hides—the truth that a community of people are carrying one among them who has died from the place of death to the place of farewell.

A Sense of Meaning. Carrying the body of the deceased from the place of death to the place of disposition is the obligation imposed on us by death. But no healthy society has viewed this merely as an unadorned journey from home to grave or seen this action simply in terms of disposal of the dead. The choreography of the funeral also symbolizes society's deepest convictions about life and death. In a funeral, we are not taking out the trash; we are doing more than just carrying a dead body to the grave or the fire. As we travel that sad pathway, we try to sing and say what this death means to us, to the dead, to all of society.

A funeral bears some similarity to an ancient Greek tragic drama. In her book *Love's Knowledge,* philosopher Martha Nussbaum contrasts going to a Broadway play to the experience of the ancient Greeks attending a theatrical performance. "When we go to the theater," she writes, "we usually sit in a darkened auditorium, in the illusion of splendid isolation, while the dramatic action . . . is bathed in artificial light as if it were a separate world of fantasy and mystery." By contrast, Greek drama was performed in daylight. The stage was in the center of the gathered community, so the ancient Greeks "saw across the staged action the faces of fellow citizens."[5]

Plays were staged, Nussbaum notes, not on ordinary occasions but during solemn civic and religious festivals "whose trappings made spectators conscious that the values of the community were being examined and communicated."[6] Therefore, attending a play was not a way of idly passing the time or distracting oneself with a few hours of entertainment. "It was, instead, to engage in a communal process of inquiry, reflection, and feeling with respect to important civic and personal ends."[7] One did not go to the theater merely to watch a play, as if the play were happening somewhere over there, but instead to become involved in the event of drama, and "to respond to these events was to acknowledge and participate in a way of life."[8]

In this sense, then, good funerals are more like Greek tragic drama than like Broadway. We do not go to a good funeral to sit in the audience and watch a presentation of interesting and moving aspects of Elizabeth's life. We go to participate, to take on our role in this piece of community theater in which, now occasioned by Elizabeth's death, we enact and interrogate yet again what we believe about life and death, what are our practical and ethical responsibilities toward each other in life and death, and who we are called now to be.

What is it that a good funeral conveys about life and death? Obviously, the communal meanings of death are specific to particular traditions. The funeral of a humanist will speak different meanings than the funeral of a Baptist, a Buddhist, or a Jew. Even so, the unadorned choreography itself of a funeral, the very act of carrying the deceased from "here" to "there," contains implicit meanings:

1. *First, the fact that a funeral ritual involves direction and movement conveys the truth that the dead are going somewhere.* From the beginning, humans have employed poetry, song, and prayer to transform the necessary taking of the dead to the place of disposition into a drama, to recast the movement from "here" to "there" in symbolic, even sacred, terms. The dead are not just being carted to the pit, the fire, or the river; they are traveling toward the next world or the Mystery or the Great Beyond or heaven or the communion of the saints or at least into the legacy of history, and we are traveling with them on the last mile of the way.

2. *Second, in a good funeral, preparing a body and carrying it to the place of disposition shows that this act involves the labor of many*

hands. The ceremonies of death, like the everyday interactions of life—gathering food and having children and building dwellings and making it through the dark nights—are things, if they are done well, we must do together and, in a deeper way, are privileged to do together. Bearing one another's burdens, in life and in death, is definitive of humanity. As Holocaust survivor Artur Sammler, in Saul Bellow's novel *Mr. Sammler's Planet,* says at the funeral of his friend Elya Gruner,

> Remember, God, the soul of Elya Gruner, who, as willingly as possible and as well as he was able, and even to an intolerable point, and even in suffocation and even as death was coming was eager, even childishly perhaps (may I be forgiven for this), even with a certain servility, to do what was required of him. At his best this man was much kinder than at my very best I have ever been or could ever be. He was aware that he must meet, and he did meet— through all the confusions and degraded clowning of this life through which we are speeding—he did meet the terms of his contract. The terms which, in his inmost heart, each man knows. As I know mine. As all know. For that is the truth of it—that we all know, God, that we know, that we know, we know, we know.[9]

In our deepest selves, Sammler is saying, we know the terms of our "contract," our mutual obligations, the humanity to be discovered in caring for each other with kindness. Kindness is not merely a thought or a nice intention; it takes material form. It is preparing a bowl of soup to comfort the weary travelers, picking up a neighbor's child at school, placing a cool cloth on a fevered brow, helping the farmer in the next field over repair the barn that the windstorm damaged. Just so, to perform, with others, the labor of carrying one we cherish and grieve to the place of farewell, is a physical manifestation of the willingness to bear one another's burdens with kindness and love.

3. *Third, the choreography of a funeral, involving a processional*

moving across the land, tells an enacted story about life, death, and hope. To accompany the dead from "here" to "there" is to enact a ritual story with a beginning, a middle, and an end. In the beginning there was Elizabeth, and in the middle there was lament and a slow walking toward a new reality, and in the end there was the letting go as we gave Elizabeth to the earth, to the other side of the river, to God.

The fact that the funeral has a narrative shape is a gift, a reassurance in the midst of the fragmentation, broken promises, unfinished tasks and, as Sammler says, the "confusions and degraded clowning" of existence, that human lives ultimately have coherence and wholeness. When the literary critic Anatole Broyard became terminally ill with prostate cancer, he wrote, "Just as a novelist turns his anxiety into a story in order to be able to control it to a degree, so a sick person can make a story, a narrative, out of his illness as a way of trying to detoxify it. . . . I would also like a doctor who enjoyed me. I want to be a good story for him."[10]

Of course, most funerals magnify this narrative unity and bring it into speech through Scripture, song, homily, and eulogy. Through our words we bear witness to the fact that, even in spite of the rude interruption of death, that most jagged-edged of human experiences, this was a life that made sense, to us, to God, to the eye of love.

The writer of the Gospel of Matthew opens his story of the life of Jesus in an odd manner: with a genealogy. He marches through the generations from Abraham forward to Jesus— Jotham was the father of Ahaz and Ahaz was the father of Hezekiah and Hezekiah was the father of Manasseh and on and on—the endless stream of human begettings. Since every single one of us stands at the end of just such a stream, we well know the wild improbabilities and chance pairings that constitute our lineage. "And my mother Martha was from Pine Bluff, Arkansas, where she fell in love at a high school dance with Robert, the boy who would turn out to be my dad. Robert was the son of Phillip, a farm implement salesman who had come to Arkansas from Missouri, where his mother Nora, when she was but eighteen, had married a steamboat captain from St. Louis she met by chance when he was visiting the home of her cousin Walter . . ."

And so it goes, the chances and uncertainties of life. If your Uncle Bill had not just barely made that flight to Los Angeles he would never have met the flight attendant who is now your aunt Nancy, and if your great-grandmother Eunice had not been prayed back from the brink when she had diphtheria at age six, she would never have grown up to marry Ernest and bear Frank, who turned out to be your grandfather. So it was with Jesus, too, a roll call of close calls and near misses and unlikely couplings from Perez to Eleazar. But when Matthew gets to the end of the string (Matt. 1:17), he takes a deep breath and looks back over the ragged list of generations he has just named:

> So all the generations from Abraham to David are fourteen generations; and from David to the deportation to Babylon, fourteen generations; and from the deportation to Babylon to the Messiah, fourteen generations.

Actually, the math here does not work. Count the names, and it does not come out to be three sets of fourteen. One New Testament scholar, in a commentary on this text, dared to ask, "Could Matthew count?"[11] But Matthew is not making a mathematical point; he is making a human point and then finally a theological point: namely that human life, which seems in its unfolding to be random, haphazard, and fragmented, has a meaningful shape when viewed in retrospect, and especially when seen from the eye of God.

In her memoir *One Writer's Beginnings,* the great Eudora Welty said that writing about her life was something like riding on a train in the mountains at night. At first, there is only the darkness and the uncertainly, but then "suddenly a light is thrown back as when your train makes a curve, showing that there has been a mountain of meaning rising behind you on the way you've come, is rising there still, proven in retrospect."[12]

This discovery of a mountain of meaning rising in retrospect is why walking in procession through the narratively shaped path of a funeral is a tacit confession of faith, faith at least in the sanctity and integrity of life. No matter how broken or shattered a life may have been, to accompany the body of that person all the way from here to there is to bear witness to the truth that this was a person of substance and there is a story worth telling about this life.

Finally, though, the wholeness of a human life is not an achievement but a gift of divine grace. The theologian Gilbert Meilaender once reviewed an autobiography written by a fellow theologian. Because the writer was a close friend, Meilaender framed the review as a personal letter. He noted that, in the autobiography, his friend seemed to be searching for the narrative key that would pull all the disparate threads of his life together and make sense of them. Meilaender expressed admiration for this quest, but then reminded his friend that the unity of our lives is finally known only by God. He wrote:

> In the end, of course, I cannot say whether you have really succeeded in finding what you were seeking in this memoir: the pattern that gives shape and unity to your life. Without in any way diminishing the pleasure I have had in reading what you have written, may I say finally that it matters not whether you've found it. The God who alone, as Augustine says, can catch the heart and hold it still knows us better than we know ourselves. He will not fail to detect the pattern and finish the story.[13]

The choreography of funeral confesses this faith in enacted form, but one does not need to be an officially religious person to walk the path of this creed, as Luke Ripley, the anxious father and tenuous Catholic of Andre Dubus's short story "A Father's Story," recognizes even as he attends morning Mass. "Do not think of me," he says, "as a spiritual man whose every thought during those twenty-five minutes is at one with the words of the Mass." He says that when he watches the priest at the altar every morning at worship he knows he will be distracted by mundane affairs—the weather, the wanderings of memory—matters that have nothing to do with the sacrament. Even so, Luke recognizes that the rhythm and structure of the Mass carry him along, even in his distractions:

> I have learned . . . both the necessity and wonder of ritual. For ritual allows those who cannot will themselves out of the secular to perform the spiritual, as dancing allows the tongue-tied man a ceremony of love.[14]

A good funeral is indeed "performing the spiritual," allowing even the tongue-tied to dance a ceremony of love. And since the ritual of the funeral is shaped by narrative, it is urgent that we tell the whole story by going the full distance with the dead, all the way to the grave or the fire or the sea.

Several years ago I was on an airport bus, traveling to give a lecture about my book on Christian funerals to a pastors' conference held on a Midwestern university campus. Across the aisle from me were a young father and his son, both wearing Mickey Mouse ears and T-shirts from Orlando's Walt Disney World. They were obviously on their way back from a vacation to the Magic Kingdom. Both were in good spirits, and the father spoke to me in a cheerful voice, "So, where're you headed?" I named the university, and he responded, "Really? That's great! What're you doing there?"

I didn't want to tell a guy wearing Mickey Mouse ears that I was going to speak about death and funerals, so I simply said, "Oh, I'm giving a lecture to a conference there."

He wouldn't let it go. "Interesting! What will you talk about?"

There was nothing to do but 'fess up. "I have written a book about Christian funerals," I admitted, "and I am going to talk to pastors about the importance of funerals."

This young father became quickly solemn. "I am the one," he said softly, "who has the privilege of washing the bodies of the dead at the little mosque I attend in Wisconsin." He paused, and then he added, "I don't understand you Christians. You don't stay to the end. You leave before things are done."

I winced because he was right. When it comes to funerals, most Christians today arrive in the middle of the play, stay for Act II, and then leave before the drama is complete, before the full story is told. Act III is a lonely ceremony left to the deceased's closest family, or sometimes the body is taken to the crematory and left in a warehouse until its number comes up for the furnace. Nobody stays to the end. But if a funeral is more than our "paying respects" or joining in on a momentary and artificial "celebration of life," if it is the bearing of the burden of the one who has died and telling the narrative of farewell and completion, then we need—for their sake, for our sake—to go the whole distance. As Thomas Lynch describes what he imagines for his own funeral,

> I want a mess made in the snow so that the earth looks wounded, forced open, an unwilling participant. Forego the tent. Stand openly to the weather. Get the larger equipment out of sight. It's a distraction. But have the sexton, all dirt and indifference, remain at hand. . . . Those who lean on shovels and fill holes, like those who lean on custom and old prayers, are, each of them, experts in the one field.
>   And you should see it till the very end. Avoid the temptation of tidy leavetaking in a room, a cemetery chapel, at the foot of the altar. None of that. Don't dodge it because of the

weather. We've fished and watched football in worse condi-
tions. It won't take long. Go to the hole in the ground. Stand
over it. Look into it. Wonder. And be cold. But stay until it's
over. Until it is done.[15]

4. *Fourth, because a funeral moves through time, it speaks the
promise of transformation.* In the stillness of a typical memorial service, the implied task is to reflect, to sit motionless and
to allow oneself to be centered on the proper memory of the
deceased. A funeral, however, is on the move, and as such it
symbolizes a different promise: at the end of the day, everything will be different and all of us will be changed.

Of course, sometimes people are just as grief-bound, just
as angry, or just as numb at the close of a funeral as they were
at the beginning. Just going through the process of the funeral
does not magically heal the wound. But like all great rituals,
funerals hold their promises in trust for us. They are embodied actions that announce what is already true. Even if the
participants have not yet arrived at that conclusion, they can
dwell fully in that truth and must still live toward it.

To walk across the landscape carrying the body of Elizabeth
involves motion taking place over time, and this movement
over the land and this passing of time signal the transforma-
tions that will occur in those of us who accompany her. Just
as a New Orleans jazz funeral starts low and goes slow, then
moves higher and strikes fire, at the end joyfully announcing the marching in of the saints, so all funerals promise an
emotional transformation and healing. It may take weeks, or
years, or a lifetime, but our walking from "here" to "there"
with Elizabeth is also a confidence that we, too, are moving
from "here" to "there" in our grief and in our hope.

In this movement over time in a funeral, we also act out
a significant moment in the recognition of our mortality and
the maturing of our souls. At the beginning of the funeral, we
embrace Elizabeth. We wash and clothe her body, we tenderly

lift her and carry her to the place of farewell, and there we let her go. A funeral moves from embrace to release, a sign that to be human we must learn to hold the living in love and to let go of the dead in hope. Most religious traditions confess that our relationships with those we love are not destroyed by death, but they are dramatically changed. Elizabeth will not be with us in the way that she has been with us until now, and when we get to the end of the funeral journey, we must open our hands and let her go.

But our religious traditions also promise that this movement over time in the funeral promises not only a change in us, but also a change in Elizabeth. We let her go not into nothingness but into the life of God. We do not know much at all about what this means, but we do know that God can be trusted and that, for Elizabeth, all is well. From our limited vision, Elizabeth has changed from one who was living and breathing to one who is now dead. From the vision of faith, though, Elizabeth is not merely changed; she has been transfigured.

The Grieving

³For my days pass away like smoke,
   and my bones burn like a furnace.
⁴My heart is stricken and withered like grass;
   I am too wasted to eat my bread.
⁵Because of my loud groaning
   my bones cling to my skin.
⁶I am like an owl of the wilderness,
   like a little owl of the waste places.
⁷I lie awake;
   I am like a lonely bird on the housetop.
⁸All day long my enemies taunt me;
   those who deride me use my name for a curse.
⁹For I eat ashes like bread,
   and mingle tears with my drink,
¹⁰because of your indignation and anger;
   for you have lifted me up and thrown me aside.
¹¹My days are like an evening shadow;
I wither away like grass.

¹²But you, O LORD, are enthroned forever;
   your name endures to all generations.
¹³You will rise up and have compassion on Zion,
   for it is time to favor it;
   the appointed time has come.

                              —*Psalm 102:3–13*

Chapter 9

GRIEF AND THE SEARCH
FOR MEANING

Thomas G. Long

Near the end of the last round of presidential primaries in 2008, the race between Barack Obama and Hillary Clinton for the Democratic Party nomination broke decisively toward Obama. Resolute Hillary supporter Lanny Davis was devastated by the prospect of her defeat. Davis had served as special counsel to Bill Clinton and had devoted much energy to Hillary's effort. He was more than discouraged; he was so grief-stricken and distraught that he entered into Google the phrase "Elisabeth Kübler-Ross's five stages of grief" so that he could map his location on the emotional journey. "Denial? Yes," he confessed. "Anger? Definitely. Bargaining? Well, OK. And depression? That's definitely what I was going through," Davis said. Only when Obama lavished praise on Hillary in his convention victory speech did Davis find himself approaching the final Kübler-Ross stage: acceptance.[1]

This incident opens Ruth Davis Konigsberg's eye-opening book *The Truth about Grief: The Myth of Its Five Stages and the*

New Science of Loss, which was received with much controversy in the world of trauma counselors, funeral home providers of "aftercare," and others who help the bereaved navigate the choppy waters of grief. Konigsberg challenges not only Kübler-Ross's tidy scheme of grief stages but also the whole idea that grief is a therapeutically manageable process that moves through any stages whatsoever.

As Konigsberg tells the story, Kübler-Ross's *On Death and Dying,* which outlined the emotional stages through which dying people move, was based on poorly grounded, idiosyncratic, and highly impressionistic research. The book might have slipped quietly into oblivion, but it unexpectedly caught fire in the public imagination. Kübler-Ross's wobbly theory assumed a life of its own in the popular imagination. People quickly seized the five stages of dying, turned them into stages of grief over death generally and then into stages of grief over any loss. Kübler-Ross the scientist occasionally tried to nuance and qualify her original claims, but Kübler-Ross the media darling sometimes played along with the runaway expansions of her ideas. "You could say the same about divorce, losing a job, a maid, a parakeet,"[2] she said in a 1981 interview.

A cottage industry of bereavement counselors and grief managers developed. New and improved configurations of the stages of grief were developed, along with treatment plans to heal the wounds. The language of rights was trotted out on behalf of the bereaved: the right to grieve and to take the necessary time to do so. Ironically, the "right to grieve" morphed, says Konigsberg, into the loss of the right not to grieve according to the necessary plan.[3] When spouses remarried "too quickly," for example, people whispered that they were short-circuiting the proper stages of healthy grief.

The problem with all this is that there is no solid evidence that these theories about grief's stages are true. In fact, the evidence we do have, says Konigsberg, points to grief as unpredictable, wild, and undomesticated in its form and intensity. It breaks like a storm over us and then calms, seemingly without reason. With the possible exception of deeply pathological grief, attempts to manage grief therapeutically are largely useless—and may harm people more than they help them.[4]

Konigsberg's views are controversial, and some pastors, therapists, and grief counselors are reacting to her book with, well . . . .denial, anger, bargaining, and the rest. When Konigsberg asked Richard Shultz, one of the first social psychologists to raise questions about Kübler-Ross's work, why the idea of five stages persists against all the scientific evidence, he said, "Because they have great intuitive appeal, and it's easy to come up with examples that fit the theory."[5]

Theologians have been raising objections to Kübler-Ross's ideas for a long time. The notion that people sail across the Stygian stream toward some tranquil stage of acceptance is neither an empirical observation nor a matter of common sense. It is, instead, just plain bad theology, a product of Kübler-Ross's smuggled Neoplatonism, which views death as the freeing escape of the soul from the "bag of dung" that is the human body. In Christian theology, however, Death is no friend, not capital D Death anyway. Small d death, which is biological death, can sometimes come as a friend, a relief from intense suffering. But capital D Death is a power pitted against all life, is in fact the destroyer of life, the breaker of promises, the slayer of love and communion. Death is not to be welcomed with an embrace but resisted and fought against as the final enemy.

Beyond this, the larger notion that grief moves through some kind of staged process toward resolution probably owes more of a debt to American optimism than to religious hope. But grief is not mainly a psychotherapeutic unfolding; it is a perilous, unruly, and emotionally fraught narrative task. We are all players in human dramas, mundane mostly but also filled with grandeur and deep pathos. When someone dies, the plot threads unravel, the narrative shatters, and those of us who are part of the story "go to pieces." ⌐When we grieve, we are not simply grieving the loss of one we have loved, we are also grieving the loss of the narrative by which we have lived our lives.⌐ We have gotten up every day counting on this person to play a part in the unfolding drama of life, but now that member of the cast is no longer present, and the play cannot proceed apace. So grief is, in part, confusion and anxiety about how to advance, how to keep living the story of life without this important person in the drama. We don't know what to say or what to do. Life stands still. The work of grief is to gather the fragments and to rewrite the narrative, this time minus a treasured presence.

A major shift among many grief psychologists of late has been to move away from thinking of grief as a cluster of treatable psychological symptoms such as depression, anxiety, despair, and apathy. The psychic distress of grief is now seen to be something like childbirth—it hurts monstrously, it's normal, and the vast majority of those who go through the experience get over the pain of it with only a little help and no lasting damage.[6] Some do not, of course, and psychological intervention can be helpful in the case of complicated grief. But for people experiencing the normal thunderclap of grief over the loss of a loved one, what is now front and center and gaining attention is the realization that grief entails a task: meaning-making. As Colin Murray Parkes puts it,

> We think, "I know where I'm going, and I know who's going with me," except that when we lose one we love, we no longer know where we are going or who is going with us. Important new understanding has come out of studies of the gradual process by which we rebuild our internal model of the world after bereavement and discover new meanings, a new narrative, and a new assumptive world.[7]

Psychologists Robert A. Neimeyer and Diana C. Sands agree. "In the aftermath of life-altering loss," they write, "the

bereaved are commonly precipitated into a search for meaning."This search can range from very practical questions (*How*
did my loved one die?) to relational concerns *(Who* am I, now
that I am no longer a spouse?) to deeper spiritual or existential problems *(Why* did God allow this to happen?). The result
of working gradually through all of these questions and the
fissures in the world from which they arise is "a revised self-
narrative."[8]

This quest for a revised narrative explains much about why
we can sometimes be mostly unmoved by the death of a neighbor down the street whom we saw almost every day, but cast
down into deep sadness and grief by the loss of someone we
never personally met and really did not know—a movie star, a
singer, or a president. The reason is that the neighbor did not
figure deeply into our personal narrative, but we did weave
threads of our life around the songs or films or ideals of the
singer, the star, or the politician.

But we do not do this task of rebuilding our life narratives alone. In the wilderness of grief, God provides narrative
manna—just enough shape and meaning to keep us walking—
and sends the Comforter, who knits together the raveled soul
and refuses to leave us orphaned. Sometimes the bereaved say
they are looking for closure, but in the Christian faith we do
not seek closure so much as we pray that all of our lost loves
will be gathered into that great unending story fashioned by
God's grace.

Twilight: After Haying

Yes, long shadows go out
from the bales; and yes, the soul
must part from the body:
what else could it do?

The men sprawl near the baler,
too tired to leave the field.
They talk and smoke,
and the tips of their cigarettes
blaze like small roses
in the night air. (It arrived
and settled among them
before they were aware.)

The moon comes
to count the bales,
and the dispossessed—
Whip-poor-will, Whip-poor-will
——sings from the dusty stubble.

These things happen . . . the soul's bliss
and suffering are bound together
like the grasses . . .

The last, sweet exhalations
of timothy and vetch
go out with the song of the bird;
the ravaged field
grows wet with dew.

Jane Kenyon

Chapter 10

ALL SAINTS, ALL SOULS
A Coda

Thomas Lynch

IT WAS 1964 AND I WAS FIFTEEN AND RIDING IN THE BACKSEAT of my father's black sedan. We had just picked up the Reverend Dr. Harold DeWindt after he'd officiated at the funeral for one of his congregants, and we were driving him to the cemetery for the graveside services. Dr. DeWindt had spent most of the decade supervising the construction and furnishing of the magnificent Kirk in the Hills, a replica of ancient Melrose Abbey, his efforts for the honor and glory of God bringing a bit of thirteenth century Scotland on forty lakefront acres of Bloomfield Hills, home to Detroit's moguls and moneyed class, the blessed and elect who liked to worship as they lived—in style.

If Melrose had the embalmed heart of Robert the Bruce buried among its holy ruins, "the Kirk," as it was called by suburban Detroiters, bore the finger prints of Harold DeWindt and affirmed the Waspish ascendancy in the order of things.

We had just left the manse by its private drive and were heading east for White Chapel Cemetery, passing in front of the Kirk, its abbey and refectory and spired sanctuary, when the churchman cleared his throat to pose his question to my father. "What sort of coffin was that you brought into church this morning, Edward?" The Reverend Dr.'s white mane and rich homiletic baritone curled to affect the accent of Oban or Belfast, along with his velvet collared cape and biretta, always made him seem like Moses to me. Surely he could part the waters and channel the voice of God.

"Black walnut," said my father. "Solid American black walnut."

The churchman's slowly shook his head side to side, disapprovingly; his voice lowered to a modest scold. "That's just not necessary, Edward; such excess, not necessary." He let pause and silence occupy the space between words to fully amplify his censure. He was enunciating the conventional ecclesiastical wisdom of the day—that money spent on funerals was a tasteless display of crass materialism, of less than spiritual reformation values. After years of raising funds and taking pledges to erect the Kirk, Harold DeWindt measured every elective expenditure against the difference it might make to "the honor and glory of God."

An "edifice complex" my father called it, and nodding toward the stained glassed, flying buttressed, pipe organed, bell towered, abundantly landscaped, and sumptuously appointed Gothic façade we'd only moments before wheeled the dead pilgrim out of, he simply replied, "Neither is that, Doctor, neither is that."

An open field, a bended knee, a willing heart—these were essential to a religious impulse. The hand-carved and, by the way, solid walnut church mouse at the foot of the baptismal font, the original oils in the narthex, the pipe organ and stained glass were add-ons and accessories that spoke to the faith and commitment of the congregation and the fund raising virtuosity of the pastor. Why spend a dead Christian's money on caskets when it might better fund the purchase of new robes for the choir or new art for the abbey's study?

Such were the fashionable contentions of the times, that year, after Jessica Mitford sold five million copies of *The American Way of Death* and John Kennedy was buried in the first televised funeral in the nation's history. The nation was caught up in the talk of funerals and their expenses and, for many of the reverend clergy, pastoral care of the bereaved became driving the best bargain they could for their congregants for caskets and mortuary accoutrements.

Over the next two decades, the clergy of many white, mainline Protestant, suburban congregations effectively threw the bodies out with the boxes. The best way to downsize the money spent on a funeral was to downsize the relative importance of the corpse. And so, for the first time in the history of the species, we started seeing funerals notable for the absence of the dead. We called these new events "memorial services."

Writing at the same time as Jessica Mitford, and often in response to her, were authors and scholars among the reverend clergy like Paul Irion (*The Funeral: Vestige or Value*), Edgar N. Jackson (*Understanding Grief* and *The Christian Funeral*), David K. Switzer (*The Dynamics of Grief*), Earl Grollman (*Living When a Loved One Has Died*), and others who took a measuredly contrary view to Mitford's, seeing the funeral as one of those ties that bound congregants to one another and to the church. They connected the funeral to other ritual enactments of life's mysteries: baptisms, bar and bat mitzvahs, and nuptials among them.

Each of these authors saw the big life events as laden with emotional, spiritual, and religious import. Edgar Jackson, an Army chaplain during World War II and a trained psychotherapist as well as Methodist pastor, regarded bereavement and grief as the necessary recovery of emotional capital that the mourner had invested in the lost loved one, a process that must be accomplished before the capital could be reinvested in a new relationship. Dr. Jackson's and other paradigms of grief and mourning made much of the role played by the funeral in confronting the reality of death and loss, providing a venue for the open expression of difficult feelings and community support, and setting in motion a process of healing of the social and psychological fabric rent by death. But these books got little notice in the wider world of reviews. So whereas Mitford's classic sold in the millions, the minister/author's sold in the dozens.

When Elizabeth Kübler-Ross, a Swiss-American psychiatrist published her best-selling, *On Death and Dying* in 1969, her "five stages of loss," originally configured around the experience of dying patients, were easily adapted to become the "stages of grief." The bereaved were accordingly seen to be working their way through and among the familiar stations of *denial, anger, bargaining, depression,* and *acceptance.* Like Mitford's critique of mortuary conduct, Kübler-Ross's model for grief recovery entered the conventional wisdom so seamlessly that three decades later, Richard John Neuhaus, in the introduction to his meditative anthology called, *The Eternal Pity,* could observe:

> Death and dying has become a strangely popular topic. "Support groups" for the bereaved crop up all over. How to "cope" with dying is a regular on television talk shows. It no doubt has something to do with the growing number of old people in the population.
>
> Evelyn Waugh's *Loved One* brilliantly satirized and Jessica Mitford's *American Way of Death* brutally savaged the death industry of commercial exploitation. Years later it may be time for a similarly critical look at the psychological death industry that got underway in 1969 when Elizabeth Kübler-Ross

set forth her five stages of grieving. No doubt many people feel they have been helped by formal and informal therapies for bereavement and, if they feel they have been helped, they probably have been helped in some way that is not unimportant. Just being able to get through the day without cracking up is no little thing. But neither, one may suggest, is it the most important thing. I have listened to people who speak with studied, almost clinical, detail about where they are in their trek through the five stages. Death and bereavement are "processed." There are hundreds of self-help books on how to cope with death in order to get on with life. This book is not one of them.

A measure of reticence and silence is in order. There is a time simply to be present to death—whether one's own or that of others—without any felt urgencies about doing something about it or getting over it. The Preacher had it right: "For everything there is a season, and a time for every matter under heaven: a time to be born, and a time to die . . . a time to mourn and a time to dance." The time of mourning should be given its due. One may be permitted to wonder about the wisdom of contemporary funeral rites that hurry to the dancing, displacing sorrow with the determined affirmation of resurrection hope, supplying a ready answer to a question that has not been given time to understand itself.

The worst thing is not the sorrow or the loss or the heartbreak. Worse is to be encountered by death and not to be changed by the encounter. There are pills we can take to get through the experience, but the danger is that we then do not go through the experience but around it.[1]

Like Mitford, Kübler-Ross's model for "staged" grief entered the conventional wisdom and common knowledge unencumbered by such critique or scrutiny. It was user-friendly, easily understood, conceptually tidy, and serviceable. A regular on talk shows and at professional conventions, Kübler-Ross was the recipient of nearly twenty honorary doctorates from the nation's finest universities, and in the space of a couple of years, the primary mission of all activities surrounding a death in the family became the wise management of grief and its stages. While it was quite helpful to regard a death as multidimensional, that is, something that happened not only to the person who dies but to the many to whom the death really matters—family and friends and fellow congregants—the concentration of energies and intentions around the neatly staged grief of stricken survivors further minimized the role the dead play in what my colleague, Thomas Long, quite properly has called the "sacred community theater" that surrounds a death in the family. And just as the religious dualism that separates body and soul and accounts for the "just a shell" mentality that dismisses the corpse once death has occurred misses the holistic ontological facts of lives, the cultural reaction to Kübler-Ross's work tended to see mortality in dualistic terms in which the dead could be disposed of summarily while the mourners must be carefully counseled through their stages toward an eventual healing. The disposition of the dead was separated from the care and treatment of the living.

This "therapeutic" model of post death activity dismissed our religious and cultural obligations to the dead—to commend them to God and a heavenly eternity by a "proper" funeral and burial—in favor of those that stressed what might be done to help uphold the living, hobbled by grief, on their road to recovery. In this latter paradigm, the corpse became unnecessary and oppressively weighted baggage, an encumbrance, freighted with suffering and pain and sadness, better disposed of so that the mourners could travel light through their "celebrations of life," hitting their stages in a timely fashion and finally achieving acceptance and recovery. In short, the narrative of judgment, redemption, and eternal bliss—stations in the ongoing journey of the soul—were replaced by narratives of therapy, healing, and recovery—points in the journey of the bereaved.

For its part, the church, ever eager to meet the mourners at the door, changed their rubrics from the somber, black-and-purple vested requiems to the white-robed, paschal-themed "witness to the resurrection" services. The liturgy shifted from the Gregorian laments of the "Dies Irae," all doom, judgment, and salvation, to the joyous hymns of Easter and homiletics of heavenly reward. And just as a "celebration of life" is easier to market than a funeral, perpetual light and eternal rest are more user-friendly than grief's fear and hopelessness.

Rarely in the religious or cultural response was there space afforded to believe like people of faith and grieve like people of flesh, which is exactly the experience that most of us have when someone we love dies—part hopefulness, part helplessness, part grudging toward God, and part grateful. This is why, after many years in funeral service, I've come to understand that a death in the family is not only or entirely a psychological event, nor only or entirely a religious event, nor only or entirely a social or retail or commemorative occasion. It is all of these and then some: an existential event involving being and ceasing to be, faith in eternity and fear of extinction, grief and belief, holding on and letting go.

And the living who do best in grief are those who do their part for the dead. By acting out our ancient obligations to the dead we get to the edge of the life we will be living without them, consoled by the promises we claim in faith, happily haunted by our dreams and memories of those gone before us. It may not be a happy ending, but it is a return to life on life's terms.

"Grief," I remember Edgar Jackson saying at a seminar, with the wisdom of a longtime pastor, "is the other side of the coin of love." And they do seem part of the one currency and coinage, and they do suggest an inescapable math: if you love you grieve. About this math we have no choice. The only way to avoid grief, it seems, is to avoid each other, form no attachments, keep to ourselves, never play for keeps. This maxim held up well enough after I'd read John Bowlby's three-volume, door-stopping study of attachment, separation, and loss, published between 1969 and 1980. The British psychiatrist's three volumes on attachment theory and maternal deprivation in childhood development, like the old Methodist pastor's simple math of love and grief, had little to add to the understanding of these mysteries Roy Orbison sang in his hit cover of Boudleaux and Felice Bryant's song, "Love Hurts," which, like "Jesus wept," managed in two words to codify the nature of grief and humanity.

∾⋙∽

We buried our mother on All Hallow's Eve. It was years ago now; still, I remember coming home from our duties at Holy Sepulchre to trick-or-treaters making the rounds in the early gloaming and rustle of leaves. We hurried our youngest boys, Michael and Sean, into their costumes and out to roam with other pint-sized ghosts and goblins for the appeasements of penny candy.

All Saints' and All Souls', these first feasts of November, have always been about brokering peace between the living and the dead among us—between pagans and faithful, Celts and Christians, new age believers and doubters-at-large—all of us humans for whom the dead are not entirely gone and the gone are not entirely forgotten. The seasonal metaphors of reaping and rotting, harvest and darkness, leaf-fall and blood-sport and killing frost, supply us with plentiful *memento mori*. Whatever is or isn't there when we die, we are likewise frightened and excited by it.

Thus, all over the Western world, from secular Europe to Mexico and South America, graves are being decorated this week with candles and fresh flowers. Picnics are being held among the old stones and markers, families are gathering round family plots to give the dead their due of prayers and remembrances. We humans are truly bound to and identified with the earth, the dirt, the *humus* out of which our histories and architectures rise—our monuments and memorials, heaps and catacombs, shelters and cityscapes—everything human is "of the earth." This "ground-sense," to borrow William Carlos Williams' idiom, is at the core of our humanity. And the stones we cut our names and dates in—each is an effort to make a uniquely human statement about death and memory and belief. *Our kind was here. They lived; they died; they made their difference. We did right by them. They were not forgotten.* For the ancient and the modern, the grave is an essential station.

But less so hereabouts, where we tend to whistle past our graveyards and keep our dead at greater distance, consigned to oblivions we seldom visit, estranged and denatured, tidy and Disney-fied memorial parks with names like golf courses or megachurches: Willowcreek and Oakland Hills.

❧

In her honors seminar, "Death in American Culture," at Gardner-Webb University in Boiling Springs, North Carolina, Professor June Hobbs takes her students on a field trip to Sunset Cemetery in nearby Shelby. Dr. Hobbs believes that cemeteries have much to tell us about ourselves. For most of her twentysomething students, it is "literally their first visit to a cemetery."

"I find this astonishing," says Dr. Hobbs. "This county had more casualties during the Civil War than any other. The dead were everywhere, the churchyards filled up, Sunday afternoons were spent visiting graves. The dead were very much a part of the community, kept alive in everyday conversations." Now they've been downsized or disappeared.

She speaks to a culture that quietly turned the family "parlor" into "living rooms," "burial policies" into "life insurance," and funerals into the ubiquitous "celebration of life," notable for the absence of a corpse and the subtle enforcement of an emotional code that approves the good laugh but not the good cry. Convenience and cost-efficiency have replaced ethnic and religious customs. The dead get buried but we seldom see a grave. Or they are burned but we never see the fire. Photographs of coffins returned from wars were forbidden by presidential fiat, and news coverage of their burials discouraged. Where sex was once private and funerals were public, now sex is everywhere and the dead go to their graves and retorts often as not without witness or ritual. Cemeteries, once part of the ecclesiastical and municipal landscape, are private enterprises, well off the beaten track.

Still, there's something deeply and uniquely human in the way we process mortality by processing mortals from one station to the next in the journey between life as we know it and the hereafter as we imagine it, in that space the dead inhabit— heaven or happy hunting ground, nirvana or Valhalla. Wherever the dead go or don't, it is the duty of the living to get them to the edge of the oblivion we consign them to. Where, we humans always ask ourselves, do the dead go? All saints, all souls share these curiosities. And all of the living are well and truly haunted by them. Where do we come from? Where are we bound? Oblivion or home? There are inklings of answers among the stones.

There is no shortage of heartache, no lapse of sadness: every day six or so thousand more Americans die. They are spouses and parents, daughters and sons, siblings and soul mates, neighbors and friends. Each bears into their hereafter the wonders of the ones they have left behind to pray for them and to them, to remember and lament.

Dr. Long and I have shared for years the sense that the religious and the community response to a death in the family had, for a variety of reasons, gone astray, leaving the bereaved hard-pressed to reinvent a wheel to work the important space between faith and feeling, body and soul, bereavement and belief, the living and dead. A death in the family remains one of the great watershed events—pressing us to consider last things and verities in ways few other moments do.

This book grew out of our hopes that first responders among clergy and funeral directors, hospice and medical professionals, family and friends—those who show up in times of trouble willing to ante up their own humanity and faith and expertise—can help the heartsore find their way again, to funerals that affirm faith, manage grief, and by getting the dead where they need to go, get the living where they need to be.

NOTES

Chapter 1: How We Come to Be the Ones We Are

1. Frederick Buechner, *Now and Then: A Memoir of Vocation* (New York: HarperOne, 1991), 87.
2. Ibid.
3. Constantine P. Cavafy, "Voices," http://users.hol.gr/~barbanis/cavafy/voices.html.
4. William Blake, "The Tyger," in *The Complete Poetry & Prose of William Blake*, ed. David V. Erdman, et al. (New York: Anchor, 1984), 24.
5. William Butler Yeats, "Under Ben Bulben," *The Collected Poems of W. B. Yeats,* 2nd ed., ed. Richard Finneran (New York: Simon and Schuster, 1996), 325.
6. W. H. Auden, "In Memory of W. B. Yeats," *Collected Poems: W. H. Auden,* ed. Edward Mendelson (New York: Vintage, 1991), 247.
7. Buechner, *Now and Then,* 3.

Chapter 2: Falling into Ministry, Learning about Death

1. Peter Berger, *The Heretical Imperative: Contemporary Possibilities of Religious Affirmation* (New York: Doubleday, 1980).

2. Walker Percy, *Lost in the Cosmos: The Last Self-Help Book* (New York: Picador, 1983), 51.

3. Peter De Vries, *The Tents of Wickedness* (New York: Signet, 1960), 136.

4. William F. Willimon, "Making Christians in a Secular World," *The Christian Century* 103, no. 31 (October 22, 1986): 914.

5. Stanley Fish, "Religion Without Truth," *The New York Times*, March 31, 2007, A15.

6. Will D. Campbell, *Brother to a Dragonfly* (New York: Seabury Press, 1977), 173.

Chapter 3: Humanity 101

1. Robert Pogue Harrison, *The Dominion of the Dead* (Chicago: University of Chicago Press, 2003), ix–x.

2. Zygmunt Bauman, *Mortality, Immortality and Other Life Strategies* (Stanford: Stanford University Press, 1992), 51.

3. John Leland, "It's My Funeral and I'll Serve Ice Cream if I Want To," *The New York Times*, July 20, 2006, G2.

4. Megan O'Rourke, prologue to *The Long Goodbye: A Memoir of Grief* (New York: Riverhead Press, 2011), n.p.

5. Ibid., 12.

6. Ibid., 13.

7. Ibid., 254.

8. Ibid., 251.

9. Ibid., 255–56.

10. Alan Ball, interview by Terry Gross, *Fresh Air*, NPR, June 25, 2001.

11. Jessica Mitford, *A Fine Old Conflict* (New York: Random House, 1977), 30.

12. Jessica Mitford, *Hons and Rebels* (New York: New York Review of Books Classics, 2004), 183.

13. Jessica Mitford, *The American Way of Death Revisited* (New York: Knopf, 1998), xiii.

14. Jessica Mitford, *Decca: The Letters of Jessica Mitford,* ed. Peter Y. Sussman (New York: Knopf, 2006), 268.

15. Ibid.

16. Stephen Schwartz and Charles Burress, "Celebrated Muckraker Jessica Mitford Dies," *San Francisco Chronicle*, July 24, 1996., A1.

17. Cremation Association of North America, "Industry Statistical Information," http://www.cremationassociation.org/?page=IndustryStatistics.

18. "Pilot," *Six Feet Under*, season 1, episode 1, written and directed by Alan Ball, HBO, June 3, 2001.

19. E-mail correspondence between Alan Ball and Thomas Lynch, May 2002.

Chapter 4: Habeas Corpus . . . *Not*

1. Martin Luther King Jr., "Letter from Birmingham Jail," *The Christian Century*, 80/24 (June 12, 1963), 768 (emphasis mine).

2. Ibid., 772–73.

3. Karla FC Holloway, *Passed On: African American Mourning Stories* (Durham, NC: Duke University Press, 2003), 16.

4. Ibid (emphasis in original).

5. Catherine Madsen, "Love Songs to the Dead: The Liturgical Voice as Mentor and Reminder," *CrossCurrents* 48, no. 4 (Winter 1998-1999): 459.

6. Catherine Madsen, *The Law of Relation, http://www.catherine madsen.com.*

7. Hiroko Tabuchi, "Japan Finds Story of Hope in Undertaker Who Offered Calm Amid Disaster," *The New York Times,* March 10, 2012, A6.

8. Ibid.

9. John 1:14 is Eugene Peterson, *The Message* (Colorado Springs: Navpress, 1996).

10. Margaret R. Miles, *Bodies in Society: Essays on Christianity in Contemporary Culture* (Eugene, OR: Cascade Books, 2008), 13–14.

11. Ibid., 14.

12. Tim Townsend, "Muslim Funeral Home will be First in Area," *St. Louis Post-Dispatch,* May 18, 2012.

13. Marykate Connor, "Comment," *The New York Times,* August 26, 2011, online version, http://community.nytimes.com/comments/www.nytimes.com/2011/08/28/magazine/*lives*-the-letting-go.html.

14. Siddhartha Mukherjee, "The Letting Go," *The New York Times,* August 28, 2011, MM58.

15. Robert Wuthnow, *After the Baby Boomers: How Twenty- and Thirty-Somethings are Shaping the Future of American Religion* (Princeton: Princeton University Press, 2010), 135.

16. "Helen Gurley Brown, 1922–2012: Gave 'Single Girl' a Life in Full (Sex, Sex, Sex)," *The New York Times* (August 14, 2012), A1.

17. Wendell Berry, *Jayber Crow* (New York: Counterpoint, 2000), 161.

18. Augustine, "On the Care of the Dead," *Retractions,* Book II, chap. 64.

19. Ibid., par. 22.

20. Ibid.

21. Ibid., par. 4.

22. Ibid., par. 5.

23. Marilynne Robinson, *Gilead* (New York: Picador, 2006), 52.

Chapter 5: Our Own Worst Enemies

1. H. L. Mencken, *The American Language* (New York: Knopf, 1984), 288.

2. Elmer Davis, "The Mortician," *The American Mercury,* May 1927, 32.

3. "The High Cost of Dying: Funeral Homes Accused of High-Pressure Sales Tactics, Fraud and Abuse," interview with funeral director, Mike Ruck, *ABC Evening News*, June 23, 2012.

4. Elaine Woo, "Obituary: Howard Raether, Funeral Industry Advocate," *Los Angeles Times,* October 10, 1999.

5. *Preneed Burial Service: Hearing Before the Subcommittee on Frauds and Mispresentations Affecting the Elderly of the Special Committee on Aging,* 88th Cong. 17-20 (1964) (testimony of Howard C. Raether, executive secretary, National Funeral Director's Association of the United States, Inc.).

6. George F. Will, "Of Death and Rent Seeking," *Newsweek* 135, no. 20 (May 15 2000): 82.

7. Ann Scott Tyson, "Some War Dead Were Cremated at Facility Handling Pets," *Washington Post*, May 10, 2008.

8. Anita Diamant, *Saying Kaddish: How to Comfort the Dying, Bury the Dead, and Mourn as a Jew* (New York: Schocken, 1999), 88.

9. Richard P. Taylor, *Death and the Afterlife: A Cultural Encyclopedia* (Santa Barbara, CA: ABC-CLIO, 2000), 134-35.

10. Michael Parker Pearson, *The Archaeology of Death and Burial,* Texas A & M University Anthropology Series, no. 3 (College Station: Texas A&M Press, 2000), 42.

Chapter 6: Funeral Directors . . . Who Needs Them?

1. Gary Laderman, *Rest in Peace: A Cultural History of Death and the Funeral Home in Twentieth-Century America* (New York: Oxford, 2003), xxvi–xxvii.

2. Jessica Mitford, *The American Way of Death Revisited* (New York: Vintage Books, 2000), xi.

3. Erika Rasmussen Janes and Lisa Scherzer, "10 Things Funeral Directors Won't Tell You," *Smart Money*, June 28, 2010, accessed at http://www.smartmoney.com/spend/rip-offs/10-things-your-funeral-director-wont-tell-you-17153/.

4. http://www.nfda.org/consumer-resources-preneed/30-bill-of-rights-for-funeral-preplanning.html.

5. Joel Stonington, "Most and Least Profitable Business Types," *Businessweek*, January 18, 2011, accessed at http://www.businessweek.com/slideshows/20110118/most-and-least-profitable-business-types.

6. Abigail Van Buren, *The Best of Dear Abby* (New York: Andrews and McMeel, 1981), 242.

7. Mitford, *The American Way of Death Revisited*, 16–18 passim.

8. "Disney's Fairy Tale Weddings," as accessed at http://disneyweddings.disney.go.com/weddings/florida/wishes/ceremony/magical/detail.

9. Gregory Jaynes, "About New York; 90 Subdued Years of Funerals for the Famous," *The New York Times*, June 8, 1988.

10. Thomas Lynch, "Socko Finish," *New York Times Magazine*, July 12, 1998, 34.

11. Laurel Thatcher Ulrich, "Vertuous Women Found: New England Ministerial Literature, 1668-1735," *American Quarterly* 28, no. 1 (Spring 1976), 22.

12. George Foy, transcript of "Do It Yourself Funerals," *Morning Edition*, National Public Radio, December 8, 1997, accessed at http://www.npr.org/programs/death/971208.death.html.

Chapter 7: The Theory and Practice of Cremation

1. Thomas G. Long, *Accompany Them with Singing: The Christian Funeral* (Louisville, KY: Westminster John Knox Press, 2009), 177.

2. Ibid., 174.

3. T. S. Eliot, "The Love Song of J. Alfred Prufrock," in *Collected Poems: 1909-1962* (New York: Harcourt, Brace, Jovanovich, 2001), 5-6.

4. Ibid., 73.

5. See Stephen Prothero, *Purified by Fire: A History of Cremation in America* (Berkeley: University of California Press, 2002), especially 15-45.

6. Long, *Accompany Them with Singing*, 177.

Chapter 8: A Sense of Movement, a Sense of Meaning, a Sense of Hope

1. These words are taken verbatim from a representative "memorial ceremony" offered by a Celebrant training agency as an example

of what a Celebrant-led service might contain. All names, however, have been changed, and some punctuation altered.

2. The story of the burial of Vera Smith is drawn from two news stories of the event: Anna Badkhen, "Tired of Waiting for Authorities to Help, Citizens Rescue the Living, Bury the Dead," *San Francisco Chronicle* (September 4, 2005) and Andrew Buncombe, "Dignity at Last for Vera Smith, the Iconic Victim of Hurricane Katrina," for Independent News & Media (November 18, 2005), both accessed at http://www.deadlyroads.com/memorial/vera_smith.html.

3. William Carlos Williams, *The Collected Poems of William Carlos Williams: Volume 1 (1909–1939)* (New York: New Directions Books, 1986), 72.

4. *The Book of Common Prayer* (Oxford: Oxford University Press, 1897), 294.

5. Martha Nussbaum, *Love's Knowledge: Essays on Philosophy and Literature* (New York: Oxford University Press, 1992), 15.

6. Ibid., 16.

7. Ibid., 15.

8. Ibid., 16.

9. Saul Bellow, *Mr. Sammler's Planet* (New York: Penguin Classics, 2004), 260.

10. Anatole Broyard, *Intoxicated by My Illness* (New York: Random House, 1992), 20, 45.

11. Raymond E. Brown, *The Birth of the Messiah* (New York: Doubleday, 1979), 81.

12. Eudora Welty, *One Writer's Beginnings* (Cambridge, MA: Harvard University Press, 1998), 90.

13. Gilbert Meilaender, "A Dedicated Life," *First Things: A Monthly Journal of Religion & Public Life*, 203 (May, 2010), 17.

14. Ibid.

15. Thomas Lynch, *The Undertaking: Life Studies from the Dismal Trade* (New York: W.W. Norton, 2009), 197.

Chapter 9: Grief and the Search for Meaning

1. Ruth Davis Konigsberg, *The Truth about Grief: The Myth of Its Fives Stages and the New Science of Loss* (New York; Simon and Schuster, 2011), 1.

2. Ibid., 9.

3. Ibid, 46-47.

4. Ibid., 123.

5. Ibid., 11.

6. Colin Murray Parkes, "The Historical Landscape of Loss: Development of Bereavement Studies," in ed. Robert A. Neimeyer et al., *Grief and Bereavement in Contemporary Society: Bridging Research and Practice* (New York: Rutledge, 2011), 2.

7. Ibid., 4.

8. Robert A. Neimeyer and Diana C. Sands, "Meaning Reconstruction in Bereavement: From Principles to Practice," in ed. Robert A. Neimeyer et al., *Grief and Bereavement in Contemporary Society*, 11.

Chapter 10: All Saints, All Souls

1. Richard John Neuhaus, ed., *The Eternal Pity: Reflections on Dying* (Notre Dame: University of Notre Dame Press, 2000), 3-4.

INDEX